# ESSAYS IN AFRICAN HISTORY

JEAN SURET-CANALE

# Essays on African History

*From the Slave Trade to Neocolonialism*

WITH A PREFACE BY
BASIL DAVIDSON

TRANSLATED FROM THE FRENCH
BY CHRISTOPHER HURST

**Africa World Press, Inc.**

P.O. Box 1892
Trenton, New Jersey 08607
(609) 695-3766

**Africa World Press, Inc.**
**P.O. Box 1892**
**Trenton, N.J. 08607**

The French originals of Essays 1–8 first published in book form in
*Essais d'histoire africaine (de la traite des noirs au néocolonialisme)*


First American Edition 1988
Originated by: C. Hurst & Co. (Publishers) Ltd.,
London, England



Printed in England on long-life paper

Library of Congress Catalog Card No.: 88-70688

ISBN: 0-86543-092-6 *Cloth*
0-86543-093-4 *Paper*

## CONTENTS



## MAPS

# PREFACE

*by Basil Davidson*

The essays which follow here are the work of one of France's most distinguished living students of Africa, at once a pioneer in the modern achievement of a scientific understanding of the continent and a fearless critic of all easy orthodoxies and accepted attitudes. If Suret-Canale is less known in the English-reading world than other French thinkers over the past two decades, this can only be because useful teaching seems always to move slowly across language frontiers and find often a slow acceptance. As it has happened, however, the English edition of one of Suret-Canale's principal works, *French Colonialism in Tropical Africa, 1900–45*, when published here by Christopher Hurst in 1971, was forthwith received as an important contribution to studies of the colonial system in the vast territories of French West and Equatorial Africa. Now we have again to thank Mr Hurst for giving us, as both publisher and translator, this new volume of Suret-Canale's work.

Written at various times, some of these essays have responded to particular debates along the way or the challenges of particular discussions, but in any case of a kind which has in no way lost its relevance to the 1980s and 1990s. Such is the case, for example, with the first essay, where the author considers the application of a marxist analysis to the elucidation of Africa's pre-colonial societies, a subject on which the last word is far from said but to which this essay adds its characteristic clarity of mind. Such is again the case with the second essay in which Suret looks at the historical and social significance of the Fula (Peul) hegemonies of the seventeenth to nineteenth centuries, another subject of crucial importance, then and now, for an understanding of the growth and variety of West African state structures.

Other among these essays have marked steps in the evolution of a coherent understanding of the processes of 'decolonisation', a horrible but useful term which has now got itself into use to describe the ending of formal empires in Africa. In this context the most influential, perhaps, has been the eighth essay here, treating the nature of 'chieftainship' within the French colonial system, and the ways in which the chiefs of the Futa Jalon, in (then French) Guinea, were dislodged by the pressures of an anti-colonial nationalism. The tenth essay belongs to the same category, and offers Suret's thoughts on what has been sometimes, if sometimes quite misleadingly, called 'development theory'. And then two quite different essays, those on Vigné d'Octon and Louis Hunkanrin, reveal other aspects of this writer's wide concerns. Here he recovers from oblivion an early critic of French colonialism, a polemicist and publicist who was seen in those days of high imperialism - unavoidably, no doubt - as an eccentric and extremist but whose voice, today, comes down the wind of time with a bracing gravity and good sense. In comparison with Vigné d'Octon there is the early nationalist of Dahomey (now the Republic of Benin), Louis Hunkanrin, whose stubborn intelligence has likewise won Suret's sympathy.

These essays are written to be enjoyed as well as to instruct. Aside from their inherent interest their value will be found, I think, to lie in their qualities of erudition, lucidity and independence of judgment. They are produced from a painstaking and even passionate attachment to the facts. This is an analyst who wants above all to know what really happened, and, if also possible, why it happened. Yet there is little use in knowing what happened and why - in so far as either can be known - unless one can set forth one's knowledge. This is a writer who knows how to share his lucidity. And then, thirdly, this is a thinker who follows no conventional or beaten track. He thinks for himself, no matter what the cost may have to be.

Now that the colonial period and the culture of outright imperialism are receding into memory, even into distant memory, it may be hard to imagine the price in personal toil and turmoil that had to be met by those who, like Suret-Canale, preferred to stand against the orthodoxies of the time. They had to expect the certainty of every sort of administrative obstacle and established obstruction in the way of their travels and researches, and yet somehow manage to persevere. They could hope for no pleasant grants and subsidies, and their tenure in any particular African place was likely to be brief. It might afterwards be claimed on behalf of the French colonial system, as of the British, that it was 'preparing our Africans, step by step, for independence'; one's experience on the ground, however, was just the reverse of whatever such 'preparation' might be thought to imply. As only one small example of that experience, I myself remember being threatened with expulsion from French Sudan (now Mali) in 1952 for having dared to interview a local nationalist leader: 'a person of absolutely no importance', I was told by the police commissioner of Bamako, but all the same the very same person, Mamadou Konaté, who afterwards became the first president of his country.

Suret-Canale has had to suffer much persecution, whether in Africa or at home, because he has always taken his own line and followed it. The nature of his use of Marx shows this independence, for it pursues no doctrines or dogmas but stands on the principles of analysis which Marx evolved for the benefit of later development 'on the spot'. As a lifelong member of the French Communist party, of course, he might well be thought to possess a willingness to bend his judgment to that party's usually authoritarian discipline. But his work denies it. Over a long acquaintance I have often disagreed with him, but I have never once discovered him following any line of thought except his own. It is perhaps in this quality of staunch independence that his principled critique of the colonial project becomes most effective.

There is much that one should say about this devoutly committed thinker: committed, that is, to the search for truth through whatever entanglements and minefields the fashion of our times may have erected in its path. Born in 1921, he was still a student - a brilliant student, one should add - when France was engulfed in the Second World War. He persisted as a student in so far as that was possible, but he persisted just as much, or more, in his refusal to stand aside from the fearsome challenges of those times. As an active patriot even during the first grim months of Nazi occupation, he was arrested by the German military authorities in September 1940 and spent the following winter in infamous jails, only to join once again, when released in February 1941, an active resistance which was then far from being any kind of widespread movement. And the rest of the war saw him in the ranks of anti-Nazi defiance.

His African years, following the war, have been spent chiefly in Senegal and Guinea, and it was there, onwards from 1946, that he prepared himself intensively for the books which he would write during the 1960s: a three-volume study of French West and Equatorial Africa (written in 1957-72), of which Mr Hurst has already given us, in English, the middle volume mentioned above; a study of the Republic of Guinea (1970); a splendid array of specialist papers and studies (some of which we have here); and latterly, a doctoral thesis on 'The Geography of Capital' in French-speaking tropical Africa, with an outline of which this present volume closes. Although by training a geographer, he is in reality a polymath - he himself would claim, no doubt, that this is precisely because of his training as a geographer - and the range of his learning reaches far beyond the limit of any introductory note. From the benefit of a long acquaintance let me add that Suret-Canale has remained a warm and genial participant in whatever challenges the years continue to bring him. It is excellent that more of his work should here become available in English.

*February 1987*

# AUTHOR'S PREFACE

This book brings together studies which have appeared in a variety of periodicals and other publications over the course of two decades. If I had to write them again today, I would naturally do so differently: they are dated, and testify both to a particular attitude and to a particular period. I still maintain and subscribe fully to this attitude, but I will not pretend that, on certain points, my understanding has not evolved and (I hope!) deepened. Those who refer to these works undoubtedly need to look also at what has been published since on the same subjects, as much to elaborate their own judgment as to discover where correction or updating is necessary.

It was the struggle for the liberation of Africa which led me to explore a hitherto unappreciated area of knowledge, the very existence of which had at times been denied. This does not lead me to claim any special merit, but I feel no inferiority complex about it either.

The marxism which has determined my attitude is not, and – unless it were to go against its own principles – would not know how to be, a means of 'measuring' various situations and periods of history. Marxism, as a scientific attitude towards historical material, can do no more than shed light on one's research. It does not give sight to the blind.

We must now define the problems raised in this collection of writings, as well as those of equal importance which have not been raised. The first study, which resumes and submits to a refining process ideas already put forward in the first part of my *Afrique Noire* in 1958, aimed to establish the nature of class in pre-colonial Africa, particularly where class antagonisms had led to the appearance of the state. 'Colonial' history and ethnology – i.e. the history and ethnology of the colonial period – had as their common failing a refusal, in the guise of a descriptive empiricism, to take these realities of class into account. Other authors, both at this period and later, did not always resist the temptation to impose on these African realities methods of analysis borrowed from other societies and other periods of history. The category 'tributary mode of production', which Marx (for want of a more precise definition at the time when he wrote) called 'Asiatic' or 'oriental', seemed to me to characterise these African societies very exactly. There have been objections to this definition; some, for example, believe it to be too general. But the very category 'mode of production' claims to do no more than 'situate' (a word used by Marx himself) social formations which are dependent upon it; it does not seek to lend itself to detailed 'deductions' – the attitude of a speculative 'philosophy' of history, an unscientific attitude which marxism rejects on principle, and which, one could say, it came into being to oppose. And in their details, the innumerable varieties of African societies present specific features, and finally typologies, which empirical study has the function of setting forth (a function it fulfils increasingly, and with success).[1]

In the framework of this mode of production, as of all others, historical evolution shows successive stages: the deepening of internal contradictions results in crises, at levels where these contradictions can no longer be radically overcome but merely reproduce themselves in other forms. The feudal mode of production experienced such crises, as did the capitalist mode. The Islamic 'revolutions' that West Africa experienced from the end of the seventeenth century to the nineteenth, but most of all in the eighteenth and nineteenth centuries, appear to me to belong to this system of evolution.

Traditional French 'colonial' historiography only took into account the ethnic aspects (the Peuls or Fulas often but not always being implied) and the religious ones. I demonstrated that it was necessary to take into account as well – and perhaps above all else – socio-economic factors relating to the class struggle, in forms which were often complex, reflecting the very complexity of these African societies and the weight of elements in their structures that were inherited from the past. These elements bring into play, to differing degrees, the totality of oppressed strata and groups in the traditional 'tribal' monarchies: tributary peasant labourers, slaves, subordinate or enslaved ethnic groups (like the Peuls), also women and young people. Numerous authors have successfully travelled by this route.

In the development of internal contradictions which have led to these 'revolutions', the impact of the trans-Atlantic slave trade on African societies from the seventeenth century onwards, but particularly in the eighteenth, has – as I understand it – played a decisive role. This point of view is now disputed by certain Western historians, who in a different connection seek to minimise the numerical importance of the trade itself in order to present its nature and its effects as having been less severe than was once claimed – as much in the number of deaths as in the treatment of the slaves on American plantations. This approach is, to say the least, not exempt from an ideological inspiration which aims to play down the responsibility of a Europe put on trial, so it is said, by anti-colonialist historiography, especially as regards Africa. Without completely denying the interest and the validity of some of its treatment of detail, I do not find the approach scientifically acceptable, and will explain why.

1. For example, the remarkable work carried out during the 1970s on pastoral and nomadic societies under the aegis of C.E.R.M.

I have not tackled here – and only mention it as a reminder – the realisation of the methods to which, over the past two decades, African history owes its most important progress. Twenty years ago, some historians wielding considerable authority held the view that there is no history which does not proceed from written sources, and that in the absence of such sources, particularly archival ones, the only African history is colonial history. In fact, more written documents exist than one might imagine, including ones of African origin, and even those of colonial origin have scarcely been exploited in an African perspective. The exploitation of oral tradition and the data provided by ethnology ('ethno-history') and recourse to linguistic and archaeological data, *inter alia*, have exposed the weakness of this prejudice, which is no less damaging in its implications for what historiography can achieve in countries possessing abundant written sources. Certainly the new methods have been narrowed down to their essentials, and they require care and a firm critical sense – just as the handling of written sources has always done. But they have amply proved their richness, even for very remote periods. Understood in this way, history demands protracted specialisation in a well-defined area; so too does a truly deep knowledge of African languages. My times in Africa – a dozen years all told – involved me in such responsibilities; and, above all, they were so often interrupted for reasons beyond my control that I was not able to become seriously involved in this area. I nevertheless believe that this kind of research can only be brought to its full realisation by African historians, who indeed are widely engaged in it already.

I have taken it upon myself in other works[2] to debunk the 'colonial' history of the conquest of Africa. Working in virgin territory, I could only mark out certain frameworks; since then, works of much greater depth have been published, and I have therefore judged it pointless to re-issue essays of mine which have clearly been outstripped.[3]

On the history of the colonial period I have included an essay confined to Guinea, and on the subsequent period a study of the so-called 'traditional' chiefdom, also in Guinea, which I hope will bear witness to the fact that a marxist approach and recourse to analysis of class realities are not necessarily 'schematic', as some would say, but rather the reverse! I have included as well a text in a rather different style – one can only call it a pedagogical style – on the teaching of African history (now, alas, almost entirely removed from French school syllabuses). This was requested from me by our Belgian collea-

2. *Afrique Noire*, I, 3rd edn, 1968.
3. E.g. my essays on Samori (*Recherches africaines*, Conakry, 1959, vols 1–4, pp. 18–22, and *Révolution démocratique africaine*, Conakry, no. 48, May 1972, pp. 199–253). Yves Person's vast and exemplary work on Samori (Dakar, I.F.A.N., 3 vols so far, 1968, 1970 and 1975) makes them virtually obsolete.

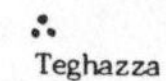


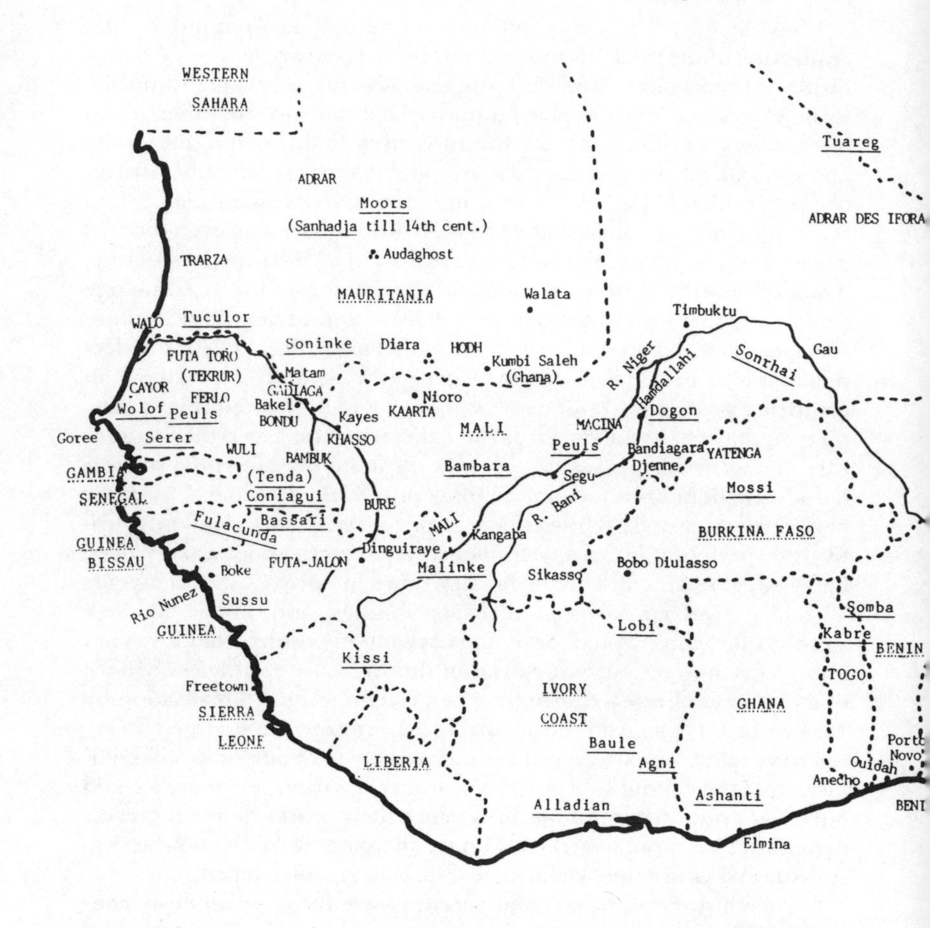


# WEST AFRICA

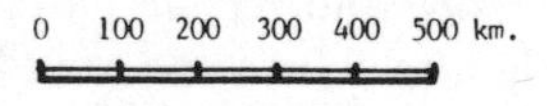


Key

| | |
|---|---|
| TRARZA | Name of country |
| Tuculor | Name of people |
| • Sikasso | Name of city or river |
| ∴ Teghazza | Name of vanished city |
| NIGERIA | Name of modern state |

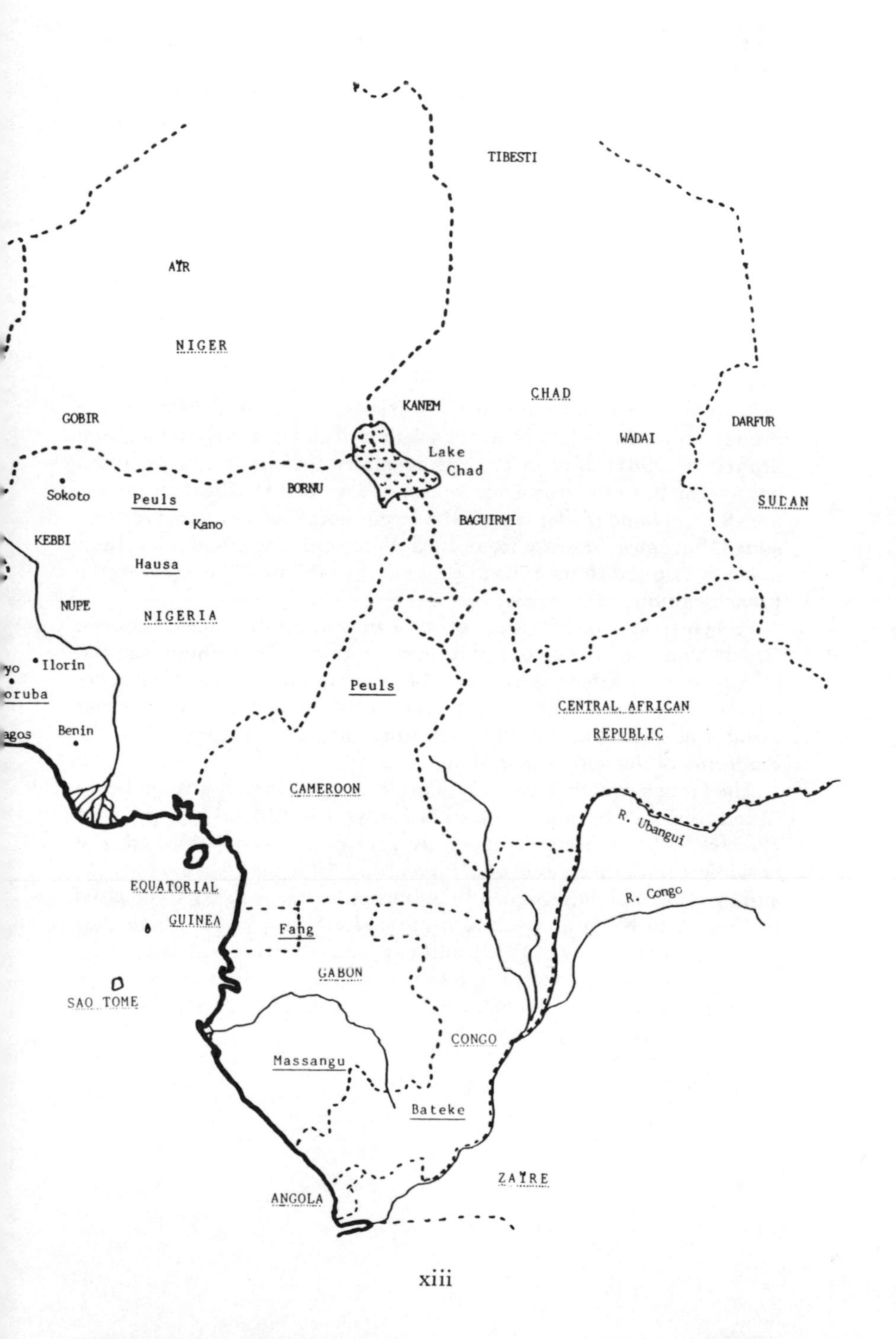
TIBESTI
AÏR
NIGER
CHAD
KANEM
GOBIR
DARFUR
WADAI
Lake
Chad
SUDAN
Sokoto
Peuls
BORNU
Kano
BAGUIRMI
KEBBI
Hausa
NUPE
NIGERIA
yo
Ilorin
Peuls
oruba
CENTRAL AFRICAN
REPUBLIC
agos
Benin
CAMEROON
R. Ubangui
EQUATORIAL
GUINEA
R. Congo
Fang
GABON
SAO TOME
CONGO
Massangu
Bateke
ZAÏRE
ANGOLA

gues. Finally, some reflections have been included concerning the neo-colonialism of the present day.

If these essays are capable of awakening the interest of readers in an undervalued field of African history and of urging them onwards to read other books - detaching them, even to a small extent, from a view which too often remains Eurocentric - their publication will not be in vain.

## TRANSLATOR'S NOTE

The translator is deeply grateful to M. Suret-Canale for his extraordinary patience and good humour in suffering the long delays in the production of this volume (the translation of all but Essay 10 had been drafted by 1981), and in answering many tedious questions about points which, in the translator's opinion, needed clarification for the non-francophone reader. As to the latter, some new notes have been added, but since these are from the author's pen, no attempt has been made to distinguish them from those that were already present in the French edition.

French-style transliteration of African and Arab names has been largely abandoned in favour of a more English style, without accents. Clarity and consistency have alike been striven for, and apologies are offered to readers who would feel more comfortable with other forms - as indeed for any imperfections that may be detected in the rendering of the author's original.

The French edition is now out of print, and will apparently not be re-issued. It should be pointed out that Essays 9 and 10 did not appear in *Essais d'Histoire africaine*; 9 has only previously been published in a periodical in the Republic of Guinea, and 10 is the 'Abstract' of the author's doctoral thesis, recently published in Paris. Essay 7 appeared in English in Klein and Johnson (eds), *Perspectives on the African Past* (Boston: Little, Brown, 1972) and is reprinted here, with minor re-editing, with the editors' permission. Essay 5 combines two separate essays in *Essais d'Histoire africaine*. The bibliographical history of each essay is given on its opening page.

*August 1987*

# 1

# TRADITIONAL SOCIETIES IN TROPICAL AFRICA AND THE CONCEPT OF THE 'ASIATIC MODE OF PRODUCTION'

*Marxism and the Study of African Societies*

How, using a marxist perspective (i.e. in a spirit of genuine scientific synthesis), should one characterise the societies of pre-colonial black Africa? This question was presented to us in 1946, and it provided the subject of numerous writings and discussions among a group of marxists who, under the direction of the central committee of the French Communist Party, were interested in African problems. Like the Communist study groups which operated in Africa between 1944 and 1951, our group included militants of both French and African origin.

When, in 1956, I was obliged to take up the question in the course of my own work, many aspects of it remained obscure. Just as the gamut of non-marxist observers had done before (and here we are not considering societies in a truly primitive stage of development, like Pygmies and Bushmen who live by hunting and gathering), one can distinguish two main types of African society. On the one hand, there were 'non-state' societies, having as their basic unit the patriarchal family in the widest sense (matrilineal as often as patrilineal) and often – though not always – organised in villages grouping together several families. Such villages constitute 'leagues' of varying extent, often within the framework of a common ethnic group (a 'tribe' or part of a tribe): these leagues are of a religious or military character and come into their own at intervals. On the other hand, there are societies which have experienced organisation with the character of a state and are endowed with a marked social stratification, but which rest on the same foundations – the patriarchal family and the village – as the societies mentioned previously. Using a terminology of approximation, we designate these two groups respectively as 'tribal' and 'feudal'.

How did these societies come into being and how did they develop? How is one to define their particular mode or modes of production? We were not then in a position to give clear answers to these questions.

Certainly the idea of the sequence: 'primitive communism, slavery, feudalism', although widespread in marxist literature, did not help us in our research. This conception had been vulgarised, and imposed in a particularly dogmatic manner, by Stalin in his work *Dialectical*

*Materialism and Historcal Materialism*, which stated the sequence without any justification on either logical or historical grounds. All the same, one must not exaggerate its influence; I for my part have always been convinced – and the most superficial examination of traditional African societies lends evidence to support it – that this schema is not applicable to tropical Africa. This view was shared by Raymond Barbé, who was responsible at that time for the work of the French Communist Party in this field, and by all the comrades who worked on those questions. At the same time, we felt incapable of advancing an alternative explanation.

To be frank, the superficiality of the work done by marxists up till that time was largely responsible for this situation. Being obliged to devote their attention essentially to contemporary problems, they had not the time to undertake the preliminary work which is unavoidable if one is to uncover and then elaborate on the documentation gathered by ethnologists – this latter being extremely scattered and often highly suspect in its interpretations, but nevertheless constituting the only possible basis for study. A solitary attempt has been made in this direction in the legal dissertation of Maurice Bourjol,[1] based on the documentation of the 'customary law of French West Africa'; this pioneering effort greatly facilitated my later work, and I am commensurately in its debt.

The work which I was elaborating from 1956 to 1958 led me to certain conclusions. First of all, I had received confirmation of the idea that the evolutionary schema: 'primitive communism, slavery, feudalism' does not apply to Africa. And, by referring to the spirit and method of marxism, I deliberately separated myself from this schema. Apropos Engels' book *The Origin of the Family*, I wrote:

> Engels' account belongs to the time in which he lived, and it is impossible to ignore the advances in knowledge that have taken place in the fields of study which he took as his own. On the other hand, the general exposition given by Engels of the evolution of human society, from the primitive community to the appearance of the state, is on the whole of value only in relation to his particular field of study (American Indians, ancient Greece and Rome, Germanic peoples). To make of this generalisation – valuable though it is within its special limits – a rigid scheme with universal application – would be to misunderstand the whole spirit of marxism.[2]

Further clarifying my point of view, I wrote:

> Marxists, basing themselves on the historical experience of the Mediterranean basin and the neighbouring regions of Europe (essentially those countries

1. 'Théorie générale des coutumes africaines', Toulouse, 1954.
2. *Afrique Noire*, I, 1958, p. 61 (1961 edn, p. 67).

which formed part of the Roman empire), distinguish two successive stages in the evolution of class societies after the break-up of the primitive community and before the advent of capitalism: slave society and feudal society.

Some have sought to attribute a general and absolute value to this succession, calling in evidence the experience of black Africa. In our view, it is difficult to accept this thesis, which does not seem to correspond to the facts, and which has nowhere had its economic validity demonstrated.

In reality, we see emerging in black Africa, on the foundations of the disintegrated primitive community (which in many of its features is still very much alive), at one and the same time the relations of slavery and those between suzerain and tributary or vassal, which one has to describe as feudal relations. (We would note in passing that we are not blind to the question of how much this terminology can add to the discussion; but it is nonetheless hallowed by frequent use.)

It seems that the mode of production which preponderates in the most advanced regions of traditional black Africa is closely comparable with that which Marx called the 'Asiatic mode of production' and of which India before the English conquest seemed to him to provide an example. It seems to us that one can in fact compare it closely with the modes of production present in the archaic periods of classical antiquity, before the relations of slavery became general, and with ancient Russia before feudal relations became general.[3]

In the 1961 edition I added: 'It offers striking analogies with [the mode of production] of China in the Chou period (11th–3rd centuries BC)', and referred to Ferenc Tökei's study 'The conditions of landed property in the China of the Chou'.[4]

We see no reason, looking back from our present vantage-point, for disowning these statements of principle. But on certain points I will seek to complete, correct and make more precise the conclusions on which I took our stand then. I had not tackled at the fundamental level the question of the 'Asiatic mode of production', partly because it was not our subject, but most of all because I did not have the use of material – marxist texts in particular – which would have made a more detailed judgment possible.

The views which I put forward on the general value of the Asiatic mode of production were given in hypothetical form because I did not possess the wherewithal to demonstrate it – and I still do not, despite the progress which has been made in this direction. In the same way, my attempted explanation of African societies and their evolution was offered with considerable care, since it had to brave specialist criticism. But, right up to the present, no objection has been made to my essential point; I was merely scolded for taking marxism as my authority and thus subscribing to *a priori* conceptions. I have called upon these critics

3. Ibid., p. 94 (1958); pp. 101–2 (1961).
4. *Acta Antiqua Academiae Scientiarum Hungaricae*, VI, 3–4, pp. 245–300.

to show me, with arguments and factual evidence, where and how I have been in error.[5] Conversely, certain specialists with viewpoints totally alien to marxism were good enough to tell me that my synthesis seemed to them to have merit.

The works produced in the early 1960s under the auspices of the Centre d'Etudes et de Recherches marxistes - by Charles Parain, Jean Chesneaux, Maurice Godelier and others[6] - have made it possible for us to move a few steps forward from our earlier positions.

Hence I propose - leaving aside all reference to the discussion concerning the 'Asiatic mode of production' - first to try and describe the essential structures of pre-colonial African society, and then to see how the results I obtain can contribute to that discussion and carry it further forward.

## *The structure of traditional African societies*

Pre-colonial tropical Africa presents three basic types of socio-economic structure, and we will attempt to summarise their characteristic features.

*The primitive community.* This is a type of society which, because of the very feebleness of the productive forces, firmly excludes exploitation of one man by another man. The primitive community resorts to hunting and gathering to provide the means of existence, but these are only able to give the bare minimum of resources necessary to sustain life. (The mode of production based on hunting and gathering is not in itself inferior in productivity, but it cannot do other than co-exist with nomadism extending over a vast area, and the accumulation of resources is impossible without any means of transport.) In these conditions there is no surplus production which an individual could appropriate for himself permanently at the expense of other individuals, and thus not even the possibility for men to exploit each other, or for society to become differentiated into mutually antagonistic classes.

In black Africa this type of society is in the process of disappearing, and even in the nineteenth century it only survived vestigially: it is, or

5. I invited the most eminent of these critics, the late doyen of American Africanists, Melville J. Herskovits, to set forth his objections in the Guinean review *Recherches africaines*. I greatly regret that he did not take up this offer, which would have opened up a true debate of value to all.
6. C. Parain, 'Le mode de production asiatique: une étape nouvelle dans une discussion fondamentale'; F. Tökei, 'Le mode de production asiatique dans les oeuvres de Marx et d'Engels'; and J. Chesneaux, 'Le mode de production asiatique: quelques perspectives de recherches' - all in *La Pensée*, 114, April 1964; and M. Godelier, 'La notion de mode de production asiatique et les schémas marxistes d'évolution des sociétés', *Cahier du C.E.R.M.*, 1964.

was, to be found among the Pygmies of the equatorial forest and among the Bushmen in Southern Africa. These last, forced to retreat into semi-desert regions, are becoming extinct. As for the Pygmies, their activity has long been integrated into that of neighbouring societies, with which they carry on continuous exchanges - all within the framework of a genuine division of labour. It is likely that this situation explains the relative poverty of their culture compared with that of Amerindians, Melanesians and aboriginal Australians whose material civilisation is comparable to theirs.[7]

The precarious nature of their living conditions obliges them to form themselves into small 'bands of hunters' (corresponding generally to a section of a clan: a group of relatives extending beyond the nuclear family), the inadequacy of whose resources stands in contrast to excessive concentrations. However, these living conditions imply a rigorous solidarity: what each individual produces by hunting or gathering guarantees subsistence for everybody. 'The rules of sharing vary from one group to another, but what is important is that in principle all the members of the group benefit from what each member catches. Set against the uncertainty of the hunter's life, this represents an important security.'[8]

The egalitarian character of the society (at the level of consumption) - the 'communism' inherent in the organisation of hunting and gathering - is imposed by the poor level of the productive forces. This level is liable to extreme variations according to environment: within the limits imposed by a more or less hostile environment, the forms of organisation are very diverse and allow of a considerable element of individualism in their make-up. One can postulate that this element of individualism is generally much greater than that which exploited classes manage to retain in class societies.

In this connection let us get rid in passing of certain misunderstandings which cause many ethnologists to deny the existence of the primitive community and of a 'primitive communism'. Projecting arbitrarily upon primitive societies notions borrowed from different social formations - e.g. certain rural areas of Europe or even the *kolkhoz* (collective farm) - they see nothing similar in the primitive societies and so reject the notion of 'primitive communism', calling it - for want of a better term - a 'marxist invention'. But in so doing they attribute to the idea of 'primitive communism' a meaning which

7. The Pygmies appear to have no language of their own (or they have abandoned it); they speak the same dialects as the neighbouring agricultural populations. The cave art of the Bushmen ceased to be practised in the nineteenth century. The organisation of kinship systems and the existence of 'totemic complexes' are not evident in the rich and elaborate forms found in Australia and North America.
8. J.-J. Maquet, *Afrique: les civilisations noires*, Paris, 1962, p. 71.

marxists have never given to it. The only definition one can give to these societies is that, because of the poor level of their productive forces, they do not allow of exploitation of men by each other, that is to say they do not allow of mutually antagonistic classes. That human anthill, the military barracks, is the archtype of the class society.[9] Nothing can be more false than to imagine men in primitive societies as deprived of individuality; Durkheim's digressions on 'collective consciousness' have grafted on to this subject some completely erroneous ideas. How, in the absence of chiefs or of any external coercive authority, the rules of social life can impose themselves and command respect is shown by J.-J. Maquet with pertinent examples drawn from the ethnologist C.M. Turnbull.[10]

*Tribal or tribal-patriarchal society.* The overwhelming majority of African societies have passed the stage of hunting and gathering and are at an altogether higher level of productive forces: namely, that of agriculture (and, secondarily, livestock rearing). Cultivation is done with the hoe (implements – the hoe, the axe and the machete – are made of iron[11]) on burnt land, and is mostly extensive, with some land remaining fallow for long periods; sometimes, however, it is intensive.

Technical details and regional variations are unimportant, but the essential fact to grasp is that the general adoption of agricultural activity (or pastoral activity: the two are generally separate), above all with the use of iron implements, has resulted in a considerable raising of productivity and the appearance of an economic surplus, or production in excess of the indispensable minimum for subsistence.

The existence of this surplus-product has allowed a division of labour and the appearance of specialised trades, which in itself is a source of increased productivity, leading to commerce. This surplus can be held in reserve in case of a bad harvest or some other disaster, or it can be used up on festive occasions, and so on. It can also be appropriated or embezzled by certain families or individuals, to the detriment of the common interest. Differentiation between rich and poor, and thence the exploitation of the mass of people by a minority and the formation of opposed classes, can now make their appearance.

Here the basic social unit is the patriarchal family, a matrilineal or

9. And that which continues to exist in socialist societies is an inheritance from class societies and has nothing to do with primitive communism, any more than it has to do with the communism of the future!
10. Maquet, op. cit., pp. 75–8.
11. But at first stone or wooden implements were used (mainly before the Christian era). How iron implements came to be used on a widespread scale, notably in agriculture, is one of the major problems in African archaeology.

patrilineal group of relatives, corresponding to the fraction of a clan tied to the land. Exactly like the 'band of hunters', it always takes in those outside the clan (spouses and sometimes in-laws). As a basic economic unit, serving as a means of agricultural production, it is not identical with a kin group in the strict sense; but it is understood by its members as a fraction of a clan, the extraneous elements being regarded as such, simply guests who are always liable to rejoin their own true kin group, but nevertheless indispensable for the very survival of the common life.

There is no private property in the form of land, as understood in Roman law or in a civil code. Land rights, collective and inalienable, belong to the patriarchal family, and are based on ancient occupation - or, in the case of cultivated or cultivable land, on ancient reclamation from the wild state. Except in certain totally uninhabitable regions, there is no 'vacant and ownerless land'; cultivated or fallow land, pasture or forest - all is appropriated, and the boundaries between different properties are firmly established and well known. As ever, there exists the possibility of quarrels over what belongs to whom, and over the exact location of the boundary.

In the restricted framework of the patriarchal family, it is the senior member of the oldest generation,[12] the patriarch or family head, who shares out the land. Being responsible for the fertility of the soil (or for the abundance of game in the hunting grounds), he alone can perform the necessary rituals, and as a result he must take upon himself the issuing of prohibitions which are sometimes highly inconvenient.

Without under-estimating the religious (or magical) aspects of the patriarchal function, it is also necessary not to under-estimate its aspects which are in fact technical. In an agricultural system which involves land lying fallow for very long periods, and where only an insignificant proportion of the agricultural land is effectively under cultivation at any one time, periodic redistribution of land is essential. It must respond to conditions imposed by the agricultural system, by the rotation of crops and by social factors: certain land remains 'collective' or 'familial' and is cultivated for the benefit of the community, while other land is in the hands of individuals. Custom, varying according to the ethnic group in question, fixes the number of days in the week which must be given to working on the family fields and on one's own personal fields respectively. In the same way, it determines their respective order and size.

The patriarchal family is often isolated and autonomous: forest encampments and *sukkalas* in the Sudanic regions constitute not only

12. The rules had to be bent if the head of the family was considered incapable of carrying out his functions.

socio-economic units but at the same time units which have their own habitat and are politically independent. But often, too, the unit which provides the habitat and the political unit is found to be the village. The 'founding' family – the family that first cleared the land – is joined by other families, who are accepted as guests. The patriarch of the founding family will have as his role the sharing out of the land, not only within the family but among the various associated families. He is the 'land chief' of the village. Along with him, there is occasionally a 'master of the water', drawn from a family with the appropriate specialisation, who performs similar functions in relation to fishing rights. The first-fruits which he exacts, or the dues to which he is entitled, have at the same time a religious significance (he takes it upon himself to break certain taboos) and the character of a material recompense for the obligations that go with his task. In gold-bearing country there was in the same way a 'master of the gold', to whom nuggets – reputedly of ill omen – were reserved, while the ordinary man had to be content with gold dust.

This system is able to function within an egalitarian and democratic framework, inherited from the 'primitive community'. Thus it will most often be in such a system where agriculture has a low productivity and only supplies an insignificant proportion of income. It was most often found among the populations of the great equatorial forest, where to clear land is extremely arduous, being threatened all the time by the forest reclaiming its own. Agricultural nomadism is frequent, the population being sparse and often scattered in 'encampments', each of which corresponds to a single patriarchal family; this isolation prevents the spread of useful techniques. The characteristics peculiar to plantation agriculture (fruit trees and tubers) make it unnecessary to establish a surplus in reserves which are liable to seizure. It is this which J.-J. Maquet has termed the 'civilisation of clearings'. All the same , it would be incorrect to draw from it a 'geographical determinism' which does not correspond to the factual data. If many foresters are thus effectively at this stage, it is in a forest milieu (at least, originally so) developed by the class societies, states and civilisations of Benin.

On the other hand, this relatively democratic organisation, in every case existing without a state, has been retained by numerous peoples of the savannas, who are often excellent cultivators of cereals. Maquet, to illustrate his 'civilisation of clearings', has taken many examples from the Kissi of so-called 'forest-clad' Guinea, who are remarkable as rice cultivators but who long ago reduced the forest which once covered their region to mere vestiges – the 'sacred groves' where the young undergo their initiation. And what should one say of the numerous Sudanic peoples (those whom the ethnologists christened 'palaeonegritic') – the Koniagi and Bassari on the Senegal–Guinea border, the Dogon of the Bandiagara escarpment, the Lobi of Upper Volta, the Kabre and Somba of Atacora, the 'Kirdi' of North Cameroon, and so on – who have the same characteristics, but are most definitely not forest people?

The development of productivity and the important factor of over-production create the possibility of exploitation and class differentiation, but not in a way which necessarily or automatically follows. A great diversity of circumstances, linked to history, make it possible for old social structures to continue in a great diversity of physical settings. Let us now examine what social differentiations can bring in their wake, even in 'societies without a state'.

As soon as there is over-production, slavery becomes possible. Originally, an enemy who is captured in war and is not immediately slaughtered is brought into the victorious group. Where productivity is weak, there is scarcely any difference between his condition – i.e. his rights and duties – and that of other members of the patriarchal family to which he is attached. He merely brings to the group an additional pair of hands. But if the level of production is adequate, the situation of the 'captive' – to use the traditional African terminology – becomes one of being exploited. He will be given the absolute minimum subsistence necessary to keep body and soul together; all the surplus which he produces by his labour will be confiscated for the benefit of the family collectivity. In concrete terms, the individual plot of land allocated to him will be small, and the number of working days which he can devote to it will be the smallest possible.

Among families, the hierarchy formerly based on the length of one's residence in the village may be duplicated – or even turned upside down – by one based on wealth. Wealth confers prestige in the first instance and from that proceeds power. The classic works of Georges Balandier revealed the role of *bilaba* among the Fang: a sort of coming together for the exchange of wealth between families – closely resembling 'potlatch', so dear to sociologists of the Durkheim school. The kings of Dahomey would originally have founded the pre-eminence of their family on the banquets which they gave for other families – their neighbours and rivals.

Now we return to the level of the patriarchal family, the village and sometimes more extended groupings – leagues with a religious or military character, at first very loosely connected and only manifesting themselves on specific and isolated occasions. Here the land chief or the war chief[13] (functions sometimes combined in one person), whom the established division of labour causes to be the recipient of certain rents,

13. Chosen for his military qualities, but originally having no authority except on the battlefield, and becoming an ordinary cultivator again afterwards.

service charges and preferential shares of booty, would be led to enrich himself and the family of which he was head, then usurp for their own personal benefit the goods of the community; they would thus become exploiters. Exploitation can be collective when it takes the form of tribute paid by one whole people to another on the basis of primacy of occupation or its opposite: rite of conquest.

One can find every means of transition from an egalitarian to a class society. Among the Fang (in Cameroon and Gabon) slavery was apparently unknown at the start of their migration; and among the Massangu of the Chaillu *massif* in Gabon, 'prisoners of war were only spared in order to replace the dead. These slaves were incorporated into families, and were only sold if they proved to be of bad character.'[14] Here we are very close to the primitive community.

Among the Kissi in the forest region of Guinea, there existed neither a state nor chiefs; the village was the highest political unit. But patriarchal slavery was widespread, and some war chiefs, operating for their own personal benefit, wielded a *de facto* authority due to the bands they had set up, the slaves they had captured in raids, and the wealth they had accumulated. In the country of the Anyi and Baule peoples in Ivory Coast, the family and village chiefs were subordinate to a veritable pyramid of chiefs who combined religious and military functions – a hierarchy perhaps inherited from the military organisation which would have been indispensable for the migration which took them from Ashanti country to their present home: chiefs of sub-tribes, chiefs of fractions of tribes and, at the top, the king, chief of the tribe. The king's actual powers, tightly controlled by the council of chiefs, are limited. Here we see the emergence of state power in embryo, notably in its judicial role: it acts as arbitrator in disputes and thus pre-empts the need for private wars and vendettas, but it has no means of enforcing its decisions, which are respected to the extent of the moral authority it wields.

In short, at the stage of development which we have just described, it is the strength of productive forces (based on agriculture and the primary forms of division of labour) which allows over-production to appear. But social organisation, the framework of productive activity, remains the same as that inherited from the preceding period: the patriarchal or village community remains close to the primitive community.

Meanwhile, various forms of social differentiation appear and their development is more or less a function of the state of the productive forces, of environmental conditions, historical circumstances and so

14. H. Deschamps, *Traditions orales et archives au Gabon*, Paris: Berger-Levrault, 1962, p. 47.

on. But the appearance of these internal contradictions has not yet led to the appearance of the state. Tribal or tribal-patriarchal society can be regarded as typifying the transition from the primitive community to the class society.

*Class society.* We thus arrive at what can be precisely termed class societies. Without falling once again into the trap of an excessive geographical determinism, we can be certain that the savanna environment - with its cereal cultivation and the need, imposed by the seasonal rhythm of the climate, for reserves and at the same time facilities for distribution, exchange and the propagation of more advanced techniques to be established - lent itself particularly to the deepening of social antagonisms. Here the surplus of production 'is particularly significant because it can consist of cereals and leguminous plants. [These] can be preserved almost indefinitely, are easy to transport and easy to quantify, and are sufficiently alike to be easily compared, these characteristics allow a source of wealth to be accumulated which is also mobile. Thus the surplus and the producer can easily be separated from one another, and then pass from hand to hand, to become concentrated in a relatively large quantity.'[15]

So we see the appearance of aristocracies and privileged classes (nobles by birth or by function) elevated above the patriarchal families (including slaves) and the villages, which remain the productive organisms and the base of the social edifice. The attributes and way of life of these aristocracies are analogous to those of feudal lords in medieval Europe.

## *Is there an African feudalism?*

Are we concerned here with 'feudal lords'? This is an expression which I have used in quotation marks, adding: 'We can see clearly that this terminology is debatable. But in any case it is hallowed by usage.'[16] Today its use seems incorrect, and we prefer to set it aside without pretence.[17]

A 'feudal mode of production' does exist: marxists and many others agreed on this point, although its exact meaning and limitations are themselves a subject for discussion. The social hierarchy in which it manifests itself is founded on connections between individuals; the hierarchy of land rights inherent in feudalism is concerned with private personal rights. Undoubtedly, Germanic tradition introduced into it certain survivals of family-related collectivity; but Roman law, with

15. Maquet, op. cit., pp. 117–18.
16. *Afrique noire*, I, 2nd edn, p. 101.
17. It was dropped from the German and Japanese editions of *Afrique noire*, I.

the support of the church (interested in eventual benefactions), appropriated it, in the sense that the holder of landed property and fiefs could give up or bequeath them without family collectivity having the power to put any obstacle in his way.[18]

Now, all those who speak of an African 'feudalism' emphasise that they understand the word in an exclusively political way. Maquet expresses the view that in the African context the word applies only to a body of political institutions.[19] We find in other authors, and even in the titles they give to their written works, the same insistence on the political nature of African institutions which they designate 'feudal'.[20]

However, neither the ties of vassalage or patronage, nor even rents or forced labour, describe the true character of feudal production adequately. Engels wrote: 'Certainly serfdom and subjection to forced labour are not a specifically medieval and feudal method of procedure; rather, we find it wherever a conqueror forces the original inhabitants of the land he has acquired to cultivate it for his benefit.'[21]

What effect does exploitation by aristocracies have on the mass of the population? The privileged strata divert to their own profit part of the production and labour of the village people under forms which were originally intended for the common benefit, especially the support of 'specialists' who were land chiefs. The working of family or village collectives as a framework for production does not change; quite simply, the common field or fields become, in part, fields cultivated for the profit of the chief or chiefs, who now regulate exactions in kind (in Africa this is the usual form). To this may be added various rents. The true significance of these was originally religious as much as economic: e.g. the lifting of a taboo, for which the chief who receives the first-fruits takes responsibility, thus opening up rights to cultivation, hunting, gold mining, and so on. However, that significance disappears and becomes exploitation pure and simple.

The religious powers of the chief - his traditional function - serve to disguise the introduction of exploitation. The latter retains the same forms, whether the chief's powers have reached out to neighbouring groups by military means or whether they are based on upstart chiefs of bands setting themselves up by force alongside the 'traditional' chiefs

18. Its only remedy is the right of pre-emption on the basis of lineage. This is sanctified by numerous customs, but it is reserved to the nobility.
19. J.-J. Maquet, 'Research definition of an African feudality', *Journal of African History*, III, 2, 1962, pp. 307–10.
20. J. Lombard, 'La vie politique dans une ancienne société de type féodal: les Bariba du Nord-Dahomey', *Cahiers d'Études africaines*, 1960, pp. 5–45, and Gomkoudougou V. Kaboré, 'Caractère féodal du système politique Mossi', *Cahiers d'Études africaines*, 1962, pp. 609–23.
21. Engels, Letter to Marx, 22 Dec. 1882.

or kings, the direct heirs of the ancient chiefs of the land.

The system of exploitation does not vary in its general principle, whatever the source of the exploiting power. The victims are exploited not as individuals but as members of a collectivity, generally a village: it is the village organisation which becomes the rule in these societies because it is an easy framework for the exaction of tribute, rents and forced labour. The village chief takes it upon himself to distribute the burden among those within his jurisdiction, and has the responsibility, at the same time as the village collectively, of fulfilling the exactions. The heavy burden of the discipline and collective obligations at the heart of the village community, far from being inherited from 'primitive communism', results rather from the integration of the community in a social system which incorporates class exploitation. The colonisers on their own account took over this handy system of exploitation, and made every effort (in which they largely succeeded) to extend it to tribal societies where it had never existed. Thus village and district chiefdoms were instituted in regions which had not known them previously, while at the same time a dispersed population saw itself compulsorily regrouped in villages so as to facilitate tax collection, forced labour and so on (notably in Ivory Coast and equatorial Africa).

All the same, the exploiters - at first, anyway - appear in a collective capacity: the king, even in the more developed states, in effect used only a very small part of his revenue exclusively for personal ends. The main part went to support his family (in the patriarchal sense) - his royal 'house' which possessed the structure of an ordinary patriarchal family though on an enlarged scale. By means of polygamy, the number of 'princes' grew, and sometimes the king entrusted them with public office. But often, as eventual candidates for the throne, these princes had their responsibilities taken from them and bestowed on the intermediate castes in the king's service[22] ('*griots*'[23] and others), or

22. In the societies of the Soninke and Malinke and those, like the Wolofs and the Peuls of Futa-Toro and Futa Jalon, which had been subject to their influence and adopted their 'model' of social organisation - i.e. almost throughout the West African savanna zone - there existed, between free men and slaves, the craftsmen - *griots* (see fn. 23 below), smiths, weavers, shoemakers, woodcarvers and so on. At once despised and feared because of their social powers (the *griots*) or magical ones (the smiths), they constituted endogamous castes, each one a separate social category.
23. The humblest category of *griots* were simply musicians and praise-singers in the service of nobles. A prince had his own personal *griot* who, besides this function, also acted as messenger or intimate adviser and as such could acquire great influence. The highest category was that of 'traditionalists' attached to great princely families, whose function was to recite from memory (in sung poems) the family's historic traditions, and so emphasise their rights and precedence.

indeed royal captives who, as members of the royal house, were given the tasks of collecting royal taxes, governing provinces, and so on. The captives (or adventurers who had ingratiated themselves into the king's retinue) often provided the formations of regular troops.

The machinery of state merged more or less with the 'royal house' and the privileged class (within which numerous gradations appeared, varying according to ethnic group and country) - this is how it appears. When the state assumes a significant size - and here we find again the mechanism which results elsewhere in the formation of a 'fief' - the king grants to his dignitaries all or part of the rents due to him in certain regions and villages. As Chesneaux has pointed out in relation to Asia, one is talking of 'false fiefs'.[24]

However, neither all the aristocratic hierarchies, nor the development of the state, are able to modify the rules concerning land. G. V. Kaboré says of the Mossi aristocracy: 'Their authority was exercised upon men and goods, without reaching landed property itself, which remained the prerogative of the indigenous people.'[25] Although the Mossi aristocracy, heirs of the conquering Dagomba who came from the south around the fourteenth century, had totally assimilated the indigenous population, it was the descendants of the latter, the Ninissi, who provided the land chiefs, and who suffered the misfortune of being deprived of all political power. In that extremely hierarchical society the condition of a 'free' tributary peasant was no longer very different from that of the captive of a patriarchal family who had not been integrated into it. Because the captives were too numerous for such integration to take place, they were quartered over a territory, often their own territory of origin, and organised themselves (or remained organised, as the case might be) in villages on the standard pattern. Undoubtedly they were no longer 'free' men; the master could draw upon their number at will for 'servants'. They keenly resented their inferior social condition, but their way of life was not appreciably different from that of any other village community.

In connection with Futa-Jalon, where the Peuls had subdued and assimilated the former indigenous people to the condition of slavery, Gilbert Vieillard noted: 'The country was divided into fiefs, but it was the people, much more than the land, which was given in fief; the fief did indeed have the tendency to become a territorial entity, but the vassals could not escape from their suzerain, any more than serfs could from their masters, by emigration - which did not cut the hereditary link.'[26] In short, chiefs or kings are never 'owners' of the land, which is

24. J. Chesneaux, op. cit., p. 44.
25. Kaboré, op. cit., p. 615.
26. G. Vieillard, 'Notes sur les Peuls du Fouta-Djalon', *Bulletin de l'I. F. A. N.*, II, 1940, p. 123.

an inalienable collective possession. At the very most, the chief or king, in so far as he embodied traditional attributes of the 'territorial chief', had the *administration* of the land, and by virtue of this, and following customary rules, could mark off the fields which would be cultivated for his profit; he could make grants of disposable land (vacant or conquered), either to establish his claim to it or to exercise his prerogatives as territorial chief there. Thus in Futa-Toro, such prerogatives were exercised by descendants either of those who had first cleared the land, or of associates of the pagan dynasts to whom concessions had been granted, or indeed of the 'Torobe' – contrivers of the Islamic revolution – who established the theocracy of the *almamys* in this region at the end of the eighteenth century. The final partition was carried out at this time by *almamy* Abdul Kader. In the scanty and therefore precious land watered by the flooding of the Senegal river, rents were tied to the land and thus assumed the character of ground rents. But the principle of collective and inalienable property stayed intact.

In the middle Niger delta the paucity of cultivable land, combined with the succession of invasions and the resulting mosaic of ethnic groups, and further combined with the co-existence of sedentary cultivators and semi-nomadic livestock breeders – all these factors have as their end-result an almost inextricable imbroglio of land systems. But the general system remains that of collective and inalienable property.

Nowhere, to my knowledge, does pre-colonial Africa show any example of a land system which allows of private rights, and which one could thus describe as 'feudal'. Perhaps this is not true of the state created by colonisation, where the privileges of chiefdom have been maintained, and at the same time it has been made easy for private landed property to come into existence for the benefit of the chiefly caste. It would be interesting to study the situation in this regard in the country of the Ashanti in Ghana and of the Yoruba in Nigeria, formerly colonised by the British. As for the former French colonies, the preponderant system of agriculture in the savanna countries (cereal cultivation on a slow cycle of rotation) generally formed an obstacle in the way of private landed property becoming consolidated.

However, the situation was not the same in a forest region where plantations were created which did indeed favour the establishment of private landed property. Thus in the forest region of Guinea, thanks to forced labour, the chiefdom was able to establish large coffee plantations, the ownership of which it duly appropriated to itself. The combination of the use of forced labour and the large private estate has the classic characteristics of feudalism, linked here to the colonial system.[27] In Ivory Coast, the same phenomenon enabled the chiefs to

27. These plantations, at least in the Kissi country, were 'nationalised' in 1958 for the benefit of local collectives.

establish large plantations for themselves; but very quickly indigenous manpower, liable to impressment for forced labour, was replaced by a workforce of wage-earners or immigrant share-croppers. But this is no longer feudalism but simply large bourgeois landed property.

In short, after having made use of the expression 'African feudalism', we believe it is necessary to renounce such terminology. The mode of production in traditional Africa was never feudal, and the use of the term in a purely political sense runs the risk of causing confusion.[28]

### *Has Africa known a mode of production based on slavery?*

Nobody, to my knowledge, has developed this thesis, and it should surely be examined. There is no denying the major social significance of slavery in pre-colonial Africa: if the institution had not already been deeply rooted there by the fifteenth century, the European slavers would never have been able to develop the trade by using African middlemen as their suppliers. Above all, the distinction between captive and free man appeared as a fundamental social division.

It was in the form of slavery that the break with primitive egalitarianism first made an unmistakable appearance, even in 'tribal' societies. But the loss of liberty did not mean in any way that the captive had an exact and uniform role in social production. Mostly the 'house captive' was incorporated into the patriarchal family, and took its name as his own; his role in production was not basically different from that of the 'free' young men of the family. When the decline in slavery had grown into a flood, the captives were organised in patriarchal families and in villages, following the customary model. They were more heavily exploited than the rest, but the method of exploitation – deduction of rent in advance or forced labour under the supervision of a 'captive chief' who was no more than the chief of a slave village – was the same.

Great agricultural estates or craft workshops dependent on slave labour were all but unknown in Africa, and their appearance was exceptional. In agriculture we know of only two cases: the kings of Dahomey used captives to work their palm groves in the nineteenth century when the difficulty of conducting slave traffic made it impossible for them to be sold on outside markets; and the Arabs created plantations in Zanzibar and other islands in the Indian Ocean by the same method, also in the nineteenth century. And in certain Sudanic towns there were workshops producing exports destined for North Africa (the leather industry in the Hausa cities, for example), where

28. This is not to say that I agree with certain ethnologists who reject African 'feudal systems' because they deny the existence in Africa of antagonistic classes!

slave labour was used on a large scale. These were late or marginal cases, and never the basis of a mode of production spread over a significant geographical area.

To summarise, the state of being a captive, although widely prevalent in Africa, was essentially a legal category, and implied no well-defined role in production such as could characterise a social class. The basic exploited class was the working peasantry, embracing at the same time 'free' tributaries and captives; while the dominant class was the aggregate of aristocracies - tribal, military and official - which included certain categories of royal captives who held public office. From this viewpoint, we are forced to accept the parallel with the medieval 'serfs' who did not identify themselves at all with the exploited class generally, since they only constituted a fraction of it; indeed, some of them had been able to integrate themselves in the dominant class, as 'knight-serfs' and 'ministerials'.

## *The economic functions of African states*

Marx had been impressed by the importance of the economic role of the state in Asiatic societies: it seemed clear that in Egypt, India and China the need to organise and co-ordinate systems of irrigation helped at an early stage to give the state a particularly robust structure. But, as Chesneaux points out, 'the question of irrigation has certainly not had the universal and permanent importance in Asiatic history that Marx attributes to it.'[29] On this point the thinking of Marx still has to be elucidated; his idea of an Asiatic mode of production was never systematically worked out. Have we never seen as equivalent to eachother, and even confused, the basic content of this idea of mode of production on the one hand, and, on the other, the particular features noted by Marx in Asiatic societies which served as his model for elaborating the idea?[30] I believe that Ferenc Tökei has correctly identified this basic content through its essential contradiction: society distinguished by the Asiatic mode of production 'developed as a class society on the basis of common tribal property'.[31]

We should not forget that the state's economic functions, whatever

29. Chesneaux, op. cit., p. 42.
30. On this subject, Günter Lewin has emphasised that Marx never stated that irrigation was one of the bases of the Asiatic mode of production. Without neglecting the importance of geographical factors, he still did not attribute to them the determining role which belonged to the relations of production (G. Lewin, 'Zu einigen Problemen der "asiatisches Produktionsweise" in der gesellschaftlichen Entwicklung Chinas', *Wissenschaftliche Zeitschrift der Karl-Marx-Universität Leipzig*, 1964, pp. 251–6).
31. Tökei, op. cit., p. 25.

importance they may have been able to assume in certain societies, are never the essential thing. The essential thing is the state's coercive role in overcoming social antagonisms and maintaining the 'social order' based on human exploitation. But those economic functions have been able to contribute to the swift consolidation of a state which, because its social antagonisms had developed only slightly, would therefore have only a somewhat fragile superstructure. In Africa this factor has also come into play, but in a different way. It is commerce, and particularly commerce in gold, which appears to have been the decisive consolidating element in the early states of tropical Africa, about which our information is slight. What do we know of the origins of Ghana, which is mentioned in Arab texts as early as the eighth century? The very word '*Ghana*', the title of a monarch after which the Arab chroniclers named the country, means 'war chief'. In fact it refers to the chief of that kind of tribal confederation, of which African history offers many examples, and which in its origins is not strictly a state. (We know that the kingdom of Ghana corresponded more or less to the population area of the Sarakolle or Soninke ethnic group.) This war chief probably had the attributes of a territorial chief at the same time; but in any case one particular attribute was certainly reserved for him, namely that of 'master of the gold' (*kaya maghan*), one of the titles which African tradition conferred upon him. What was this attribute?

Gold-bearing alluvia are still exploited today in the upper valleys of the Senegal and Niger rivers, in the setting of the patriarchal community. The work is done during the period of the year after the harvest. To start work on a new site requires the same ceremonies as does the start of agricultural work. The family head and, above him, the territorial chief share out the rights. The supreme territorial chief – here *kaya maghan* – was entitled to the nuggets: the biggest, a block of unrefined gold weighing a considerable amount, was attached to the royal throne. The miners contented themselves with gold dust, which was found in much greater quantities than today. In the gold workings of Siguiri the discovery of a nugget is still considered an evil omen which must be exorcised by appropriate ceremonial.[32] Besides the nuggets, the 'master of the gold' probably collected a tithe on the gold dust too – just as the successive sovereigns of these regions have done.

The fact that gold was being exploited presupposes that already to some extent it was being traded: Ghana is first mentioned in Arab writings as the 'land of gold'. What is certain is that contacts with the Arab world gave a great boost to this trade, which had the effect of cementing Ghana's state structures. Arab or Berber merchants came in search of

32. See G. Balandier, *Afrique ambiguë*, Paris: Plon, 1957, p. 73.

gold to the capital Khumbi Saleh, a double town which included both the residence of the king and his household (the royal town) and, at some distance, the commercial town inhabited by Muslim merchants (the king and the local population were pagans). The indigenous traders, ancestors of the present-day *dioulas* (itinerant traders of West Africa), brought the gold to the capital from the mines, which were some distance to the south, and there exchanged it for goods such as salt or copper brought in by the Arab or Berber merchants. On this occasion the king would levy the taxes, of which El Bekri in the eleventh century gave us the schedule. In this connection the 'war chief' had the task of ensuring the security of the transactions.

It was this economic function connected with commerce which seems to have played the decisive role in the founding of most states in black Africa: Mali (which later took over from Ghana), Gao and Kanem-Bornu. We are less well-informed on the Benin states (the Ife civilisation), which left no written records of their development before the fifteenth century, but their works of art in bronze and brass testify to the importance of the trade for which they were the point of contact, since the copper which they used was imported. All these West African states relied visibly on being joined to a tribal confederation, with a king who was also a war chief at its head, and to a market whose security it guaranteed and from which it derived an important part of its revenues. The capital, as we have seen, was both a royal residence and a market-city.

It seems very probable that the East African states on the Indian Ocean littoral (*Zendj* to Arab authors) – we refer here to African states, not the Arab factories on the coast – had an origin similar to that of the West African states. To gold they could add ivory and iron as export products for the Arab world.[33] Must one deduce that the state in Africa owed its appearance to the fact of contact with foreigners? This hypothesis loses force from the existence of the Mossi states, which have sometimes been termed 'feudal' simply because they had an essentially peasant basis, and their regular fighting units were made up of a highly structured military aristocracy, the mounted '*Nakomse*'. Their rise was long believed to date from the tenth century, but the most recent research seems to show that it could not have been much earlier than the fourteenth century.[34] Commerce does not appear to have played any part in their formation.

We do not think that there is any need to look for the reproduction of a model borrowed from Asia in the organisation of East African

33. See Basil Davidson, *Old Africa Rediscovered*.
34. See Yves Person, 'Tradition orale et chronologie', *Cahiers d'Études africaines*, 1962, pp. 462–76.

states;[35] one can only note some superficial points of resemblance which result from a community originating in kingship, which itself derives from the 'territorial chiefdom'. Furthermore, it is clear that African kings were not deified. There were, on the other hand, gods who were conceived in the image of kings, but while in Egypt and elsewhere this process had long since reached its conclusion, it had seldom gone that far in tropical Africa. Most 'gods' (rather, what we incorrectly call gods) do not receive honour comparable to that accorded to kings. . . .

Delafosse had already observed of the Mossi states: 'It appears certain that the Mossi empires were always protected from any influence that was not African, and hence one can deduce that the political institutions which are characteristic of them, and which are found in almost the whole of black Africa, are of indigenous origin.'[36]

### *The role of the state in class exploitation*

Even if the economic functions of the state are not everywhere apparent, are we obliged to believe that the role of the state as an instrument of class exploitation is a decisive element in the Asiatic mode of production? The representatives of the exploiting class exercise their authority in a way that follows from the public functions previously exercised in the name of the collectivity and for its benefit: functions which are religious, economic (in the division of land) and military. The share of the over-production appropriated by the exploiting class was previously paid by way of compensation or wages for tasks carried out in the framework of division of labour. In a famous passage in *Antidühring*,[37] Engels showed the absolutely general nature of this phenomenon. But one must be careful not to confuse public functions with state power. The essence of the state, we must repeat, is the exercise of an authority set above society as a whole to maintain and perpetuate a class domination. Class exploitation had already appeared embryonically in tribal society, without the state existing. At the outset, as Engels noted, it did not at all imply the use of coercion, but rested on 'free consent and custom'.[38] Only when the schism into antagonistic classes has been clearly achieved, and the interests of the dominant class enter into open conflict with those of the masses, does the state appear and become a necessity. From that point onwards, the public functions exercised by the dominant class in the name of the collectivity assume a state character; their exercise contributes to the consolidation of state

35. Question raised by Chesneaux, loc. cit., p. 49.
36. M. Delafosse, *Les Noirs de l'Afrique*, Paris: Payot, 1921, p. 64.
37. F. Engels, *Anti-Dühring*, Moscow, 1978, ch.IV, p. 219.
38. Ibid., p. 199.

power, and to feeding the illusion that this power is wielded for the collective benefit, 'above the level of class' (even when this exercise of power is henceforth diverted into a direction favouring the dominant class).

In short, the state is not the cause of class exploitation; it is its consequence. As an element in the superstructure, we do not believe it could form part of the definition of a mode of production. All the same, we believe that the appearance of the state is significant in the Asiatic mode of production in so far as it reveals how mutually antagonistic classes, in the precise definition of the terms, are constituted. In tribal societies, class antagonisms are only manifested in an embryonic state, and are not yet characteristic of the relations of production. In the 'Asiatic mode of production', a dominant class appears, detached from the work that is directly productive; and at the same time as the state, at this elementary stage of its evolution, makes its appearance, the dominant class – its authority derived from the exercise of public office – becomes effectively identified with the state apparatus. This helps to give the state the appearance of having a role that is out of the ordinary, not in an illusory sense but as a particularly visible and striking phenomenon. Yet this role has resulted from the characteristics of the Asiatic mode of production, not as an element helping to shape them.

## *Is there an African despotism?*

If – as we believe – the state cannot be a determinant of the character of a mode of production, even less susceptible to being so considered is the form in which political power is exercised. The despotism on which Marx insisted in relation to Asiatic societies is not implicit in the mode of production. If by despotism one is to understand an absolute and arbitrary authority, one has no choice but to reject the notion of an 'African despotism'.

The confusion was the work of the colonisers. Their vision was clouded by the pomp and ceremony surrounding African kings, and by their preconceptions concerning 'oriental despotism', and they thus often believed themselves to be dealing with absolute monarchs. 'Very few administrators', wrote Governor Labouret, 'realise how very slight is the power of local chiefs, in spite of their considerable influence. They act towards these auxiliaries as if they were actually despots. . . . This process of command would, at a pinch, succeed with autocrats, of whom there are some in Africa. With individuals who are not, and never have been, tyrants it is doomed to failure.'[39]

39. H. Labouret, *À la recherche d'une politique indigène dans l'ouest africain*, Paris: Eds du Comité de l'Afrique française, 1931, p. 94.

Just as the family head or patriarch is no more than the manager of the family wealth, and is strictly controlled by the adults in the group, so the village chief (by which we understand here a traditional chief, not one imposed by the administration) is also strictly controlled by the assembly of free men and the council of elders (heads of families). And, just as in traditional African kingship, it is the aristocracy – consisting of the royal family, the princely families connected with it and the nobility of office-holders (even if of slave origin) – which uses and closely controls the royal power through oligarchical councils (the council of the royal family, the college of electors, and the council of elders or dignitaries).

As heirs to the religious attributes of the erstwhile land chiefs, the kings have kept their ancient responsibilities and liabilities: if the harvest fails or a military defeat is suffered, they are often judged incompetent and are consequently deposed or sometimes killed. Among the Yoruba, the ritual murder of the king remained the rule: the Alafin of Oyo, the supreme political chief, was submitted to the authority of a council of high office-holders (forming a noble caste) who decided each year whether the Alafin could continue to reign or not. If the decision went against him, he was presented with a parrot's egg, which signified that he must end his life. But this nobility of office-holders (*Oyo Misi*) was itself in a state of dependence in relation to a highly exclusive secret society, the *Ogboni*, which admitted only certain elders (of either sex) who belonged to the tribal aristocracy.[40] The kings were subjected to a multiplicity of prohibitions, the most common being that against seeing or crossing water (a river or the sea) and against eating or talking in public: they communicate with their subjects hidden behind a curtain or screen, often through the medium of a herald who repeats questions and answers.

Despotism or tyranny only appeared late, when military adventurers founded empires of which the state structure was fragile. The essence of the state was not so much the king – whose apparently despotic behaviour mostly reflected his obedience to custom – as the machinery of which he was the chief or the supreme embodiment: the royal house, the court, ministers, the military and administrators. If by despotism one understands the personalisation of state power, that is another thing. With only very rare and insignificant exceptions,[41] no

40. P. Morton-Williams, 'The Yoruba Ogboni cult in Oyo', *Africa*, XXX (Oct. 1960), pp. 362–74.

41. The 'Lebuk republic' of Cape Verde was no more than a confederation of villages which had rejected the authority of the king (the Damel of Cayor). Certain trading towns that were not capital cities (e.g. Djenne and Timbuktu) were constituted on a republican basis at certain times, but were in a position of vassalage or dependence in relation to the neighbouring kingdoms.

great African state has ever been a republic. The very concept of the state is inseparable from the monarchical form.

But is this peculiar to Asia and Africa? To say nothing of the tendency to personalise state power which survives today so tenaciously even in the most advanced countries - was the Middle Ages easily able to conceive of a state without a prince to rule it? It would seem that it was classical antiquity, with its system of slavery, which first isolated the abstract notion of a state - *res publica* - in the form of a city. The Roman empire began its obliteration, and its resurgence had to wait till modern times.

### *The Asiatic mode of production and stagnation*

I shall not dwell on this question, which was dealt with by Maurice Godelier,[42] but be content to observe that the internal contradiction peculiar to the Asiatic mode of production - class exploitation *versus* collective ownership of land - can not be resolved in a progressive direction by itself. Under this system, the sharpening of class exploitation, far from destroying the structures that are based on collective ownership of the land, has the effect of reinforcing those structures: they constitute the framework within which the over-production is creamed off - the essential condition of exploitation. However, evolving within its own limits, class exploitation can lead to the liquidation - temporarily, at least - of the dominant class and its state, and a regression to the tribal-patriarchal stage: this pattern appears to have been reproduced in Africa over and over again. Most often, it will end in replacing an aristocratic structure by another structure, different in form but analogous in content. The 'Islamic revolutions' of the Peuls and the Tukulors in the eighteenth and nineteenth centuries seem to have been of this type. Thus, in the country of the Hausas, the *jihad* of Usman dan Fodio and his Peul and Tukulor followers depended on a rising of exploited captives and peasants against the traditional Hausa aristocracy; but the result was the substitution of a new aristocracy of Peuls and Muslims for this ancient tribal aristocracy.[43]

Within the system, but marginal to its fundamental contradiction, the development of the private fortune - of which commerce is the main constituent - tends generally to make this contradiction explode by suppressing one of its two elements, namely by the dissolution of collective ownership of the land and the conversion of land into a saleable commodity. If this development does not come to pass, the alternative result is effective stagnation, or arrival at an impasse. (It would

42. M. Godelier, op. cit., pp. 31-4.
43. D. A. Olderogge, *Zapadnay Sudan v XIX vv. Ocherk po istorii i kul'turui*, Leningrad, 1960.

be interesting to know whether ancient Egyptian society could show such an example.) In Marx's view, the economic self-sufficiency of Indian village communities caused the changeless nature of Asiatic societies.[44] It remains to be discovered whether that self-sufficiency was as genuine as Marx believed it to be.

It seems to me that in Africa this apparently cyclical evolution contained an element of progressive modifications, which led cumulatively to qualitative changes: here obstacles were created by factors of history (trade, leading to a sharpening of social contradictions, but based on a regression rather than a development of productive forces) and of geography (low population density and an abundance of disposable land).

As to Asia and pre-Columbian America, it would be fitting to examine whether the significance of changes in the political system is strictly limited to the political sphere or whether they become transformed into deeper changes. Perhaps this examination could lead to the characterisation of several levels or several types within the Asiatic mode of production.

I continue to believe that the fundamental structure of the Asiatic mode of production is of a system of production based on the rural community, which owns the land collectively to the exclusion of any form of private property, co-existing with human exploitation - exploitation which can be very varied in form, but which always operates through the community. Thus defined, the notion of 'Asiatic mode of production' - a form of words clearly in need of revision - takes on a universal value applicable to a stage of development through which the majority of human societies have passed, and of which pre-colonial Africa offers us examples spread over much of its territory.

But this very general notion embraces numerous variants - in the different forms taken by human exploitation, by the development of antagonistic classes, and by the functions assigned to the state and the degree of perfection attained by the state's machinery. In this sense, the Asiatic societies to which Marx referred constitute one variant of this mode of production, while the African societies which have reached the stage of development described above constitute another. Studies devoted to other parts of the world and other periods of history could show us if there are yet other variants - something I regard as highly probable.

44. K. Marx, *Kapital*, Moscow, 1983, vol I, bk. 2, p. 318.

# 2

# THE SOCIAL AND HISTORICAL SIGNIFICANCE OF THE PEUL HEGEMONIES IN THE SEVENTEENTH, EIGHTEENTH AND NINETEENTH CENTURIES[1]

## *The Black African state in the sixteenth and seventeenth centuries*

The sixteenth century marks an important break in the history of Black Africa. The Middle Ages had seen the blossoming of an original civilisation. On the decayed foundations of the primitive community, which had reached a more or less advanced stage, there began to develop class opposition; slavery (in its patriarchal form); the formation of an aristocracy from the 'chiefdom' - in other words, members of the village community with specialised functions of an economic, religious and military nature (respectively territorial and war chiefs);[2] and the appearance of towns (Timbuktu, Djenne, the Hausa cities, the cities of Benin) with a notable development of commercial activity but not using money. (As money equivalents, cowries[3] and a variety of merchandise were used - pieces of woven cotton, wrought-iron bars, blocks of salt, measures of millet, livestock or slaves; there was no general standard of money equivalence.)

There are striking similarities between the economic and social formations of the Germanic peoples at the time of the invasions, and those of the Greeks of the archaic period (before the sixth century BC). However, Africa showed notable differences in the elements influencing the form of the productive forces. First, the use of the wheel either for transportation or for irrigation was unknown, although wheeled vehicles criss-crossed the Sahara well before the Christian era. Secondly, agriculture - generally extensive, but also at times intensive - only utilised various forms of hoe and not the plough, which moreover was ill-suited to the special climatic and soil conditions of tropical Africa. And thirdly, agriculture and livestock-breeding

1. The original version of this chapter appeared in German with the title 'Zur historischen und sozialen Bedeutung der Fulbe-Hegemonie (XVII-XIX Jahrhundert)' in *Studien zur Kolonialgeschichte und Geschichte der nationalen Befreiungsbewegung*, vol. 2, Berlin (East), 1960, pp. 25-9. A corrected and updated French version was published in *Cahiers du C.E.R.M.*, 1964.
2. One can compare the most advanced African societies of that time with those in Asia which Marx studied and took as his model for the 'Asiatic mode of production'.
3. Shells found in abundance in the Indian Ocean.

remained on the whole separate, suited to different ethnic groups.[4]

It was within this economic framework that the first great states of black Africa developed: Ghana (4th[?]-13th cent.), Mali (13th-15th cent.), the Songhai empire of Gao (15th-16th cent.), and the cities of Benin which appear to have reached their apogee in the thirteenth and fourteenth centuries.

The African upswing was to be brought brutally to a halt, directly and indirectly, by the transformations which were affecting Western Europe. First there was the development of the trade in slaves destined for the American colonies, the role of which in the accumulation of capital in Western Europe is well known. Africa's destiny as a 'commerical reserve for the hunting of people with black skins'[5] was not finally sealed till the end of the sixteenth century. The Portuguese, who had sighted the coast during the fifteenth century, had at first wanted to procure gold and spices, and with this in view had penetrated the continent very early; even at the end of the sixteenth century, some adventurers still hoped to create another Brazil in Africa.[6]

Although the question of why Africa's development took the course it did has never been satisfactorily answered, some reasons suggest themselves: the high density of population, the existence of societies at a sufficiently advanced stage of evolution to have, at times, an embryonic state organisation, but still close enough to the primitive community for tribal institutions to give it a considerable power to resist intruders, even those with firearms - these circumstances put obstacles in the way of the populations being enslaved or exterminated by a handful of *conquistadores*. Evidence of this is the fact that Portuguese attempts to set about exploiting the gold seams in the interior (Bambouk and Boure) or organise production of pepper (Guinean pepper or *malaguette;* once thought to be of inferior quality) were checked. On the other hand, the existence of relations with the character of slavery, and of an agricultural technique that was both advanced and well adapted to tropical conditions, indicated an ideal source for the supply of labour to replace the exterminated populations of the Caribbean and Brazil, whose more rudimentary state of social evolution and lack both of slavery and of habits of agricultural work corresponding to the needs of the colonisers would have excluded the possibility of their being utilised in this way.

The slave trade paralysed the development of productive forces in

4. Among exceptions are the Serer of Senegal, who combined agriculture with livestock rearing. But this combination was only manifested in the use of manure in cultivation, not by the use of draught animals in agricultural work.
5. Marx, *Kapital*, Moscow, 1983, vol. 1,bk. 1, ch. 31, p. 702.
6. 'L'Afrique noire entre hier et aujourd'hui' (colloquium), *Annales: Économies, Sociétés, Civilisations*, 1958, no. 1, pp. 64-6.

black Africa, first by the demographic blood-letting and the enormous loss of productive manpower that resulted from it.
According to W. E. B. DuBois, the loss amounted to 100 million in less than four centuries, comprising on the whole the youngest and most vigorous elements;[7] J. D. Fage more conservatively puts the number at 30–40 million.[8] Having remained static since the seventeenth century, the population of Africa, which had then probably represented one-fifth of the world total, did not represent even one-thirteenth by the nineteenth century. But the trade was pernicious above all because of its economic and indirect social consequences.

In exchange for slaves, Europe gave Africa nothing but shoddy trade goods of a derisory value, adulterated alcohol, and firearms and gunpowder – these last, ironically, were to intensify the hunt for slaves. Confining themselves to the role of intermediaries, the slavers made the Africans themselves their suppliers, and thus the agents of their own ruin: the most lucrative occupation ceased to be productive activity but became instead the war to gain possession of slaves for trade, with its train of material and human destruction.[9]

It was above all the littoral (the Gulf of Guinea, the Congo and Angola) and its immediate hinterland that felt the evil consequences of the European trade. The Sahel and Sudanic regions only suffered attenuated effects, but they nonetheless suffered, if by a less direct route, the negative results of the great transformations in the Western world and the Mediterranean in the fifteenth and sixteenth centuries.

The great Sudanic empires of Ghana, Mali, Songhai and Bornu were created through the beneficial effect of commercial and intellectual relations with the Arab world. In exchange for gold and ivory, the Sudan received salt from Teghazza in the Sahara and, above all, merchandise produced by the Arabs – textiles, handicrafts, manuscripts.[10] This brought about the prosperity of urban centres such

7. W. E. B. DuBois, *The Negro*, London, 1915, p. 156.
8. J. D. Fage, *Introduction to the History of West Africa*, Cambridge, 1955, pp. 82–7. More recent publications have estimated the number of individuals transported to the Americas at 9–10 million, thus going back to the figure proposed by the Abbé Raynal at the end of the eighteenth century. If one takes account of the losses caused directly or indirectly by the trade (those killed in slave raids, or dying *en route*, either overland or on the sea voyages), this figure can be multiplied several times. This agrees with Fage's estimate of the cumulative population loss.
9. From the point of view of the productive forces, the connection with America was not without certain positive results. It led to the introduction of new and more productive plants for cultivation in Africa – e.g. maize, manioc and groundnuts. However, this was only a diversification of the species raised, or the replacement by more productive plants of local varieties which were then abandoned. It was not a 'revolution' in the productive forces capable of offsetting the effects of the trade.
10. Leo Africanus, in the sixteenth century, noted that in Timbuktu handwritten books from Barbary [the Maghreb] were sold – at a greater profit to the merchants than other goods.

as Timbuktu and Djenne. Relations with the Arab world were secured *via* two major routes. In the west, from the Niger and Senegal rivers, caravans reached the salt mines of Teghazza and ended at Sidjilmasa (in the Tafilalet, southern Morocco), from which the gold reached the Maghreb and Spain. In the east, from Gao or Bornu, various routes reached the coast of Tripolitania and thence Tunisia and, most important of all, Egypt.

The seventeenth century was to complete the ruin of these arteries of exchange. In Morocco, as throughout North Africa, the end of the Middle Ages was marked by the decline of urban, mercantile civilisation. The resulting decay encouraged attacks by the Portuguese and Spaniards who, after the reconquest of their own lands by the Arabs, went on to the offensive in North Africa and established themselves there. As masters of the Moroccan littoral, the Portuguese took the place of the caravan drivers as intermediaries between northern and black Africa, going by the sea route to Cape Verde and beyond to sell merchandise once imported from the Maghreb. This diversion of the traditional commercial circuit made itself felt also in an inverse sense: the establishment of the fortress of Elmina on the Gold Coast attracted away from the Arab world, if not all the gold of the Sudanic region, then at least that of the southern mines.[11]

In North Africa this Christian attack provoked a popular reaction and a reawakening of Islam, but this form of Islam was not that of the town-dwellers and merchants but a feudal and rural form, of religious brotherhoods, *marabouts* and feudal warriors. In Morocco the movement resulted in the overthrow of the Merinids; the Saad dynasty (a Sherifian one, i.e. claiming descent from the Prophet) replaced them and drove out the invaders. However, Sidjilmasa was destroyed, and Morocco was isolated by a blockade mounted by both the Christians and the Turks. It was undoubtedly to replenish a stream that was drying up that the new ruler of Morocco sought to lay his hands on the sources of Sudanic gold. Sultan Moulay Ahmad Al Mansur (known as El-Dehebi, 'the golden'[12]) first tried to seize the salt-pans of Teghazza, a dependency of the Songhai empire, and then sent a formation of 1,000 Spanish turncoats, armed with muskets, who seized Timbuktu, Gao and Djenne, and destroyed the Songhai empire in 1591.

11. See F. Braudel, 'Monnaies et civilisations. De l'or du Soudan à l'argent de l'Amérique', *Annales, Économies, Sociétés, Civilisations,* 1946, 1, pp. 9–22, and *La Méditerranée et le monde méditerranéen à l'époque de Philippe II,* Paris, A. Colin, 1949, pp. 364–9. Also R. Ricard, *Études sur l'histoire des Portugais au Maroc*, University of Coimbra, 1955.

12. 'Probably the proverbial riches of the Sudan never attained the value of the Portuguese ransoms, which earned Al Mansur the title of "golden".' See C. A. Julien, *Histoire de l'Afrique du Nord*, Paris, 1951, vol. II, p. 215.

The Spanish-Moroccans were not able, any more than the Portuguese, to lay hands on the gold mines – they were too far away. Their descendants confined themselves to making frequent raids throughout the Niger valley. The principal effect of this was to complete the ruin of the Saharan trade (in the eighteenth century a large caravan left Morocco for Timbuktu only once every two or three years[13]), traffic in slaves constituting a large proportion of what remained.

The routes of the central Sahara, terminating in Tripoli, were less frequented; but there too the traffic dwindled and partly changed its character. Tripoli was no more than a staging-post on the way to Egypt. The Portuguese, after destroying the maritime ascendancy of the Arabs in the Indian Ocean, went on to destroy the Egyptian fleet in 1509, and blocked access to the Red Sea and the Persian Gulf. Egypt, deposed from its role of commercial intermediary between the Christian West on the one hand and India and the Far East on the other, fell eight years later to the Turks. The latter would now guarantee the defence of Islam, under threat from the Christians, as far as the Maghreb: Barbary pirates from the Aegean seized Algiers in 1516 and linked their destiny to that of the Ottoman empire. The Turks occupied Tripoli in 1551 and Tunis in 1574. Over the Arab world, a vast area of commercial exchange, a feudal empire was installed where commerce languished and was largely in foreign hands. Here again, slave traffic took first place, and in addition supplied concubines and eunuchs to the Ottoman harems.[14]

Thus the dilapidation of the commerce of Egypt and the Maghreb – originally due to internal causes (ossification and feudalisation of the Islamic world) but hastened by the attacks of the Europeans – had repercussions on the commerce of the Sudanic region, which lived solely by its relations with the Arabs. The urban centres like Timbuktu were weakened. Hence the great empires of the old type disappeared. These had been associated with urban markets and been supported by Islam, deriving their resources from taxes on trade and tribute from their vassals. They had been relatively stable;

13. Cf. Marcel Emerit, 'Les liaisons terrestres entre le Soudan et l'Afrique du Nord au XVIIIe et au début du XIXe siècle', *Travaux de l'Institut de Recherches sahariennes*, Algiers, 1954, vol. IX, pp. 29–47.

14. It still needs to be noted that this traffic never had the importance of the European slave trade, contrary to the opinion of many bourgeois historians, who would like the responsibility for the latter shared with the Turks and thus attenuated. But the Turkish trade existed only to provide a domestic slavery, not a productive one. The trade towards the East did not grow to an appreciable size till the nineteenth century, when it served to supply a plantation economy on the East African coast, for the profit of Arab navigators, who had resumed the position from which the Portuguese had once ousted them.

Ghana and Mali were in existence for centuries, and were capable of maintaining order in the interior,[15] probably due to the survival of ethnic institutions and military democracy.

Islam was in retreat, parallel to the towns losing their influence and an upsurge of new states that were essentially peasant and pagan (while Mali and Songhai drew their support from the towns and from Islam). The Mossi kingdoms and the Dogon and Gourmantche revived and stepped up their attacks on the Niger valley. At the same time the Serer, who had been driven back into the south of Senegal, freed themselves. In the middle of the sixteenth century the Peul chief Koli, with an army of Peul and Malinke followers, seized Tekrur and there set up a state ruled by the pagan Peul dynasty of the Denianke. Mahmudu II, the '*mansa*'[16] of Mali, appealed in vain to the Portuguese to suppress it. Already penetrated in the north-west, what was left of Mali was also in retreat in the north-east. With the collapse of the Songhai empire, it hoped at first for a re-conquest, and with the help of the Peuls of Macina, the '*mansa*' Mahmudu III tried to recapture Djenne: it was the firearms of the Spanish-Moroccan pasha of Timbuktu that stopped him in 1599.

About 1660 the Bambara peasants, a branch of the Malinke people who had been the bedrock of the Mali empire, rebelled and formed the rival kingdoms of Segu and Kaarta (Nioro), both fiercely pagan. Biton Coulibali, who created the Segu kingdom, raised a professional army of slaves, with corps of engineers and a flotilla to deploy on the Niger, consisting of Somono fishermen. In 1670 he finally drove Mali back to the upper Niger (the Keita, descendants and heirs of the '*mansas*' of Mali, withdrew to the village of Kangaba, where they continued to maintain themselves right up to our time, but in the reduced role of petty local princes). He then extended his authority to Djenne and imposed his overlordship to Macina and Timbuktu where the '*Arma*' aristocracy, descendants of the Spanish-Moroccans of Songhai who had become completely or partly negrified,[17] were reduced to paying him tribute as they already did to the Tuaregs. After Biton Coulibali, the Diara dynasty, installed in 1750, maintained the power of the Segu kingdom. The Hausa cities profited from the collapse of the Songhai empire around 1600 to shake off the tutelage of the king of Kebbi,

15. Ibn Battuta praised the security of Mali in the fourteenth century: 'Throughout the length and breadth of the country, a perfect security prevailed; one could live there and travel about without fear of theft or depredation.'
16. *Mansa* was the title borne by the monarchs in the Mali empire, and which is borne by kings in the Malinke country generally.
17. Nominated at first by the Sultan of Morocco but in fact independent, the Pashas of Timbuktu were, from 1612 to 1660, elected by their soldiers. The '*Arma*' aristocracy soon ceased to speak Spanish and adopted the Songhai language.

reject the interference of Bornu in their affairs, and so restore their independence.[18]

The period which began with the sixteenth century did not only show symptoms of regression, although these certainly predominated. It also saw the appearance of a new type of state, with a standing army as its nucleus.[19] These states obtained a growing proportion of their resources from raiding and hunting for slaves, and they imposed tribute on their subjects and vassals which became ever more burdensome and was often levied by military means. It was an unstable and in some ways a barbaric form of state, but it was, in a word, more advanced than its predecessors. The Bambara state of Segu was one example and the old state of Bornu, by adapting to new conditions, was another. The king of Bornu, Idris III (1571–1603) managed, with firearms obtained from Tripoli, to raise a battalion of slave musketeers. With this help, he was able to extend the boundaries of his state so that it covered a greater area than ever before in its history: for a time it covered the entire shore of Lake Chad, Kano in the west, the Aîr massif, and the desert as far as Fezzan. After his time, however, ties with the tributaries slackened. It was on similar foundations that the states of the central Sudan – Bagirmi, Wadai and Darfur – were consolidated at the beginning of the seventeenth century.

How is one to explain this evolution? If urban activity – especially that of the old traditional centres – was in jeopardy, the extension of trade – European and Muslim – brought about a development of commercial relations, which indeed had a special character: in the absence of any monetary equivalent, the slave served increasingly as the unit of account, along with the head of cattle, the block of salt, and cowries. European goods were imported on an increasing scale, both through European trade warehouses and through the instrumentality of the Ottoman empire.[20] As the result, the process of social differentia-

18. From this point on, we will leave out of consideration the forest and littoral regions, whose evolution shows some original features. One was a decline of the old civilisation and ancient states (the cities of Benin and the Congo kingdom; another was the establishment in the eighteenth century of the animist warrior kingdoms of Ashanti and Dahomey, which preserved in their organisation many strongly pagan features. The latter of these was evidently connected with the development of trading on the coast by European concerns.
19. Such an institution had appeared from the end of the fifteenth century in the Songhai empire under Askia Mohamed, former lieutenant to the usurper of the throne, Sonni Ali (1493–1529). Up till then, the emperors of Gao, like the rulers of Ghana and Mali before them, had resorted to levying their free subjects in order to make war. Askia Mohamed created for the first time a professional army made up of slaves and prisoners-of-war, units of which, distributed throughout the empire, fulfilled the role of police, backed up by a flotilla on the Niger.
20. It was through the Ottoman empire that the first money came to be introduced into Africa at the end of the eighteenth century. This was the silver Maria Theresa dollar.

tion into opposed classes continued to deepen, and spread more widely. The dissolution of the tribal organisation of the society was speeded up. But the basis for this was a decline in productive forces, where the social differentiation merely redoubled the misery of the masses and was anything but a way forward.[21]

### *The origin and ethnic characteristics of the Peuls*

From the eighteenth century onwards, the states ruled by the Peuls played a leading economic and social role. We have already seen them make an appearance with the state of the Denianke, but their role there was only temporary and they became involved in an animist counter-attack; in effect they established the overlordship of a pagan dynasty in Futa-Toro, where Islam had put down deep roots, perhaps since the time of the Almoravids. However, the Peul states of the eighteenth and nineteenth centuries were champions and propagators of Islam. They form a distinct phase in the history of black Africa, even if their movements in the sixteenth and seventeenth centuries had prepared the way for it.

In order to clarify the conditions for this transition to a new stage, we have to recall briefly what we know of the origin and ethnic character of the Peuls. The subject has spawned a vast literature of variable worth, in which an overheated imagination has sometimes supplied the deficiencies of hard information. It is true that the subject excites the imagination particularly because the Peuls occupy a special and undoubtedly unique place in West African ethnography. They call themselves *poullo*, pl. *Fulbe* (other West African peoples use a variety of such denominations: Fullâni for the Moors, Afuli for the Tuareg, Fula for the Malinke, Tsilmigo [pl. Silmisse] for the Mossi, and so on). The area they inhabit is not clearly defined; they are to be found from Cape Verde to Chad and the borders of Ubangi-Chari, from the desert to the edge of the equatorial region (Ilorin in Nigeria). All those who speak their language or are integrated into their economy number about 4.5 million people.

The principal reason for this dispersion is their economic specialisation. The Peuls are (or were originally) pastoralists who raise cattle. The zone which is best suited to their activity and which forms the axis of their homeland is the Sahel. Here and there they almost reach the desert itself and thus acquire pastureland to which they have access during the rainy season; but here they are at the limit of what they can

21. We should note in passing that this process remained relatively gentle and limited in scope. It was left for the imperialist colonisation of that time to accentuate and deepen it so that it assumed considerable proportions.

achieve by husbandry, and run up against the pastoralists of the Sahara (Moors and Tuaregs). To the south, they are able to penetrate deeply into the Sudanic zone to which, as a rule, they come back in the dry season - but for this they need the compliance of the sedentary cultivators, the masters of the soil. But beyond this, at the approach to the forest zone, the tse-tse fly[22] bars the way. As nomads, they are not strictly on home ground anywhere, except where they have established themselves by conquest and become sedentarised. They do not form a solid homogeneous population anywhere, and co-exist with other peoples.

Are the Peuls a race or racial type apart?[23] If by Peuls we mean the 4.5 million people mentioned above, most of whom have long been intermingled with the people among whom they co-exist, certainly the majority have no physical characteristics that distinguish them from other black people. If, however, we consider the most 'pure' groups, who have remained faithful to their primitive social organisation, there is indeed a dominant physical type which sets them somewhat apart from other blacks in West Africa ('plainsmen' and 'forest-dwellers'). The most prominent traits would be a slightly above-average height (169-171 cm.), a marked dolichocephaly (long head), long legs, a coppery-brown skin colour, absence of prognathism, a narrow and sometimes aquiline nose, black but always wool-like hair, and very poor dentition with a high incidence of tooth decay.

This racial type is not unique - it is also found, with some differences, in East Africa (the Ethiopian type) - and is one of several variants of the African negro race. It displays similarities with the morphological traits of the white race - hence the hypothesis that it has resulted from an ancient and very thorough intermingling between black and white; however, this is not proved, and in any case its essential morphological traits enable it to be considered a variant of the black race.[24]

22. Carrier of trypanosomiasis (sleeping sickness). However, the barrier was not as impenetrable as was sometimes supposed; the Peuls broke through it on occasions, even if it meant abandoning the zebu in favour of the Guinean ox (*ndama*).
23. In 1978 I commented on the above: 'Today I would not use the terms "race" and "racial" to designate these physical types, which are nonetheless impossible to define precisely. The progress of biology in the past twenty years has definitely shown up the impropriety of the term "human races".'
24. H. Vallois (*Les races humaines*, Paris, 1944) considered that a 'primitive stock' existed there, 'which is not clearly differentiated, either in a black or in a white direction. This would explain why the general Ethiopian type is so different from the Mulatto type. Crossing of blood was only a secondary occurrence.' It is generally agreed that the Ethiopian sub-race should be regarded as one of the variants of the black race, with which it shares at least one element: skin-colour.

This fact, together with the colonialist mentality to which the natural inferiority of the black race was a fact admitting of no argument, explains how what J. Richard-Molard has justly called 'fantastic lucubrations'[25] have developed concerning the origin of the Peuls. It is not difficult to grasp how these arose. In so far as these shepherds formed a dominant aristocracy in certain regions (not in all, as we shall see), the way was clear for racists to ascribe reason to an imagined 'white origin' - however black they might have become subsequently - in the style of *nachgedunkelte Aryer* (Aryans who were black after the event) of the late Dr Goebbels.

But where did these imagined whites come from? Some traditions hold that they came from the east (these traditions are found among all the peoples of West Africa, and their historical or mythical truth has never been established). As we shall see further on, this could possibly be the recollection of a genuine migration. But it is much more likely to reflect the normal preoccupation of Islamised peoples to attribute to themselves ancestors of Arab origin. The over-excited imagination of our authors then made them descendants of the ancient Egyptians, brought there in a long migration, or Hyksos, or indeed Israelite shepherds. . . . None of this has any foundation, any more than the still widespread idea which would make the Peuls, with the Mauritanians, the Tuaregs and the Ethiopians, a branch of the supposed 'Hamite' race. This concept of a Hamite race is a monstrosity, of the same ilk as the 'Aryan' race of the Nazi theoreticians. It confuses - in a way which permits any sophistry - notions of race which are radically different from the only useful sense of the word (i.e. the biological sense) and notions of language and civilisation (social order). If the term 'Hamitic' has a meaning, it is simply that of a family of languages covering the greater part of North Africa, especially that part inhabited by whites, but without the linguistic boundaries always coinciding with those between races. Today, linguists are inclined to reject this term in favour of 'Hamito-Semitic', a linguistic totality embracing several groups - the Semitic, ancient Egyptian, Berber and Cushitic.[26] The American specialist J. Greenberg[27] proposes the addition of a fifth group, the Chadic, including Hausa and the languages related to it (Kotoko etc.).[28]

25. J. Richard-Molard, *Afrique occidentale française*, Paris: Berger-Levrault, 1956, p. 97.
26. See M. Cohen, *Les resultats acquis de la grammaire comparée chamito-semitique* (lectures at the Institute of Linguistics of the University of Paris, 1933), Paris, 1934, and 'Langues hamito-sémitiques et linguistique historique', *Scientia*, 6th series, 86 (1951), pp. 304–10.
27. J. Greenberg, 'Étude sur la classification des langues africaines', *Bulletin de l'I.F.A.N.*, series B, XVI (1954), pp. 83–142, and XVII (1955), pp. 59–108.
28. The question was raised by Marcel Cohen and other specialists, but without their believing it possible to settle it once and for all.

They have also tried to amalgamate with the so-called Hamitic race not only the whites of North Africa (most of whom now speak Arabic), who from an anthropological viewpoint link up with the Mediterranean sub-race which through other causes occupies parts of Southern Europe, but also the blacks of the Ethiopian sub-race, some of whom undoubtedly speak Cushitic dialects while others speak Semitic dialects (Arabic in Chad and Amharic in Ethiopia) and yet others, like the Peuls, speak a language related to those of the West African peoples - and all the while the Hausas, who are black (but not of the Ethiopian type), speak a language which integrates with the Hamito-Semitic family. . . . One thus sees the inextricable muddle when biology (racial in the only accurate and admissible sense of the term) is confused with linguistics and sociology.

It is true that laborious attempts have been made to link the Peul language - and thence the whole gamut of black African languages - to ancient Egyptian. The most notorious such attempt was made in the early 1940s by Homburger,[29] and more recently the same author has pressed the hypothesis still further in seeking to make the black-African languages derive, through ancient Egyptian, from the Dravidian languages of India, corresponding to the area covered by the civilisation of Mohenjo-Daro.[30] Unfortunately Homburger is a specialist in neither Hamito-Semitic nor Dravidian languages, and the greatest authority in Hamito-Semitic comparative linguistics, Marcel Cohen, discounts this thesis completely.[31] It is even more disturbing to find Homburger reinforcing these linguistic arguments by invoking 'the traditions which point to the Sahara or Egypt as the cradle of the rulers who gave to the ancestors of the blacks of today their present culture [*sic*]'.[32] The colonialist mentality pointed out above (the idea that the blacks of Africa suffer from a congenital incapacity) is all too visible here, even if it is not completely conscious. One can only agree with the Marquis de Tressan, that 'these essays of Homburger have unconsciously held back the understanding of Africa.'[33]

29. L. Homburger, *Les langues négro-africaines*, Paris, 1941.
30. L. Homburger, 'L'Inde et l'Afrique', *Journal de la Société des africanistes*, XXV (1955), pp. 13-18, and *La langue et les langages*, Paris: Payot, 1951. We should be aware in this connection that we have absolutely no *knowledge* (whatever the probabilities) of whether the founders of the Mohenjo-Daro civilisation spoke a Dravidian language. . . .
31. M. Cohen, in 'Compte rendu des "langues négro-africaines" ', *Journal Asiatique*, 1943-5, pp. 382-7, notes particularly that Meroïtic is not an altered form of ancient Egyptian (this being one of the elements of Homburger's 'demonstration') but a Cushitic language.
32. L. Homburger, *Les langues négro-africaines*, p. 337.
33. M. de la Vergne de Tressan, 'Du langage descriptif en Peul', *Bulletin de l'I.F.A.N.*, XV, 2 (1952), pp. 636-59.

The Senegalese historian Sheikh Anta Diop has taken up this thesis again to apply to comparisons between the Egyptian and Wolof vocabularies.[34] Hitherto linguists have remained unconvinced by these comparisons; they are based on a vocalisation of ancient Egyptian which is open to dispute since ancient Egyptian had no notation of vowels, which means that we are ignorant of their exact value. For the rest, the most recent scholarship leads to the placing of the Peul language in the black African family of languages; Greenberg integrates it with the vast Nigero-Congolese family, which embraces most of the languages of black Africa. Its relationship to Serer and Wolof seem well established, and it seems admissible that Peul, together with those and several other languages, constitutes a 'Senegalo-Guinean' group, centred in the far west; Peul shows a very marked archaism.[35]

The only concrete evidence supporting the theory of the Peuls' eastern origins is archaeological, provided by the cave drawings of the Sahara. The cattle herdsmen represented in these drawings have numerous similarities with the Peuls of historical times; the physical type shown in silhouette, hair dressed in the form of a crest or in tresses and a bun, hemispheric huts, style of life etc. These drawings enable one to reconstruct an itinerary from the Nilotic region as far as Hodh, passing to the north of Tibesti, eastern Tassili, Hoggar and Adrar des Iforas – in a time when the Sahara still offered sufficient pasturage. The population movements of which we see a trace here took place, at the earliest, in the sixth or fifth millennium BC. Their occupation of the Sahara seems to have lasted until the time of the early Egyptian empire. It is highly probable that these 'cattle herdsmen' were the forebears of the Peuls, although a number of obscure points remain. (E.g., why had the 'historical' Peuls lost every trace of their ancestors' tradition of cave art?)[36]

After a considerable interval, historical tradition shows us the Peuls, before the sixteenth century, living as nomads in the Termes (Hodh region), today semi-desert but once the heartland of the Ghana empire. In this region (Mauritanian Adrar, Trarza and Hodh), they co-existed with the nomadic Sanhadja nomads (ancestors of the now

34. Sheikh Anta Diop, *Nations nègres et culture*, Paris, 1955, and 'Histoire primitive de l'Humanité. Evolution du monde noir', *Bulletin de l'I.F.A.N.*, XXIV, 3–4 (1962).

35. M. de la Vergne de Tressan, *Inventaire linguistique de l'A.O.F. et du Togo*, Dakar, Mémoires de l'I.F.A.N., 30, 1953.

36. Cf. Henri Breuil, *Les roches peintes du Tassili-n-Ajjer* (Pan-African Congress of Prehistory, Algiers, 1952), Paris, 1955, – . 65–220; Henri Lhote, 'L'extraordinaire aventure des Peuls', *Présence Africaine*, XXII, Oct.–Nov. 1958, pp. 48–57, and, by the same author, *A la découverte des fresques du Tassili*, Paris, 1958. A clear synthesis of existing knowledge on the question can be found in R. Cornevin, *Histoire de l'Afrique*, I, Paris, 1962, pp. 49–50, with an original map of the probable migrations (p. 45). This author also notes wisely that 'the cave art of the Western Sahara enables us to presume, but not be certain, that this was the prehistoric route of the herders of bovidae towards Futa-Toro' (p. 50).

arabised Moors and authors of the Almoravid conquest of Morocco and Spain at the end of the eleventh and beginning of the twelfth centuries) but also with black agriculturalists, the Bafur, from whom, through differentiation and migration, the principal ethnic groups of the eastern Sudan are descended (the Wolof and Serer, the Sarakole, and the Manding and Bambara).

The linguistic relationship of the Peul language with Wolof and Serer gives some force to the hypothesis whereby the Peul, like the 'Bafur' with whom they co-existed, spread out from this region of the Western Sahara towards the west, south and east and thence, borrowing the savannas and steppes for the purpose, as far as Adamawa and Chad. In the view of J. Richard-Molard, this theory could well stem from an illusion: it was the French who, having made the acquaintance in Senegal of the 'Har Pular' (speakers of Pular, the Peul language), went from there to Chad, met the 'Har Pular' again throughout their route, and attributed to them historically the same itinerary as they had followed themselves.[37] Richard-Molard's opinion comes up against a fundamental objection: the thesis of a migration from west to east is not an invention of French colonisers, but was formulated by travellers of the preceding period such as Clapperton[38] and Barth[39] following information obtained on the spot.

It will still be objected that the Peuls appear in history travelling from west to east, which confirms the theory of the migration; it is true that wherever the Peuls appear in history, they were already well established, even if they were later reinforced by migrations from the west. But from this one may conclude simply that the flow of migration had begun much earlier (perhaps around the end of the first millennium, and at the same time as the dispersion of the 'Bafur'), and continued in the period for which we have historical evidence.[40] Historical tradition, which appears coherent at this point and which we have no reason to doubt, retraces this migration in a very logical manner.[41]

To conclude, the hypothesis of the Peuls having a 'western' origin, and having migrated from the western Sahara as far as the borders of Chad, appears virtually proven. On the other hand, the hypothesis of a previous Peul migration from the Nilotic region rests only on presumptions: physical similarities between the Peuls and the peoples of East Africa, and the evidence of cave drawings in the Sahara. Even if it had been completely verified, it would by no means justify gratuitous

37. J. Richard-Molard, *Les langues négro-africaines*, op. cit., p. 96.
38. Hugh Clapperton, *Journal of a Second Expedition into the Interior of Africa*, Philadelphia: Carey, 1829, p. 253.
39. Heinrich Barth, *Travels and Discoveries in North and Central Africa, 1849–1855*, vol.1, London: Longmans, Green, 1857; reprinted London: Cass, 1965.
40. Barth states that, coming from the banks of the Senegal river, they already formed an important element in the population of Bornu by the sixteenth century.
41. Cf. Cornevin, op. cit., pp. 353–4.

speculations on 'cultural transfers' from Egypt which excluded Egyptian evidence and the chronology established by prehistorians.[42]

Now let us return to what is known beyond doubt. There still exist today – notably in the Senegalese Ferlo but in other regions too – Peul groups (the 'Burure' Fulbe[43]) who have remained faithful to their primitive organisation. What is striking is the extreme archaism of their social organisation, which has remained much closer to primitive communism than that of the agriculturalists, leaving aside the 'palaeonigritic' Lobi, Kabre, Tenda *et al.* With them the ethnic organisation retained its full vigour, having the clan – originally matrilineal – as its basis. As everywhere, the clan was subdivided into extended families, groups of relatives capable of numbering up to several hundred; but even though, among cultivators, the extended family is the economic unit if not always the domestic one, among the Peuls it is divided into very small fractions. As a rule, the basic groups scarcely ever numbered more than ten people, e.g. in two (usually monogamous) households. This dispersal is probably due to the actual living conditions of the 'Burure'. With extraordinary powers of endurance, braving the extremes of summer heat as well as the winter cold, they infiltrate in the rainy season as far as the least habitable savannas or steppes: the Nigerian Sahel and the 'deserts' (so named because they lack drinking water, not because of the climate) of Ferlo, of the area enclosed by the Niger bend to the south, of the Dahomey borders and of Upper Volta. They live there in solitude. At the end of the dry season, they are compelled to move near to rivers or wells, and enter into contact with agriculturists, the masters of the soil, in order to gain authorisation to occupy the pasture lands. Permission is normally given without trouble; the Peul herds bring their own manure for the fields, and certain exchanges take place (grain for milk products).

But the Peul is free and proud; although poor, he is hostile to any stranger and scornful of the cultivator (who does him a good turn). A tolerated but often ill-treated guest, he is suspicious and flees at the slightest alarm. If he cannot avoid an attack, he will resist with desperate courage, but if there is previous warning he will not wait for it; even less will he be the aggressor. His power of resistance consists in his showing that he can always elude capture, as the colonial tax-gatherers were to discover. There were few slaves or people of comparable status

42. A much more convincing explanation for the similarities is the existence of a common Saharan area of civilisation in the Neolithic age, part of whose populations (the herders of bovidae) migrated westwards and then southwards, while others moved towards the Nile valley (Cornevin, op. cit., pp. 59–60).
43. 'Burure Fulbe' is the plural of 'Bororo Peul'.

(most were recruited from among black agriculturalists, even if they had adopted the Peul language): *matiube* or *rïmaibe* (agricultural serfs), *laobe* (joiners or wood-carvers) and *waïlube* (smiths) were only found in significant numbers at a more advanced stage of social evolution.

There was no political superstructure. At the level of the fraction or clan, the chief (*ardo*), usually the senior member of the oldest generation, was no more than the spokesman for the group, and was under the strict collective control of the adult members. The 'Bororo' Peul remains (or remained till very recent times) fiercely pagan.

Archaism extended to dress. The 'Bororo' Peul goes about practically naked, with a leather apron covering the loins, and, like palaeonigritic people, the head adorned with a large funnel-shaped straw hat. (It was Islam that introduced cotton clothing.[44]) Their houses are rudimentary, being made of straw on a hemispheric frame which can easily be dismantled - sometimes they are no more than shelters made of branches - and an enclosure of thorny branches protected the pen of the young animals from predators. This is the 'Bororo' Peul of today, and this is how he lived before his encounter with history. But once history intervened, he appeared in an altogether different guise; now sedentarised, he became a member of a warrior aristocracy which was an ardent disseminator of Islam, the support of powerful states, and master of the black cultivators who were thus reduced to servitude. It was from the eighteenth century onwards that this extraordinary mutation occurred - at different times according to locality, and never total. (Alongside the Peul aristocrats were 'Burure' who, as we have seen, retained their primitive organisation; they had often been enslaved.)

We must now again take up the thread of historical development, before we try to explain the conditions and causes of this transformation.

## *The Peul hegemonies and their historical significance*

As we have shown above, the first historical mention of the Peuls was at the beginning of the sixteenth century. The Peul chief Tenguella lived nomadically with his group of Termes in the region of Nioro and Diara. He revolted against the authority of the Songhai *askia*, then suzerain of the region, and attacked the king of Diara,[45] who had accepted this suzerainty, probably with help from the *mansa* of Mali.

44. However, the use of pantaloons coming down to the knee, and of the *bubu*, at first natural-coloured and then blue, became widespread from the eighteenth century, even among the pagan Bororo. Cf. Mollien, *Voyage dans l'intérieur de l'Afrique*, Paris, 1820, I, pp. 140-1.

45. One of the successor-states which arose in the wake of the dismembered Ghana empire.

The army of *askia* Mohamed, commanded by his brother Amar, marched against him and pursued him as far as Diara, where he was defeated and killed (1512). According to legend, his son Koli Tenguella, who was supposedly descended from the *mansas* of Mali through his mother, took refuge with the remnants of his army in Badiar, to the north-west of Futa-Jalon.[46] From there, with his Peuls and numerous Manding followers, he later returned to the north, conquered Futa-Toro (the ancient Tekrur) which was governed by officers owing allegiance to the kingdom of Diara, and there founded a pagan Peul state in 1559. The Denianke dynasty held on to power there till 1776, persecuting the Muslims.[47] Although it is difficult to confirm the details, this account seems to indicate that remarkable social transformations had taken place, at least in certain Peul fractions; hitherto they had not produced groups of warriors organised for offensive warfare and conquest. It is worth noting that these fractions invariably entered into a combination with Manding elements: the title borne by the Denianke was no longer the Peul *ardo* (which was still used by Tenguella) but the Malinke title *silatigui*.[48] On the other hand we should also note that the formation of this military state in Futa-Toro, in the general economic context that we have defined above, seems to coincide with the disappearance of towns (Tekrur, Sila) mentioned and described by medieval Arab travellers; their very sites are unknown to us today.

The process which led to this military state being formed was not completely new. We find in its most rudimentary stages the elements of the dissolution of the primitive community. At the very heart of this community (the tribe or the clan), certain associations establish themselves, suitable for mobilisation in military expeditions. These associations are based no longer on blood ties but on an agreement to work in

46. According to the chronology proposed by Delafosse. However, the Portuguese chronicles mention one Koli, king of the Fulas in the second half of the fifteenth century, who could conceivably be the same person; perhaps there were several Kolis.
47. This, at least, was the version put about by the initiators of the 'holy war' which defeated the Denianke. In fact, documents published after this essay was first published show that in the seventeenth and eighteenth centuries the Denianke were Muslims themselves [1978].
48. *Silatigui*, in Mande, means 'chief of the road', i.e. leader of the immigration from Badiar. This did not prevent Mali, having at first supported the efforts of Koli Tenguella (against the usurpations of Songhai), from being disturbed by his progress: *mansa* Mahmoud II appealed to King João III of Portugal against Koli Tenguella's incursions on what he still considered part of his empire. In 1534 João III contented himself with sending not an army but merely an ambassador, Peros Fernandes.
49. A typical example of this can be seen among the Bamileke of Cameroon, where traditional associations, either of a religious character with pagan (*komze*) origins or

mutual alliance;[49] in time they bring together groups which are ethnically diverse but which work together either on a basis of equality or in a patron-client relationship. Only at a more developed stage can they result in the subjection of whole peoples by a dominant fraction.[50] In practice, the transition from a tribal aristocracy, formed within the community, into this aristocracy of conquerors often takes multiple forms. There can be no doubt that qualitatively this stage of evolution is new; without disappearing, ethnic ties give way to ties of a new type – contractual, between patron and client, between lord and serf or vassal – even if these latter ties try to achieve 'sanctification' by means of a magical assimilation with the ethnic ties (a blood pact). The internal evolution of the societies favours the establishment of these groupings of conquerors: they visibly attract a number of men who have become socially uprooted, above all young men from poor families or to whom the growing authority of the family and tribal chiefs has become burdensome.

The arrival of the Peuls in Macina, on the banks of the Niger, was accomplished with less disturbance. It was about the beginning of the fifteenth century that these Peuls, who also came from Termes under a chief of the Diallo clan, installed themselves on the Niger with the permission of the governor who wielded his authority in the name of Mali. But the Dialube chiefs of the Peuls, despite their hostility to Islam, accommodated themselves willy-nilly to the overlordship successively of Mali, Songhai, the Spanish-Moroccans of Timbuktu, and finally the Bambara. In any case, immigration here was on a larger scale and resulted in the sedentarisation of these ancient nomads.

In a general context of economic and social regression, which they turned to good account, the former nomads can be seen to have undergone a considerable development in their social organisation; they had become a dominant aristocracy (locally, at least), and first assimilated and then subordinated agricultural serfs (*rimaïbe*) and artisans grouped in castes – the offspring of the peoples who had formerly occupied the country. Parallel to this, Peul pastoralists were infiltrating into other regions further south (Futa-Jalon) and further east (Yatenga, Gobir and as far as Bagirmi). We have mentioned the great uncertainty

---

based on age sets, co-exist with contractual warlike associations of limited size, going back two or three generations (cf. R. Delarozière, 'Les institutions politiques et sociales des populations dites Bamiléké', *Études Camérounaises*, Douala, no. 25–6 (1949), pp. 5–68, and no. 27–8, pp. 127–76).

50. The same process was already present in the earliest formation of the Songhai empire of Gao, at least from the reign of *askia* Mohamed onwards, and even more in the formation of the Bambara kingdoms in the same period; and it seems to have been present also in the establishment of the conquering *ribats* among the Sanhadja Berbers, the instruments of Almoravid expansion.

which exists concerning these movements, and it is not impossible that Peul elements were present in these regions at a very early date. Pagan Peuls were established in Futa-Jalon from the tenth century - if the local *tarikhs* are to be believed.[51] It seems very much as if these movements attained their greatest volume in the seventeenth and eighteenth centuries; in any case it was then that, in a number of cases, they resulted in sedentarisation.

What were the conditions in which this happened? This is the moment to look at the role of livestock-raising in the evolution of societies. We know that Engels (following Morgan) considered its role to be decisive in this evolution; he also placed it chronologically before agriculture.[52] He saw in it the origin of private property and of male dominance and their social consequences (animals were the concern of men - following from the sexual division of labour which made hunting their domain as well). This conception is linked to that developed for the history of Asia at an earlier period and for the Mediterranean world, where the birth of the classical civilisations was ascribed to Indo-European and Semitic pastoralists. It is known today that these pastoralists, mere conquering minorities, superimposed themselves on earlier agricultural civilisations that were highly developed, which they destroyed while assimilating a great part of their store of knowledge. The example of black Africa shows a more complex state of affairs than one would tend to think. Thus male domination became established very quickly in purely agricultural societies; conversely, among pastoralists descent frequently remained matrilineal (e.g. the primitive Peuls), and women frequently enjoyed extensive freedom and social authority (e.g. the non-Arabised Berbers and the Tuaregs).[53]

51. It scarcely needs to be emphasised how suspect these *tarikhs* (local chronicles) are, with their vested interest in demonstrating the great length of time the present lords of the country have resided there. Louis Tauxier (*Moeurs et histoirè des Peuls*, Paris, 1937, p .73) refuses to admit that the Peuls came to Futa-Jalon before the end of the seventeenth century (1694, to be exact), after which massive contingents arrived, from Macina and Senegal. The earlier movement led by Koli Tenguella went no further than Fuladu (Badiar). But one wonders if certain elements of the Peul culture of Futa-Jalon, of Malinke origin, are to be explained not solely by borrowings from the indigenous Diallonke but also by an earlier fusion with Malinke elements. (This could easily be explained in the case of Peuls who had come from Fuladu, but less so in the case of those who had come directly from the north.) In addition, Portuguese documents attest to the presence of Peuls in the south of present-day Guinea (Conakry) and the north of Sierra Leone from the mid-sixteenth century. Cf. A. Teixeira da Mota, *Nota sobre a historia dos Fulas - Coli Tenguela e a chegada dos primeiros Fulas ao Futa-Jalom* (2nd international conference of West Africanists, Bissau, 1947), Lisbon, 1950, V, pp. 53-70.
52. F. Engels, *The Origin of the Family*, London: Penguin, 1985, p . 54.
53. This was also true of the Sanhadja Berbers of the Western Sahara before they became Arabised. Ibn Battuta (op. cit.) notes the fact with precision concerning the

And the fact remains that livestock-raising played a privileged part in social evolution. Introduced among cultivators as a supplementary resource, it speeded up the process of social differentiation. As Vieillard noted of the Hausas, 'To be a man was in itself capital in its essential form: to be part of a numerous and vigorous family, and to have slaves; then animals assumed some importance because they had the best exchange value.'[54] On the other hand, within pastoral societies livestock-raising produces the conditions - the *possibility* - of a more rapid evolution. In the agricultural societies of black Africa, this evolution is held back (right up to the present time) by the general persistence of collective land rights to the exclusion of private property; and it is held back too by the relatively fixed nature of the custom which determines the proportion of family fields to individual ones, and of the days and half-days of labour which must be reserved for one or the other. All attempts to modify it meet strong resistance.

Among the pastoralists, however, although collective grazing rights are precisely defined (even in the Sahara) and are stoutly defended when necessary, always retaining their collective character, the animals themselves can easily pass from collective to individual ownership; no proportion between the one and the other has been prescribed.[55] As wealth is accumulated - above all in livestock - and the inequality of its division becomes marked, a rapid mutation can take place at the appropriate time. The mutation often seems to have been stimulated by the development of exchange through contact with pre-existing urban centres.

An example of this can probably be seen in the Almoravid expansion. In the western Sahara during the tenth century, several populations were co-existing: the black cultivators of Ghana who controlled access to the gold-bearing regions in the south, acting as commercial intermediaries; Islamised Berbers - traders originally from North

---

Messufa of Iwalaten (Walata) in making a comparison with the Indians of Malabar.

54. G. Vieillard, *Coutumiers juridiques de l'A.O.F.*, III: 'Coutumier du cercle de Zinder', Paris, 1939, p. 144.

55. The only detailed study of this question that we know of is by Marguerite Dupire: *Peuls nomades*, Paris, 1962. It relates to the nomadic Peuls in the Republic of Niger. According to this author, there is no hard evidence for collective ownership of animals by the extended patrilineal group; the animals were merely given the same markings. Ownership of animals is strictly personal - with the head of the family, however, managing the herd belonging to his wives and his children without property of their own, sometimes with considerable freedom to dispose of the animals. This is true, at least, as regards the animals belonging to the children; the parents-in-law take a close interest in those of the wives, whose families or children enjoy the rights of inheritance.

Africa and others sedentarised locally, who together made up the populations of Ghana's vassal towns in the Sahara (Aoudaghost, Walata etc.); and finally the veiled Sanhadja Berbers of the desert – nomadic stockbreeders, only slightly Islamised – who were vassals of one or other of the groups just mentioned, and had the appearance of 'poor relations'. Now it was these poor relations, organised in a religious and military brotherhood (*ribât*),[56] who were transformed in the eleventh century into extraordinary conquerors: converted to a strict form of Islam by the reformer Ibn Yassin, they attacked and subdued in turn various Sanhadja fractions, and in 1054 sacked Aoudaghost because it insisted on maintaining its allegiance to the pagan ruler of Ghana. Finally they took possession of Ghana itself in 1077[57] and compelled the ruler to embrace Islam. During this time other groups conquered Morocco and then Spain.

Another striking historical parallel is that of the Arab conquest. The description given by Ammianus Marcellinus of the Arabian desert Beduins at the end of the fourth century recalls in a remarkable way the primitive Saharan pastoralists and the 'Bororo' Peuls.[58] Two and a half centuries later, these same Beduins, transformed by internal processes (the result of contact with the commercial and caravan centres of Mecca and Medina) and disciplined by Islam, were to embark on world conquest. With the Arab empire they were to create the framework for one of the great civilisations of history, at the very same time as they left behind in their country of origin certain groups who were only to raise themselves slowly above their primitive level.[59]

The case of the Peuls, meanwhile, is rather different. Here the catalyst which made the way easy for their abrupt transformation was not the presence of trading cities; as we have seen, those to which they had access were stagnant or declining, and the Peul states established themselves essentially in areas that were completely rural. But we have emphasised that, despite the weakness of the trading cities, the consequences of the slave trade had the effect of accentuating the process of social differentiation throughout the whole of rural Africa.

It is here that one is made aware of the Peul's role as a specialist in stock-rearing. As Vieillard noted in the passage quoted above, it was in the absence of urban activities and of money as a means of exchange,

56. Hence the name *Al Morabetîne*, corrupted to Almoravid = those organising themselves in a *ribât*.
57. Both the fact and the date (advanced by Delafosse) are disputed.
58. Ammianus Marcellinus, *Res Gestae*, bk. XIV, 4, 3–6. Ammianus, a Syrian by birth who had done military service in the east, gives here a first-hand account.
59. W. Montgomery Watt's *Muhammad at Mecca*, London 1953, and *Muhammad at Medina*, Oxford, 1956, illuminate convincingly the way that these mutations took place.

and in the absence too of individual land-holding that would have allowed a monopoly in land to develop, that livestock became for a minority group of black cultivators a path to enrichment and the principal means of accumulating - or, better still, hoarding - the wealth they had acquired.[60]

Richard-Molard rightly notes:

In most of the northern Sudanic region, the black peasant likes to own animals; it ennobles him.[61] But he would judge that by tending them he suffers an impairment of his honour. The opposite is true of the Peul. Here one has recourse to the specialist, the humble *pullo* in the village. Half-starved, bound by a contract which assures him of grain, and a share both of dairy produce and of the annual increase in livestock, he takes charge of the livestock that is held in common and disappears into the wilderness to present himself again once the crops are harvested, at the moment when it is opportune to graze his animals on the next season's *lugans* (fields ready to be cultivated). He thus penetrates deep into the Sudanic region during the rainy season. Little by little, he builds up his own herd. Better still, he gives his daughters, who are the most beautiful girls in French West Africa, to the owner of the land. There they never forget that their situation must benefit the *pullo*, who, having become 'negrified' and having enslaved the peasants, will be the future master of the locality.[62]

This is, on the whole, a correct picture, but one lacking in precision. The Peul - as the guardian of accumulated wealth, and having within his care what is the essential mark of wealth in his peasant milieu - becomes increasingly conscious that he has economic control

60. Richard-Molard did not understand this when he wrote: 'A *pullo* is someone, whatever the colour of his skin, who has an obsessive passion for oxen, however useless to him they may be. For Mediterranean and Western man, *pecus* = *pecunia* (livestock = capital). It is the same for the Saharan. For the black, too, animals always serve a purpose of some kind, even if it is to fulfil some religious ceremony. But nothing of the kind applies to the Peul, as yet untouched by "civilisation". The horned animal serves no purpose for him whatever. It is he who serves the animal. This is "ox-mania" that does not even become "ox-worship"' (Richard-Molard, op. cit., pp. 95–6).

    Richard-Molard here makes a wrong generalisation by applying the idea of (productive) capital, strictly in its modern sense, to historical periods and societies for which it had no meaning! The ox is the 'Bororo' Peul's means of existence; and if his herd of cattle is not an absolute necessity for the sedentarised Peul, it remains for him, as for the cultivator who purchases cattle, a means whereby he can realise and save his wealth. Lucien Febvre had already drawn attention to the acquisitive character of livestock-rearing at certain stages of social development (L. Febvre, *La terre et l'évolution humaine*, Paris, 1922, pp. 350–3).

61. A note of caution here: Richard-Molard saw only the psychological aspect of the phenomenon, without observing its economic and social content. The social consideration that attaches to ownership of animals is the result of the wealth to which it bears witness.

62. Richard-Molard, op. cit., p. 98.

over a key sector. But he is always an interloper, a guest who is merely tolerated, and subjected to numerous vexations by the landlords, which he suffers less and less willingly. At times, none the less, he has stayed in this semi-sedentary situation, as the serf or vassal of the peasants, he is, says Richard-Molard, 'the Peul against whom this policy [which he invokes above] has not succeeded'. His setbacks have not affected him. In the countries where there were highly structured peasant states - like the kingdoms of the Mossi or the Bariba - ruled by a military aristocracy in the true sense, the Peul remained a subordinate, and even tended to assimilate himself. Sometimes he adopted the language and type of dwelling of his masters. All he retained was his pastoral specialisation. The same was true of the Fulakunda of the Casamance-Guinea borders (Fuladu) in the course of their absorption by the Malinke, but for other reasons which are less clear.

Where the Peul became master, it was not by his own doing, as the passage of Richard-Molard cited above would lead one to suppose; a veritable revolution was needed. Neither the ethnic organisation, nor the animism to which hitherto it had remained grimly attached, provided the framework in which the revolution to which the Peuls aspired could be accomplished. Conversion to Islam furnished an ideology and at the same time rules of social life perfectly suited to this transformation, as they had been earlier for the Almoravids in Africa itself, and of course for the Arabs at the time of the Prophet.[63] The role of the *marabouts* of Mauritania, teachers of the future chiefs of Futa-Jalon, and that of the Peul-speaking Muslim Tukulors who, under Denianke domination, had kept the flame of Islam alight, were not all-important here; they simply brought to the Peuls the ideology best suited to the social and political movement in which they were actors. This conversion to Islam was accompanied by the Peuls (or, to be more exact, certain groups and certain families) being constituted into a warrior aristocracy. This was the process whereby the revolutions in these very diverse regions came about, simultaneously or successively. In each region a similar situation had been created.

It was a revolution, first and foremost, which from 1727–8 made Futa-Jalon into a Peul state, aristocratic, military and theocratic. Here, as in the earlier venture of Koli Tenguella, very diverse elements (Sussu, Sarakolle, Tukulors and Malinke from Upper Senegal) joined themselves to Peul elements which had infiltrated long before or come

63. On this subject see W. Montgomery Watt, *Muhammad at Mecca*, op. cit., which contains interesting views on the role of nascent Islam as a religious reaction to a similar social situation (development of wealth and social differentiation; the inadequacy of the ideology associated with the old ethnic structures). This work also contains some incorrect views. Cf. the criticism in M. Rodinson, 'Mahomet et les origines de l'Islam', *Cahiers rationalistes*, no. 164 (1957), pp. 173–83.

from Termes and Macina. They were quickly assimilated, and reduced the indigenous Jialonke cultivators (related to the Malinke) to serfdom. The climate of this southerly but mountainous region was well suited to pastoral activities, which remained of great importance and the only aristocratic ones, even if they did not have the leading place. Indeed from that time forward, the aristocrats invariably entrusted the care of their herds to 'Bororo Fulbe' who had remained loyal to their primitive organisation and often to paganism, and had been reduced to a vassalage that was punctuated by revolts. For the ethnic structure, which passed on to a second design and did not disappear, they substituted a territorial organisation: a confederation of nine provinces (*diwâl*), themselves subdivided into 'parishes' (*misîde),* these last governed by a *lamido* or *ardo*, the province by a superior *lamido*, and the confederation itself by an *almamy* (*Al Imam*) chosen from the middle of the nineteenth century onwards for a term of two years from the Alfa and Sori families alternatively.[64] Although a Muslim religious and political chief, the *almamy* had also inherited his office from the ancient agrarian kingships, as the rites observed at his investiture showed.

Then in Futa-Toro a group of Muslim Tukulors, the Torobe,[65] inspired by the *marabout* Suleimane Ba, overthrew the pagan Peul Denianke dynasty. *Almamy* Abdul Kader won a final victory over the last of the *silatigui*, Sule-Bubu, and in 1776 established a theocratic state in Futa-Toro, with the form of an elective monarchy. The similarity to Futa-Jalon is in fact no more than superficial - for the Tukulor victors, although they were *har pularen*, were also black cultivators, while it was Peul pastoralists who had suffered defeat.

The explanation we have sketched above cannot easily be invoked here, and we must look for other influences: the weakness of the pagan Peul monarchy which was dependent on a handful of adventurers and had not been able to consolidate an ideology suited to the times; and the existence of a peasant population at a much more advanced stage of development than most others, influenced by the long-standing activity of the towns and by the traffic of the Senegal river, and penetrated since early times by Islam.[66] On the other hand, it was Peul Muslims in

64. However, let us note, with G. Vieillard: 'The country was divided into fiefs, but it was the people who were given in fief, much more than the land. The fief, certainly, had the tendency to become territorial, but the vassals did not escape from the power of their suzerain by emigrating, any more than serfs could thus escape from their master; the hereditary tie was not broken' ('Notes sur les Peuls du Fouta-Djalon', *Bulletin de l'I.F.A.N.*, Dakar, I, 1939, p. 123).
65. Plural of *Torodo*, a man who prays to God.
66. Works published after this essay was first published show that the decisive factor was a national movement of resistance to the encroachments of the Moors, which had been tolerated or even requested by the Denianke. [1978]

Bondu who, soon afterwards, achieved a very similar revolution and created a third theocratic state, also governed by an *almamy*.[67]

We should not assume that these theocratic states were tyrannies. These monarchies were elective, and Mollien has already noted: 'The government of Futa-Toro is an oligarchy, *and the people themselves are not without power*.'[68] Just as at Futa-Jalon, the councils of elders, controlled from the bottom of the ladder by general assemblies of free men, played a decisive role. In this connection Vieillard writes: 'Under the *ancien régime*, political life was intense. Every decision that had to be taken, in the confederation and in each *misîde*, required consultation; *disondirde* – to consult one with another – occurs in the chronicles at every turn.'[69] Although a source of weakness in so far as it encouraged dissension, this persistence of institutions inherited from the simple tribal period (which also recall the 'military democracy', as defined by Engels in archaic Greece and among the Germanic tribes) certainly gave them a superiority over their rivals, and assured them of a coherence which the latter did not possess.[70]

A little later, in 1810, a band of Muslim Peuls led by Sheikh Hamadu Bari (Seku Hamadu) deposed the pagan chief (*ardo*) of the Diallo clan, whom the people blamed for his submissiveness and inertia in the face of exactions from the Bambara and Tuareg overlords. It seized Djenne and even for a short while Timbuktu, and built a new capital, Hamdallahi (meaning 'praise to God'), on the right bank of the Bani river. Thus the Peul kingdom of Macina came into being; with a solid administration and well-organised system of finance, it lasted till 1862.[71] About the same time, in 1801, the Peul shepherds of Gober revolted against their Hausa masters. Aided and

67. The extremely mixed population of Bondu in fact comprised a large proportion of Tukulors. [1978]
68. G. Mollien, op. cit., I, p. 193. Emphasis added.
69. G. Vieillard, op. cit., p. 131.
70. Among West African peoples that had passed beyond the tribal stage, only the Peuls showed some signs of military democracy: everywhere there is evidence of assemblies of free men advising and controlling the chiefs, even where the Peuls were in a subordinate position (e.g. those who were vassals of the Mossi kingdom of Yatenga – see L. Tauxier, *Le Noir du Yatenga*, Paris: Larose, 1917). But it is very probable that they existed among other peoples. Vieillard noted that the word *tekun*, which among the Peuls of Futa-Djallon meant electoral colleges and deliberative assemblies, 'is a Diallonke word, undoubtedly borrowed by the victors from the vanquished. Among the Diallonke of Sangalan, *tekun* means "age sets" on active service, which play the most important role in the village community' (Vieillard, loc. cit., p. 132).
71. See Ch. Monteil, *Djenné*, Paris: S.E.G.M.C., 1932, and above all the admirable work of Amadou Hampaté Ba and J. Daget, *L'Empire peul du Macina*, The Hague/Paris: Mouton, 1962 (new edn).

abetted by a group of warriors from the Peul and Tukulor countries (Macina and Futa-Toro), the scholarly Osman dan Fodio had himself acknowledged first as Sheikh and then as Caliph of the believers, and set up a vast empire over them. From the capital which he established at Sokoto, he soon dominated the Hausa country, the Kebbi and the Nupe. His progress was halted before Bornu where a native sheikh, Mohamed El Amin El Kanemi, saved the old dynasty; but it was to make himself the power behind the throne in the mean time that his son, in 1846, deposed the slothful Sultan and took his place. Stopped at this point by the resistance of Kanemi, Osman's authority, at least on the religious level, reached as far as Cameroon: there indeed the Peuls of the high plateaux revolted in their turn under the leadership of the chief whom he had instituted, Adama, and created another Peul empire bearing the latter's name - Adamawa.

How, while clearly in a minority, did the Peuls under Osman dan Fodio manage to overcome the Hausa states, firmly structured as they were, and with an old civilisation, and furthermore converted to Islam (superficially, at least) since the fourteenth century by traders of Malinke origin? D. A. Olderogge has shown that the Peuls combined their attack with a revolt of Hausa peasants (slaves and tributaries) against the Hausa aristocracy. All they finally succeeded in doing was to substitute themselves for it and impose on the populations an even heavier oppression than they had known before.[72]

Osman dan Fodio, more a mystic than a warrior, left the direction of military operations largely in the hands of his brother. His son and successor Mohamed Bello (1843–55) had to suppress, at the beginning of his reign, a general revolt of enslaved people. Mediocre as a soldier, he was a punctilious administrator and a brilliant man of letters, author of many works in Arabic. After his time, never-ending revolts and growing independence on the part of provincial governors weakened the empire of Sokoto.

All in all, the Peul hegemonies, in an unfavourable economic context and despite their heavy oppression of subject peoples, contributed some positive elements. The military chief was no longer simply the leader of an armed band; he was also a religious chief, and could not pretend to any dignity without being versed in the Scriptures - '*Modibo*' '*Thierno*' and '*Karamoko*'[73] for the most learned after

72. D. A. Olderogge, *The Western Sudan from the 14th to the 19th centuries*, Moscow: Publishing House of the Academy of Sciences of the U.S.S.R., 1960 (in Russian).
73. Local terms (the Peul '*Thierno*' = Malinke '*Fode*') corresponding to religious titles bestowed as a function of the bearer's Koranic knowledge: the ceremony for bestowal, which included the giving of a turban, implied that the recipient assumed obligations with regard to his religious conduct. The significance of the terms became honorific, and they were often used as fore-names.

the *almamy* or the Caliph. Preoccupation with religion led to religious teaching becoming universal; at the beginning of the nineteenth century, Mungo Park, when he crossed the Bondu, observed that no village was without its Koranic school. Doubtless the instruction was of a low standard; at the bottom of the ladder, they would confine themselves to deciphering the Koran and learning it by heart without understanding its meaning, but at the top, knowledge was at the level of medieval scholasticism, transmitted by the universities of Mauritania. This civilisation certainly did not have the brilliance which Timbuktu had known (in an urban setting) some centuries earlier. But it was better than the void which European colonisation brought in its place. Writing in Arabic, Peuls and Tukulors created a literature - in their own language but transcribed into Arabic script - consisting of chronicles and poetry (the latter sometimes spoilt by an excessive concern to imitate Arabic forms and prosody).

### *The great venture and the defeat of El Hadj Omar*

Soon after the Peul hegemonies were established in the east, a new empire established itself in the west. Its hero was El Hadj Omar Saïdu Tall, one of the great figures of nineteenth-century Africa. In a certain way, his venture prolonged that of the Peul and Tukulor politico-religious reformers of the previous period. It both surpassed and opposed it, and we shall look at it in terms of this paradox.

Omar was born around 1797 in the neighbourhood of Podor in Futa-Toro, the fourth son of the *marabout* Saidou Tall. The family of the latter belonged to a group of Torobe (see above, p. 47) who had overthrown the Denianke some time before. At the age of twenty-three he made the pilgrimage to Mecca; there he had himself received into the brotherhood of Tijaniyah and returned not only with the title '*El Hadj*', then very rare in black Africa, but with the warrant of Caliph of the Tijaniyah of the Sudan. These titles, and in addition his genuine scholarship as a Muslim man of learning, earned him a triumphal welcome home. El Kanemi, master of Bornu, and then his compatriot Mohamed Bello at Sokoto heaped him with honours, gifts and women (Mohamed Bello gave him two of his daughters as legal wives). The Peul king of Macina also received him with honour, but less warmly; this king, Seku Hamadu, a rigid and austere Muslim, disapproved of the pomp which surrounded the scholar-pilgrim and, perhaps most of all, understood the danger which Omar's prestige presented for his established powers - he was even tempted to have him assassinated after his departure from Hamdallahi.[74] The pagan king of Segu reacted

74. This statement comes from champions of Omar, probably anxious to excuse the fate of Seku Hamadu's grandson and successor, who was conquered and put to death by El Hadj Omar's followers.

even more unfavourably; after receiving him, he first arrested, then released him, and later tried to have him murdered after his departure. On the other hand, the chief of Kangaba - a member of the nearly 1,000-year-old Keïta dynasty and heir by a remote line of descent to the *mansa* of Mali - gave him a cordial reception, as the *almamy* of Futa-Jalon had done. The latter offered him a place of retirement in his dominions, and allowed him to found a *zauïa* there (a religious-military community, analogous to the *ribâts* which gave rise to the Almoravid movement). At the same time, Omar exploited the gold of the Siguiri region. After an official tour in Senegal, which he used for propaganda and recruitment, and in the course of which (in 1847) the French commander at Bakel gave him a frosty welcome (as did certain indigenous monarchs, for similar reasons), he established himself at Dinguiraye and built a fortress there.

How is one to explain the personal prestige of this pilgrim and at the same time the anxiety he aroused? For societies where the old ethnic organisations were breaking up on all sides, incapable of serving as a framework for new social realities, Islam provided a new religious, political and social framework which was better adapted for the purpose; but it did not remove the contradictions in the countries where it was implanted, at least not for everybody. The old ethnic institutions continued to resist, and the substitution of a new military and religious aristocracy for the old tribal nobility - when ultimately the two could not combine - only succeeded in removing one contradiction, which was then reborn in a slightly different form.

In the Muslim brotherhoods, which had been widespread up till that time (the Qadiriya predominating at the beginning of the nineteenth century), there existed between the generality of adherents and the religious chief a great number of mystical grades to which only a few privileged individuals could aspire. In fact, these grades reserved for a minority, consisting of a small number of families, the direct and total contact with the religious chief from which mystical and material benefits flowed. They perpetuated under Islam, in a new form, the privileges of the tribal aristocracy (or those which benefited the initiates of the higher grades of the animist secret societies: the Guinean *porro*, the *komo* of the Manding and the *oro* of Benin).

The Tijaniya broke these barriers and established direct contact between the simple adherents and the Caliph, and it gave to all the vision of attaining to higher things through courage or learning (or, better still, both). From this fact it derived a revolutionary and relatively democratic character (within the brotherhood).[75] It attracted all those, especially the young, who were oppressed by the social, family

75. The reference here, of course, is to the Tijaniya of the Sudan and not of North Africa, the two having very different characteristics.

or feudal set-up – all those for whom a growing internal differentiation between rich and poor spelt ruin. This was particularly the case in the Senegal river valley, and in Futa-Toro, heartland of the Tukulors. From there the prodigious success of El Hadj Omar; the respect – and fear – he inspired among established authorities because these were at a stage where civil and religious society had become confused; the progress of the brotherhood; the growing authority of the Caliph – all these prepared the way for the seizure of political power. One could perhaps say, with Richard-Molard: 'In three-quarters of a century, the landmarks of Muslim Peul power had become so solidly based and so widely distributed that the way seemed clear for the realisation of a Peul-Islamic hegemony over the savannas of West Africa. [. . .] Without France, most of West Africa might have fallen into the hands of a Torodo chief.'[76] We do not share this view, since it allows too little importance to the limits imposed on El Hadj Omar by the social milieu, which explain, far more satisfactorily than French intervention, the relative failure of his venture. Undoubtedly he rose to prominence on ground prepared by earlier Islamic Peul movements, compared to which he represented a superior stage. But he came into violent collision with the whole 'established order' of Islamic Peul states, as with the old agrarian and animist kingdoms; and because of the economic and social condition of the country, he could not overcome the contradictions on which he had relied for support in order to succeed, contradictions which re-appeared after him in a somewhat different guise.

As soon as he assumed the headship of state at Dinguiraye, El Hadj Omar came up against the declared hostility of the *almamy* of Futa-Jalon, whose predecessor had supported his first steps. From 1850 till 1854 he destroyed the agrarian kingdoms of the Keïta and the Bambara of Kaarta (the capital of which was Nioro); then he turned west against the Muslim kingdom of Khasso whose capital Medina resisted[77] and was finally relieved by the French governor of Senegal, Faidherbe, in 1857. Colonial historiography took this episode as a basis for crediting Faidherbe with having delivered the final blow which made the efforts of El Hadj Omar unproductive. This does violence to the facts, because El Hadj Omar immediately attacked French positions far in the rear in Bondu and Futa-Toro, his own country. In 1859 he made an abortive attack on the French post at Matam, but nowhere was he defeated outright by the French forces. Meanwhile, he met the open hostility of the established aristocracy, the Muslim Torobe chiefs

76. Richard-Molard, op. cit., pp. 68–9.
77. The resistance of the little French fort at Medina, under the command of the mulatto Paul Holle became part of the popular hagiography of French colonialism.

from whose ranks he himself had emerged. The people were on his side, and many young men joined his armies; some chiefs, under popular pressure, went over to him.[78] But most of the chiefs, against their people's wishes, resisted him furiously and appealed to the French.[79] Without them, Faidherbe would certainly never have dislodged him from Futa-Toro.

French-controlled Senegal, where more than anywhere else the traditional social patterns had disintegrated, is probably where El Hadj Omar would have found conditions best suited to the creation of a stable state; but the very factor which had created these conditions – the French presence – also stood in his way. Without artillery, he was powerless against French outposts armed with cannons.[80] Deluded by his compatriots, El Hadj Omar turned east, and having returned to Nioro, went on the attack against the pagan Bambara of Segu and the Muslim Peuls of Macina whose alliance he had sought before his attack on Medina. He destroyed their states and seized Segu

78. These were the turncoats who made up his forces, and who formed the original nucleus of the Tukulor population which today spreads throughout the Sudanic region: 50,000 from Bakel to Mopti across the Sahel of Nioro; 55,000 throughout the Bondu, the valleys of the Sine and the Salum and the Gambia; and 11,000 around Dinguiraye, the original base. This accounts for more than one-third of the total Tukulor population (300,000). Archinard had driven out those who had settled in the Segu region, and brought them back under escort to Futa-Toro. The importance of the exodus of their subjects suffices to explain the displeasure of Futa-Toro's traditional chiefs.

79. See Paul Marty, *L'Islam en Mauritanie et au Sénégal*, Paris: Leroux, 1915–16, pp. 276–7 ('Les groupements tidianïa dérivés d'El Hadj Omar'); also A. Gouilly, *L'Islam dans l'Afrique occidentale française*, Paris, Larose, 1952, and 'Vie d'El Hadj Omar' (transl. Saleno), *Bulletin du Comité d'Études historiques et scientifiques de l'A.O.F.*, nos 3–4 (1918), pp. 405–31. The latter records that one of his brothers had a dream in which he saw the Prophet Mohamed, who gave him this message for Omar: '. . . Finally, tell him that he should have nothing to do with the inhabitants of Futa in Senegal, because they are traitors' (p. 423). The explanation of Tukulor commentators, namely that these words refer only to the inhabitants of Bossea, is hardly convincing.

Cultru's *Histoire du Sénégal du XVe siècle jusqu'à 1970* (Paris: Larose, 1910) follows the same line: 'Perhaps at first he thought that he would dominate the whole of Futa in Senegal. . . . But the chiefs whom he disturbed showed themselves hostile. One of the chiefs of Bosseyabe tried to assassinate him'(p. 334). Also, 'From Medina to St Louis the blacks spoke of him and fixed their hopes on him; he had to be the instrument of vengeance for their race against the Moors, *their liberator from the tyranny of chiefs*' (p. 335 – emphasis added).

80. In 1855 El Hadj Omar had sent a letter to the Muslim inhabitants of St Louis; as the *Annales sénégalaises* (Paris, Maisonneuve et Leclerc, 1885) observed, ' . . . in fact, he had many supporters even in St Louis' (p. 104). It says too that the people of Futa-Toro and Bondu 'had been roused to a state of fanaticism by his emissaries, and were prepared to do whatever he commanded at the first word' (p. 103). In 1862 his supporters unleashed a general rebellion in Futa-Toro.

in 1861 and Hamdallahi in 1862. But he did not succeed in crushing their resistance: the Bambara carried on the fight in the bush, and the Peuls of Macina rose up, besieged him in Hamdallahi from which he managed to escape by setting it on fire, and ended by killing him in a cave in which he had taken refuge, in 1864. His nephew Tidiani succeeded, in spite of great difficulty, in gaining the upper hand with the help of the Dogon highland people who were pagans and traditional enemies of the Peuls. Installed at Bandiagara, he upheld the Tukulor hegemony till the conquest by the French. El Hadj Omar's son and successor Ahmadu, who remained at Segu, concealed the news of his father's death for a long time, and for more than a generation, fostered by the circumstances of his disappearance, the legend persisted that he was still alive and would one day return - as was later believed of the Mahdi. This is enough to show what El Hadj Omar represented for the people in the regions of Senegal actually under French domination or imminently threatened by it.

It should not be forgotten what desperate opposition El Hadj Omar met with from his rivals - most of all the aristocracy of Futa-Toro and the Peul aristocracy of Macina; thus he should not be represented as having received his support from the network of Peul power, since it was the Muslim Peul states that resisted his overlordship most strongly, and the Peuls of Macina - not Faidherbe - who caused his downfall.

The state which he created, and to the headship of which his son Ahmadu succeeded, was not long in showing other signs of weakness. Apart from the continuing resistance of the conquered aristocracies, there were limits to the egalitarian sentiments of the Tijaniya. Among the *talibe* (disciples and lieutenants) of El Hadj Omar there were men of numerous ethnic origins who remained indissolubly tied to their master by the common faith.[81] But ethnic rivalries were so persistent that, with Tukulors forming the greater part of his army, they finally worked against him and his successors, especially in the Niger region of the Sudan where the Tukulors were merely a conquering minority. *Talibe* and fighting men whose destiny was linked to his soon constituted a new aristocracy as oppressive as the old ones.

After his death, the furious struggles among his own sons impeded attempts to resist French penetration. In 1890, when Archinard took Segu, there was this paradox: in Senegal the railway workers and traders went on strike and took part in demonstrations, so that a general Muslim uprising was feared. On the other hand, in Ahmadu's

81. We only need to cite the example of the Bambara chief Bandiugu Diara, a convert, who died heroically defending Wossebugu against the French attackers on Ahmadu's behalf.

Sudanic states no coherent resistance could be organised; a short time before, his brother Muntaga had preferred to blow himself up rather than let Ahmadu enter his fief of Nioro, and his other brother Aguibu, with the defence of Dinguiraye in his hands, went over to the French, as did the Bambara. It was not long before those who took this action came to repent of it bitterly. Aguibu, whom the French 'promoted' to be king of Macina, was soon 'retired from his post'; and the descendant of the Bambara kings enthroned at Segu, who took his role more seriously, was shot after a few months for 'high treason'. So these puppets made way for 'direct administration'.

We can summarise as follows. In relation to the intervention of France, which had the material means of obstructing him, and was soon to extend its stranglehold, El Hadj Omar had arrived too late on the scene to act as a unifying force. On the other hand, in relation to the Niger region of the Sudan, he had arrived too early: the social conditions there had not matured sufficiently for him to be able to overcome the obstacles inherited from the past. That is the significance of his tragic end.

Moreover, this point is of relevance for the whole of black Africa. At the time of the European imperial conquest, the social condition of Africa was such that it could not put up any serious opposition to it. This was not due to any lack of courage; the history of the conquest is studded with acts of heroism and fierce resistance by African peoples and their chiefs. But these acts could not alter the course of history.

The virtues of ethnic solidarity, which had given the first African states their staying power, were dying. But not only was it impossible to overcome the divisions and hatreds between peoples, which they inherited from their tribal past, but they became more acute as social differentiation progressed, so that hatred between one people and another and one family and another were compounded by hatreds between overlords and subjects. The European conqueror was given a perfect scenario, making use of Africans in his own profitable conquests, whoever the enemy of the moment might be, and playing on personal, family or tribal animosities. The unwise 'collaborators' of yesterday would be crushed in their turn under the iron heel of colonisation. The fierce and prolonged resistance which the conquest sometimes met could be dealt with piecemeal; it was never necessary to meet a unified national resistance because the social conditions made it impossible. By a vengeful reversal of history, it was colonisation itself which created the conditions for them to find unity and emancipation – not before it had subjected the populations to a martyrdom lasting three-quarters of a century.

# 3

# THE CONTEXT AND SOCIAL CONSEQUENCES OF THE AFRICAN SLAVE TRADE[1]

There was a time when the slave trade between Africa and America had its open defenders and even eulogists. In 1784 the Chambers of Commerce at Nantes did not hesitate to praise this form of business and to enumerate with great objectivity the reasons why it was so remunerative (the word used was *interessant* = 'interesting', in the sense of providing interest on capital). 'The African commerce', said this body, 'is the most advantageous in the kingdom, the most abundant source of wealth entering the state. Without it, America, deprived of slaves, would become unfruitful. The trade in blacks is the basis of all our shipping; it is what provides the hands for cultivation in our islands, and brings us in return an incredible mass of trade goods such as sugar, coffee, cotton and indigo, as much for consumption in the kingdom as for foreign trade.'

Those who undertook this most advantageous form of commerce were proclaimed fine men and benefactors of the state, if not of all humanity, and Father Rinchon (see below, p. 63) even tells us that when a group of speculators in Brussels decided to launch out into operations on the coast of Guinea, a journalist had proposed that this admirable initiative should be rewarded and that a statue be raised in their honour. Weuves, in his *Réflexions historiques et politiques sur le commerce de France avec les colonies d'Amérique, par M. Weuves le jeune, négociant* (Paris: L. Cellot, 1780), wrote: 'One dares to say that these merchants are worthy of recognition by kings: they deserve to be placed alongside illustrious men of all kinds and singled out like them with honours, such as are only due to true upholders of the state.'

If interest on capital or state approval were here cited as the justification, others did not stop short of according it divine sanction. Even the great Bossuet loftily condemned those who questioned the propriety of slavery: 'To abolish slavery', he wrote, 'would be to condemn the Holy Spirit, who, through the lips of St Peter himself, requires slaves to remain in their present state and not to oblige their master to free them.' In the West Indies, Father Labat[2] held up to ridicule some

1. This text, which appeared in *Présence africaine*, no. 5 (1964/II), pp. 127–50, was transcribed from a tape-recorded lecture. The reader is asked to excuse its 'spoken' style, the shortcomings of which have not been completely eliminated by some correction of points of detail.
2. Jean-Baptiste Labat (1663–1738), a Dominican missionary in the West Indies, was

doctors of the Sorbonne who had become involved in disputing the legitimacy of slavery. Father Labat wrote: 'The colonists say that the doctors who have given their opinion neither reside in the Islands nor have shares in the Companies – if they did, they would have decided very differently.' Still in the nineteenth century, Father Libermann, who revived the order of Holy Ghost Fathers, did not go so far as to defend slavery but justified it as a supplementary form of original sin which was the burden of the black race: 'Moral blindness and the spirit of Satan are too deeply rooted in this people, and the curse of their father still lies upon them; it is necessary for them to be redeemed by pains made one with the pains of Jesus, which alone are capable of expiating their brutalising sins . . . in order to have God's curse washed away.'[3] Besides these approving voices, there was also dissent well before Abbé Raynal at the end of the eighteenth century, but because the critics were reprobated, we have scarcely any record of their opinions. However the polemics of Bossuet and Father Labat against them show clearly that they existed.

The nineteenth century saw the triumph of slavery's opponents, not all of whose abundant writings on the trade can be said to have proceeded from a spirit of undiluted humanitarianism. Some of these works, containing diatribes on the chains, whips and nudity associated with the trade, seem to owe more to perverted eroticism than to humane feelings of censure regarding an evil practice. But in the end slavery was officially condemned, and indeed it was in the cause of abolishing slavery that Africa was subjugated. At this moment a number of opinions gained currency which have not yet disappeared. These grew to form the elements of a kind of mythology, the features of which we shall now examine.

First, we are told that African slavery and the transatlantic trade, while undoubtedly horrible and deserving of condemnation, are still typical of a traditional phenomenon. The Europeans, between the fifteenth and the nineteenth centuries, only did what Phoenicians, Arabs and Turks had done before them. Secondly, this Arab and Turkish slavery was surely on a bigger scale and much more horrible than that carried on by Europeans. Those principally responsible for the horrors of slavery were the Arabs and the Turks – and the Africans themselves. This was a theme often heard at the time of the conquest.

It is said that the conquest had as its object the freeing of the unfortunate Africans from the bonds of slavery – and incidentally from false religions. It was the heyday of the French anti-slavery society, founded

---

the author of several important works on that region in the early eighteenth century.

3. G. Goyau, *La France missionaire*, Paris: Plon, 1948, II, p. 177.

by Mgr Lavigerie, archbishop of Algiers, and blessed by Pope Leo XIII who, in his letter *Inter innumeras sollicitudines* (1892), gave his blessing to colonial France, which was to be 'admired for setting off to distant lands where by the expenditure of her treasure, the labours of her missionaries and even the cost of her blood she spreads at once the fame of France and the blessings of the Catholic religion'.

Today the view that the slave trade is one of the basic causes of Africa's historic backwardness has numerous adherents, and this has caused a new crop of myths to spring up. First, this idea is challenged as foolhardy and without scientific basis, and the result of 'political passion'.[4] The trade was not as terrible as is made out, and could not have claimed many more victims, or removed many more men from Africa, than fratricidal wars. Secondly, it would be false to see in the abolitionist movement of the nineteenth century the effect of economic factors; it was a pure upsurge of opinion, running counter to economic factors.

Are slavery and the African slave trade the product of African tradition? Certainly slavery existed in Africa, for without it the purchase of slaves would have been impossible, but it existed wherever differentiation into opposing classes – the exploiters and the exploited – had appeared, and indeed this is true of every continent. The forms of slavery peculiar to Africa were embryonic: 'house' slavery – closer to adoption and distinct from the kind practised in Greece and Rome – was the predominant form. Trading in slaves only impinged on convicts, the anti-social elements who were sold so that society could get rid of them, or prisoners of war who in earlier times had been killed. In each case, sale had been substituted for the death penalty, whether that penalty had been a 'statutory' punishment or an inevitable consequence of the victim's situation.

What was the exact number or proportion of slaves in Africa? We have little exact information. Mungo Park, in his accounts, estimated three slaves to one free man, but he adduces no precise information to support this. Barth estimated that in Kano province, which was the centre of a thriving slave trade, the proportion was one to one. It is difficult to know whether either Mungo Park or Barth included mere tributaries in their definition of slaves; probably they did. Barth did not mention personages owning a great number of slaves except among the Peuls of Adamawa – this he explained by the recent date of the conquest – and he did not say how they were used. The only large-scale slave-owners cited by the Arab chroniclers were among the merchants of the Saharan and Sahelian towns, for whom slaves visibly served as a form of circulating capital.

4. H. Brunschwig, *L'Avènement de l'Afrique noire*, Paris: Armand Colin, 1963, p. 16.

In 1904 the Poulet report estimated the number of captives in French West Africa at 2 million, out of a population of about 10 million. In this connection one must note that the events of the conquest, the occupation of the great Sudanic centres, and the taking of Segu, Sikasso and other towns, far from reducing the number of slaves, almost certainly caused it to increase. It is difficult now to establish what proportion of the people were kept in captivity, but it is immediately obvious that it cannot be compared with the situation in Italy under the Romans or in fifth-century Athens, where slaves represented the great majority of the population.

Now we come to the thesis that the enslavement of blacks by the Phoenicians, Romans and others was the prelude to the modern slave trade. Examination of the relevant texts shows absolutely no sign of a truly significant traffic between Africa and the Roman empire. The few reconstructions that one has been able to find on this subject turn out to be imaginary. It is clear that certain products which were or could have been of African origin - ivory, gold dust, ostrich feathers - were to be found in Carthaginian markets, but all these products could have come from North Africa or at least from its borderland with the Sahara, which was not then desert as it is today; there were elephants in North Africa and gold deposits in the Sous area of Morocco. As for slaves, who were in any case very exceptional, they could well have come from the Northern Sahara where there was a widely distributed black population at that time (it is still in evidence today). The oft-repeated hypothesis of caravans of black slaves crossing the desert to get to the markets at Carthage is supported by no hard evidence, and is no more than a largely conscious attempt to justify the trade by presenting it as part of the mainstream of tradition. When the number of black slaves in Rome seems to have reached its height - at the time of the Antonines in the second century AD - their possession was a luxury and a mark of distinction among the aristocracy. However, they were a rarity, and the raids into the Saharan borderlands, notably among the Garamantes ('Berbers', but with black skins), were enough to keep this luxury trade supplied.

Our contention here is confirmed by Stéphane Gsell, now a somewhat forgotten author but one whose authority is irrefutable. In his *Histoire ancienne de l'Afrique du Nord* he wrote as follows concerning the conflicts between Garamantes and Ethiopians in which the Romans intervened several times on the side of the Garamantes:

Did they bring these unhappy [Ethiopian prisoners] to the gates of Syrtes to sell them as slaves? Were other blacks brought from the Sudan, destined for the same fate? This is what we do not know. There were certainly blacks in Carthage, and it is likely that the Carthaginian trade sold them to the Greeks and Italians; but they could have come from less far away, from the southern edge of Barbary where 'Ethiopians' [i.e. blacks -- J. S.-C.] lived in antiquity. There is no proof that the Carthaginians took much from the heart of Africa; it was largely by means of piracy, war and the slave trade that the Mediterranean countries supplied the slave market.[5]

In conclusion, not only was there no tradition of a black slave traffic flowing to the Roman empire, but this type of slave (whose provenance was almost certainly North Africa and Egypt) was rare and exceptional. The majority of slaves in the empire came from the 'barbarian' lands of Asia and Europe: orientals and, later, Germans. What need was there to go to the far-away Sudan to look for an item of merchandise which could so easily be found closer at hand?

We now pass on to the question of the Middle Ages and the Arabs. The view that this trade existed in the Arab period appears to me valid, and is certainly supported by evidence. There is no doubt that during the period of greatness of the Ghana and Mali empires, there were black slaves, obtained in raids against independent tribes, being sold in the Arab world. But here again there is no evidence in the writings of Arab authors that this commerce, which existed everywhere at that time, especially around the Mediterranean and in the Western world, was on a particularly large scale. It was no more important, and probably much less so, than the slave traffic which supplied the Arabs from Europe, where, untroubled by scruples of conscience, Christians sold to the infidels pagan Germans and Slavs picked up in raids on the outer confines of the Christian world. In the tenth century, Ibn Haukal mentions, among other export items carried from the maghreb to the East, mulatto women - destined for harems and 'to become the mothers of several sultans' - and 'eunuchs brought from the land of the blacks and from that of the Slavonians'.

At this time the castration of eunuchs for the Arab world was one of the most thriving commercial activities in the northern French town of Verdun, and for a long time in Venice the same commerce was carried on at the expense of Slavs from the Adriatic, who incidentally gave their name to the institution: it was at this time that the word 'slave'[6] replaced the Latin *servus*, or serf, bringing with it a modification in the meaning. This commerce could not be conducted on a large scale because in the Arab world, unlike colonial America, slavery did not play an important part in production; it served above all to supply the harems and great houses with concubines and personal servants. One should note too that it was not a one-way traffic: among their court

5. Stéphane Gsell, *Histoire ancienne de l'Afrique du Nord*, Paris: Hachette, 1929, IV, p. 140.
6. From medieval Latin *sclavus*, 'identical with the ethnic name *Sclavus*, Slav, the Slavonic races having been reduced to a servile state by conquest' (*O.E.D.*).

pages the emperors of Mali had white slaves bought in Egypt.

Another error follows from this, namely that of overestimating, to the point of giving it a decisive role, the slave trade after the tenth century in the direction of the Arab lands or the Ottoman empire, where for the same reasons its importance was reduced. This trade, furthermore, left no appreciable trace among the population, and did not become important till the nineteenth century, when it supplied a plantation economy on the coast of East Africa, where the Arabs had once again taken the place which the Portuguese had once seized from them. Around 1840, some 15,000 slaves were traded annually in the market of Zanzibar. According to Livingstone, and on the basis of data provided by the English consul Rigby, the Customs-house in Zanzibar registered 19,000 slaves passing through from the Niassa region alone. This is not an inconsiderable number, but it is little compared with the American trade in the eighteenth century. Here one should add a word on the significance of the Arab slave trade in Zanzibar. The regime of slavers in the island was protected throughout the nineteenth century by the English, who had been so punctilious over the suppression of the trade. Only in 1845, bowing to public opinion at home, did England demand of Seyid of Zanzibar that he should limit his slave trading to the interior of his African possessions - which was no hardship since the essential purpose of the Zanzibar trade was to supply labour to the clove plantations which constituted the staple of the country's economy. The complete abrogation and prohibition of this trade, in principle, had to wait till 1873, but even then the big plantation, slave-based in fact if not in principle, continued its existence under the protection of British imperialism till 1964.

I will now broach another objection which no one has made to me but which I shall make myself. In Mesopotamia at the end of the seventh century there were a sufficient number of *zendj* slaves, as they were called - in other words, slaves of African origin - to provoke slave revolts which continued for nearly two centuries. This phenomenon, it should be noted, was localised in the plains of Iraq, the seat of the Caliphate and thus the focus for the whole Muslim world. In addition, we can be certain that it was a popular movement, being associated with slaves of African origin who were there in large numbers, agricultural workers, and native Chaldaeans (who were sufficiently Islamised to give the movement a religious colouring). In short, the movement was not one that could be described as racist or racial; it was rather an insurrection of the exploited (for this is what they were, whether of African or Iraqi origin) against their exploiters. The present-day rulers of Iraq still recall this movement of the seventh and eighth centuries in their revolutionary traditions. If one is going to ask how important was the slave trade with Iraq as its destination, one must also ask how great is the African component - the black component - in the population of Iraq today. It exists, no doubt, but there is little firm evidence for it. One is led once again to affirm that even if Iraq attracted a larger importation of slaves than any other Arab land, this contribution from Africa was ultimately of little importance, and impossible even to compare to that which went to America.

Let us now turn to what I shall call the 'second wave' of mythology. In an article called 'Histoire passée et frustration en Afrique noire',[7] and even more in his book *L'Avénement de l'Afrique noire*,[8] Henri Brunschwig questions the general attitude of Africans who attribute their continent's backwardness to the slave trade:

Africans are perfectly willing to blame their low population density and the backwardness of their civilisation compared with other continents on this continuous removal of youthful and vigorous elements. Perhaps they are right, but this emigration only represented 1 or 2 per cent per year of the continent's total population, and the regions which it affected are the very ones where today the population density is greatest.

Can one say that the blacks would have been more numerous without this tapping? Birth and mortality rates depend on conditions which are too varied and complex for one to be so confident in drawing this conclusion. The European emigration to the New World in the nineteenth century did not impoverish the countries from which it came; their populations have not ceased to grow as the result. In Africa drought, epidemics, internecine wars, and the ways and customs which do not encourage the survival of small children would perhaps have kept the population at a modest level even if there had been no transatlantic trade.

We have been encountering . . . one of those frequent problems in the history of the black race which political passion has sought to resolve precipitately, but which scholars hesitate even to raise because the data seem so uncertain.[9]

What is one to think, first, of the arguments regarding debility in terms of numbers? If we look at the sources, it is certainly difficult to appreciate the importance of the blood-letting suffered by black Africa. The present figures for the black population in America do not on their own allow one to evaluate the importance of the transportation correctly. On this matter Father Rinchon notes:

One question arises: how is it that the negroes introduced in such large numbers into the [West] Indies were never able to reproduce themselves sufficiently to prevent further recourse to the trade? (It is a fact that in the island of Santo Domingo, into which 2,200,000 slaves were imported in a space of fifty years, there are only 600,000 blacks today.)

7. *Annales, Économies, Sociétés, Civilisations*, Sept.-Oct. 1962, pp. 873-84.
8. See note 3, above.
9. Brunschwig, op. cit., p. 16.

This question was also asked by Fénelon, governor of Martinique, in a letter to his minister, dated 11 April 1764: 'One thing that astonishes me is that the population has not been able, since the colonies were founded, to produce the wherewithal to dispense completely with consignments for the coast of Africa, by forming at least a solid core whose continual reproduction would prevent it from always being placed at the mercy of these consignments.'

Fénelon goes on to set forth his view of the lack of development of the black population: malnutrition, the excessive workload of pregnant black women, and the diseases frequently suffered by black boys and girls (referred to in the French-speaking Caribbean islands as *négrillons* and *négrittes*, the latter word also being used of young black women). Rinchon continues:

Even their 'animal' education is not attended to at all – in particular, one sees them in the fields exposed all day long to the fierce rays of the sun. Degrandpré [a slaver] estimates the annual mortality of blacks in Santo Domingo at 30,000, and births, together with new arrivals by transportation, at 44,000. The slave trader added: 'It must be admitted that we do speculate on the excessive amount of work they do, and we would not be afraid of making them die of fatigue if the value that we obtain from their sweat equalled the cost of their purchase.' Without the trade, the slave population of the Caribbean islands would end by disappearing completely within about forty years.[10]

What Rinchon tells us proves that the present black population level in the Americas does not allow us to evaluate fully the importance of the transportations. This view is borne out by Gaston-Martin:

Hilliard d'Auberteuil[11] wrote of Santo Domingo, which he knew well, having lived there for twelve years: 'Since 1680 more than 800,000 negroes have been brought into the country. Now [in 1776] there are no more than 290,000. A third of the negroes from Guinea usually die in the first three years after their transplantation, and the life expectancy of a negro in the country, given his heavy work, cannot be put at more than fifteen years.'[12]

These few quotations are food for reflection. Unfortunately the statistical data on the importance of the trade are fragmentary. At the end of the eighteenth century the number of those transported

10. Dieudonné Rinchon, *La traite et l'esclavage des Congolais par les Européens,* Paris: Vanelsche, 1929, pp. 97–8.
11. Born at Rennes in 1751. During his stay in Santo Domingo he was an advocate at Cap Français (today Cap Haitien), and on his return to Paris he published the strongly critical *Considérations sur l'État présent de la colonie française de St Domingue* (2 vols, 1776). The furious hatred towards him which this aroused probably led to his assassination in 1785 when he returned to Santo Domingo.
12. Gaston-Martin, *Histoire de l'esclavage dans les colonies françaises*, Paris: Presses Universitaires de France, 1949, pp. 124–5.

to the American continent every year was in the neighbourhood of 100,000. Father Rinchon, for his part, estimates that 13,250,000 were transported from the Congo alone. W. E. B. DuBois estimates the transportations as follows: in the sixteenth century 900,000; in the seventeenth 2,750,000; in the eighteenth 7 million; and in the nineteenth 4 million – around 15 million in all. Taking account of the uncertainty of the figures, he believed that at least 10 million Africans were transported to America. Charles de la Roncière puts their total for the seventeenth and eighteenth centuries at 15 million, with another 5 million for the half-century 1798–1848, based on British parliamentary papers – hence a total of at least 20 million.

We do not have the means to analyse these figures, but we must emphasise that they do not reflect the true demographic loss suffered by Africa. To the number actually transported the much greater number of other victims of the trade has to be added: those killed in the course of slave raids and wars for the hunting of slaves, those who died on the long marches to the coast, and those who died on board the slave ships. DuBois estimated that for one slave who set foot in America, five men were killed in Africa or died at sea. He thus concludes that the American trade took 60 million men from Africa, adding that with the inclusion of the east-bound traffic (based on estimates which, as already explained, we believe to be greatly exaggerated) it reached a figure of 100 million.[13] Ducasse, in his book *Les Négriers* (The Slavers),[14] advanced a figure of 150 million.

Let us now consider a more recent author, the English historian J. D. Fage. He estimates that deaths *en route* can be put at one-sixth, which would increase the number transported from 15–20 to 18–24 million. Finally, because of the modest size of these figures, and including those who lost their lives in the slave hunts, he proposes a total between 30 and 40 million.[15] This is indeed a moderate figure. One could clearly discuss at length the contribution to the overall mortality of the ancillary operations of the trade – if they can be so named. We will simply hold to the view that the actual losses must have been at least double the number of those who actually disembarked in America – perhaps more. There is no touchstone by which we can be more precise. Thus, even if we cannot be certain, the minimum loss represented by the trade still remains a very considerable figure.

Let us now move on to other arguments. We would say that the zones from which the slaves came – essentially Benin and the Congo – were originally among the most populous in Africa, and we

13. W. E. B. DuBois, *The Negro*, London: Williams and Norgate, 1915, p. 155.
14. A. Ducasse, *Les Négriers*, Paris: Hachette, 1948.
15. J. D. Fage, *Introduction to the History of West Africa*, Cambridge University Press, 1955, pp. 82–7.

are asked to conclude that the trade did not bring in its wake a noticeable depopulation. To turn the question round the other way, if Benin (i.e. the country of the Yoruba and the Fon) provided so many recruits to the trade, was that not because it was already one of the most populous regions? The depopulation of the Congo is evident enough.

Concerning Gabon, H. Deschamps raised the question in his book *Traditions orales et archives au Gabon*:[16] '[The trade], where it existed, was a means of maintaining custom and of procuring goods, at the same time as getting rid of undesirables. On the other hand, the populations which furnished the most slaves are today the most numerous.' There is a point here which should be discussed. We know, for example, that the people of Libreville, the Mpongwe, usually had many villages of captives, who were always originally from the interior. It was these who introduced the Bwiti, a secret society originating with the Mitsogo. Can one imagine that the inhabitants of these villages, coming from a people as important as the Mitsogo, can all have been sold off as undesirables, or must one think that in spite of everything it was the result of wars between peoples and tribes for the acquisition of captives? The question answers itself, and we turn to the second point.

Deschamps tells us that the traditions he collected did not go beyond the nineteenth century, when the trade was already declining fast. Brunschwig has shown the wasting away and degeneration of the coastal populations of Gabon who enriched themselves by the trade in the eighteenth century and had seen the activity disappear in the nineteenth century - while in other regions such as Dahomey it had continued up till 1850. Gabon, however, was never at any time an important supplier of slaves for trade: most came from the Congo or the regions close to the estuary - Loango and Angola.

Thirdly, the present-day demography of Gabon is the result not of the trade but of the slaughter caused by colonisation in our own time. From this point of view, the losses resulting from the trade are insignificant compared with the ravages of the colonial system which prevailed in French Equatorial Africa during the last sixty years of its existence. The requisitioning of labour for wood cutting, the gold mines and public works enfeebled the population; famine too did its work, most notably in 1925 but also at other times. Men were constantly being commandeered and separated from their families, the result being a fall in the birth rate and the spread of venereal disease, since those men could only find relief among prostitutes, most of whom were infected. In the villages, where only women, children and old men were left, they even requisitioned the food supplies to feed the workers.

The declining population of Gabon, where the level of fertility was

16. Paris: Berger-Levrault, 1962, p. 140.

seriously affected, is the consequence of these events, which took place entirely in our own time. Here one can cite many an author of the most orthodox colonialist views, such as Bruel or Éboué; I shall content myself with a reference to Colonel Lotte of the medical service, who, writing of the demographic situation of French Equatorial Africa in a professional journal,[17] gave some utterly horrifying information on the demography of Gabon. He based his assessment on an index established for the Belgian Congo, namely the number of living children per 100 adult women. When it stands at around 150, a population is in a state of advance; at 130–150 it is stationary, and below 130 it is regressing. In Gabon regression was to be found everywhere, even in the richest and most prosperous region; at Woleu N'Tem, in the Oyem district, it was 105; at Mitzic 50; in the Estuary and the Ogowe region, at Port-Gentil 81; and in Libreville 47. In these last regions, Lotte tells us, an 'accelerating demographic collapse' was taking place. The *circonscriptions* (districts) of Mouilla (113) and Chibanga (126) were below the stationary level. He concluded: 'The demographic situation in Gabon appears to be exceptionally grave. The present generation, already whittled down to the limit in the regions of forest exploitation and labour recruitment, will not be replaced.' I will not dwell on the point, since it is not our subject; but such a situation, and its causes, do not appear throughout the investigation by Deschamps, and I do not think that without considering this situation one can draw conclusions on the demographic effects of the slave trade from the present state of things and persisting memories of the immediate past. It is clear that this situation has completely blotted out the consequences which the trade in the eighteenth century could have had on the population.

Yet the demographic question is not the fundamental one. Let us consider Brunschwig's second argument, which was a comparison with Europe. This writer only considers the demographic aspect and forgets its economic and social context. The slave trade was less serious in its strictly demographic and numerical consequences than in its economic and social ones, which he does not face at any point. How does one explain the phenomenon of the trade? Why were the blacks called in to replace the exterminated indigenes in the tropical plantations of America? It was because they in particular had had habits of work and were practised in methods suited to tropical agriculture. These methods were unfamiliar to the American Indians, even the most evolved, with the exception of those of the *Altiplano* who for their part could not acclimatise themselves or work in the tropics; they were unfamiliar too to European expatriates, a labour-force still widely used

17. *Revue de Médecine tropicale*, no. 3 (1953), pp. 304–19.

in the seventeenth century (these hired men, of peasant origin but only used to the agricultural practices of the temperate zone, could not adapt themselves to agricultural work in the tropics).

Let us look again more closely at this social context. What were the pre-Columbian American societies? We will leave out of our consideration the Aztecs and Inca peoples of the *Altiplano*, in whose society class differentiation had already developed, but who were incapable of working in a tropical climate: they were to be used as slaves or as a servile workforce for forced labour in the gold and silver mines of the Andes, and agriculture was carried on in an economy based on serfdom but only for local consumption - its products, with few exceptions, being non-exportable. As for the populations of the low-lying tropical regions, the hot lands of Central and South America, they were familiar with certain forms of cultivation, notably of maize, but for them agriculture was only subsidiary; these people were at the stage of the primitive community, and still lived mainly from hunting and gathering. They thus showed themselves to be ungovernable and unutilisable, often responding to enslavement by suicide - those collective suicides of which Spanish authors have left us horrifying descriptions. They were exterminated. In Africa, on the other hand, class differentiation was beginning to show itself, and agriculture was the basic resource, the principal source of production. It used a technique which was already at an advanced stage, and adapted to tropical conditions. The attempts to populate the West Indies with white volunteers had been a failure, but not because of the climate. Some groups - such as the fishermen (originally Breton) of the Îles des Saintes, a small group of islands near Guadeloupe - adapted themselves perfectly to the climate and became firmly established. The problem was lack of adaptation in habits of work; the blacks had an agricultural civilisation already well adapted.

It was in just this sense that in Brazil in 1827 '*Brigadeiro*' da Cunha Matos, a convinced slaver, affirmed the civilising character of Africa in relation to America. It was even said in the Brazilian Chamber of Deputies by Bernardo Pereira de Vasconcelos in 1843: 'It is Africa that has civilised Brazil.' In effect, a whole material civilisation, including nutritional practices, was implanted in tropical America, not only in the African populations but in many cases among those of European origin. It was an imported African material civilisation.

The social situation in Africa, on the other hand, was the following:
1. In the Sudan regions especially, but equally in certain regions of the Gulf of Guinea, Benin and the Congo, there existed enough states or military organisations to frustrate all attempts, in Africa itself, at direct implantation and exploitation of labour. Why, therefore, was this labour transplanted? And why were slave plantations not established in

Africa? It was because the social conditions existing there did not allow a slave-based colonisation by Europe to take place without major difficulties. It was, simply, unrealisable at that time. So when Henri Brunschwig tells us that up till the nineteenth century Africa had nothing to offer but its manpower, it is impossible to agree with him. Absolutely nothing in the climate and natural conditions need have prevented these plantations of tropical products, which were actually created in the West Indies and Brazil, from appearing in Africa. Natural conditions had no bearing on the case; it was the social conditions that prevented this implantation from happening.

2. At the stage of social development which Africa had attained, whether in the societies where class differentiation had resulted in the setting up of organised states, or in so-called 'stateless' societies, slavery, even if in its domestic form only, had made its appearance everywhere. It had infiltrated the whole way of life and become a fully-fledged institution, so that the slave trade was relatively easy to set in motion.

3. Finally, the social state of Africa did not allow of unification and resistance by the gamut of peoples against the European enterprise. On the contrary this enterprise – the slave trade – came about with the support of the ruling social strata.

So what are we to conclude? The trade began by paralysing the development of the productive forces in black Africa, in the first place no doubt through the enormous numerical loss in the labour force which resulted from it, but above all, and fundamentally, through the indirect economic and political consequences. In effect, Europe gave Africa, in exchange for slaves, nothing more than merchandise of paltry value, shoddy goods over-valued because of their seeming rarity and exoticism in African eyes, gunpowder and arms destined to be used largely in the hunt for slaves, and adulterated alcohol. These were the principal trade goods.

Europe was generally able to manage without involving itself directly in the hunt for slaves. To purchase the slaves from the Africans themselves held out many more advantages and was infinitely less risky; it was in this way that the Africans became the architects of their own ruin, to the sole benefit of the slavers. Instead of productive activity, making war became the most lucrative occupation for them, with its train of human and material destruction – war for the acquisition of slaves to trade; the slave-hunter ran the risk, if his luck changed, of becoming a captive himself and making the same journey, his legs shackled, along the corpse-strewn routes to the ports down which he had previously driven his brothers.

It was at that time, and only at that time, that insecurity – incessant wars and raids breeding misery and famine – became a permanent feature of black Africa. We need only compare this with the state of security attested to by Ibn Battuta in the fourteenth century, which he himself contrasted with conditions then prevailing in the Arab world. Relations with Europe and colonial America undoubtedly brought only negative consequences for black Africa. As in Europe, new plants were introduced - maize, cassava and groundnuts - but this only diversified existing species or substituted more productive plants for local varieties which were later more or less abandoned. Thus the American groundnut replaced the *voandzeia subterranea*. However, this was not able to cause a revolution in the productive forces which could compensate for the baneful effects of the trade. On the other hand, the extension of the trade developed commercial relations of a particular type, with the slave as a unit of exchange like a head of cattle, a bar of salt, or a handful of cowries. The result was that the differentiation of society into antagonistic classes continued to deepen and widen. But it was on the basis of a regression of the productive forces that this differentiation was, in a unique way, a source of misery for the masses and in no way a factor promoting civilisation or progress.

In this sense, the social context of emigration - if one dares use that word to refer to the African slave trade - is absolutely different from the social context of the European emigration of the nineteenth and early twentieth centuries. The latter was a consequence of the development of capitalist society, of a progress accelerated by productive forces in the capitalist framework. And without impeding that progress, and proportionately less than if there had been a large natural population increase, it allowed a temporary attenuation of some of the contradictions at the heart of European society resulting from it. By contrast, the African trade was not the result of an internal process of development, but of external need and intervention; it had not been something which had run parallel with, or followed, progress in the productive forces. Clearly it could only have been introduced, as we have already said, by reason of the social condition of Africa, where slavery in its patriarchal form existed almost everywhere. But let us repeat that in this social context it brought in its train only a regression of productive forces, in various forms and for reasons which we have pointed out and which Henri Brunschwig altogether fails to take account of. There is the heart of the problem. The exact amount of the population loss and the statistics of the trade in this or that region are secondary compared with this.

Now we turn to a final point - a final myth: that of the origins of the abolition movement. For Brunschwig, the abandonment of the trade 'seemed to owe more to a moral revolution than to economic imperatives'.[18] What should be one's reaction to this statement? It seems to us

18. H. Brunschwig, op. cit., p. 211.

that the abolition of the trade can be explained very simply. It came within the framework of the triumph, at the beginning of the nineteenth century, of so-called liberal capitalism, of free competition, in which commercial capital was no longer privileged (as it was in the seventeenth and eighteenth centuries, particularly capital devoted to colonial trading operations) but became dependent on industrial capital. We are speaking of a time when European capitalism, with Britain leading the way (was it by chance that Britain also led the abolition movement?), was conquering the world market. The exploitation of the colonies seemed to proceed by the same mercantile methods. However, colonial trade no longer operated on its own account, swindling the European consumer the same as the native people of the colonies, sheltered by monopolies and privileges; trade was now no more than the intermediary of the industrialist, who gladly connived at the exploitation of the colonies, but with shared profits and no privileges for the trader. For triumphant, industrial capital, the equality of the rate of profit was the sign of fair dealing between capitalists – a 'just profit' for the trader, corresponding to the capital employed; if there was additional profit to be made, the industrialist, who provided the merchandise to sell and bought the primary products from the colonies, certainly intended to have his share of it. Free competition here replaces Providence in bringing about this distributive justice.

From this point of view the slave trade with America, and slavery on the plantations, seemed to be the continuation of an intolerable privilege. Thus English industrialists, who in the first half of the nineteenth century reduced their own workers to unimaginable misery, exhaustion and degradation, condemned slavery as an abomination in the name of humanity. With equal disinterestedness, the captains of industry in New York and Boston, in mid-century, pursued the abolitionist campaign until the slave-owning South was crushed.

We find the same legend repeated (and perpetuated by Brunschwig) whenever we read of the supposed disinterestedness of the explorers. From the end of the eighteenth century, Houghton and above all Mungo Park opened the way for the penetration of the African market. When the littoral offered only poor opportunities for European commerce, it was proposed to open up direct access to the markets of the interior which were believed to hold greater potential. We know that European goods penetrated there, but they did so through intermediaries who enjoyed a *de facto* monopoly: Egyptians and Tripolitanians towards the north-east, the coastal populations of the Gambia in the Congo, the Jack-jacks (Alladians) of the Ivory Coast, the Brassmen of the Niger delta, the Bateke of the Congo and many others took a part of the legitimate profits which ensured free competition for European capital.

One could refer, one by one, to the works published by the explorers; in every one of them the commercial preoccupation is clear. This is not to say that the explorers in their personal capacities were directly interested; but all their works show that one of their major concerns was to evaluate and sound out the markets which could be opened up to European commerce. It is true particularly of Barth, who was working for the British, and René Caillié shows the same concern. That said, we do not intend to ascribe to the anti-slavery phenomenon - the abolition movement - a narrowly economic and technical interpretation. There is no doubt that when Wilberforce and Granville Sharp launched the abolition movement at the end of the eighteenth century, they acted from no personal motive and were conscious of obeying only moral imperatives. But it is impossible to believe that the birth of such a movement at such a time and not before, especially in England, was a matter of pure chance. Their ideas reflected, on this particular point, the 'liberal' ideas of the most advanced of the bourgeoisie.

'The proof that economic motives are not enough', writes Brunschwig, 'is that the humanitarians were to take a century to win their case.'[19] This is to overlook that there are no absolute economic imperatives and that contradictory interests are always present. Brunschwig is right to say that 'their ideas [those of the early abolitionists] were in advance of their time',[20] but not a century in advance as he seems to think. After the end of the Napoleonic wars they were to have the active support of the entire English bourgeoisie (excepting the particular groups interested in the trade, especially slavers) and above all the industrial bourgeoisie, which was in the process of becoming the determining element. But, beyond the humanitarian theme, Britain was provided with an opportunity to establish its commercial monopoly under cover of suppressing the trade.

From 1807, when England started to tread the path which led to its prohibition of the trade, till the 1860s, when all trading in slaves was in irreversible decline, the struggle between opposed forces and interests continued through numerous vicissitudes. It is certain that the period following the restoration of the Bourbon monarchy in France in 1815 saw the total closure of certain traditional markets (Santo Domingo and the British West Indies) and the partial closure of others (the southern United States) - although organised 'farming'[21] of slaves, notably in Virginia, mitigated the shortages in certain regions caused by the abandonment of many fortified trading posts on the African

19. H. Brunschwig, op. cit., p. 22.
20. Ibid.
21. I.e. breeding with a view to the eventual sale of their offspring.

coast. But this recession was not universal. The trade was not officially outlawed south of the Equator till 1842, and although Brazil was obliged, by a convention signed with the British government in 1826, to outlaw the trade with effect from 1831, the Brazilian trade continued to thrive and actually grew in volume, reaching its record volume in 1848.[22] Ouidah, Porto-Novo and Lagos on the Benin coast remained active slave trading centres, the principal entrepreneurs being Afro-Brazilians (de Souza at Ouidah and Domingo Martinez at Porto-Novo).[23] So too did Angola and the Congo, where the Portuguese were entrenched, and – of less importance – the 'Southern Rivers' where slavers of North American origin operated.

The seizures of slave ships by the anti-slavery fleets in 1846–7 accounted for no more than 4 per cent of the total of slaves exported from Africa, and the operating risks were more or less balanced by the rise in the selling price, which had doubled in Brazil. This traffic was carried on almost exclusively under the Spanish, Portuguese and United States flags. In Brazil, 1850 marked the decisive turning-point. The government resigned itself to putting the prohibition of the trade into effect in order to stop the increased (and often arbitrary) seizures of merchant vessels by British fleets.[24] The traffic to Cuba seems to have continued a little longer, and apart from that it was carried on in camouflaged forms. Thus in the French West Indian possessions during the Second Empire, to placate the planters whose slaves had been freed in 1848, a decree of 1852 authorised the recruitment of 'volunteers'. This practice called forth repeated protests from the British.[25] In 1857, the Marseilles firm of Régis obtained a contract to supply and transport 14,000 such 'volunteers', wound up its establishments on the Ivory Coast and in Gabon to raise funds for investment in this enterprise, and set up a depot at Banana in the Congo, slaves being too costly at Ouidah. This traffic went on till 1865, and was 'severely condemned by the English and even by the Portuguese'.[26]

22. The number of slaves imported into Brazil annually between 1788 and 1829 varied from 18,000 to 65,000. The annual average between 1841 and 1845 was around 20,000. However, the importation rose to 50,000 in 1846, 56,000 in 1847 and 60,000 in 1848 (José H. Rodrigues, *Brasil e Africa*, Rio de Janeiro, 1961, ch. VI, 4).
23. On the subject of the 'Brazilians' of Dahomey, see Pierre Verger, *Les Afro-Américains*, Dakar: I.F.A.N., 1952; J. F. de Almeida-Prado, 'Les relations de Bahia (Brésil) avec le Dahomey', *Revue d'histoire des colonies*, 1954, pp. 167–222; C. W. Newbury, *The Western Slave Coast and its Rulers*, Oxford: Clarendon Press, 1961, pp. 36–44; and J. H. Rodrigues, op. cit., ch. VI, p. 5.
24. From 54,000 in 1849 and 23,000 in 1850, the importation fell to 3,000 in 1851 and had virtually ceased by 1857.
25. Cf. the collection of documents entitled *La Fondation de Dakar* (ed. J. Charpy), Paris: Larose, 1958, p. 148.
26. Chanoine L. Jadin, 'Le rôle de la marine française au Congo', *Bulletin des séances de l'Académie royale des Sciences coloniales*, Brussels, 1958, p. 1353. On the role of Régis,

On the other hand, the trade was kept up and developed in East Africa around Zanzibar, where the Sultan, an ally and protégé of the British, had introduced the clove tree, and whose plantations accounted for 90 per cent of the world's clove production at the end of the nineteenth century.[26] Britain, so energetic in her attacks on the trade in the west, here proved remarkably complaisant, the heart of the matter for her being to keep a check on American planters. As long before as 1827, '*Brigadeiro*' da Cunha Matos, deputy for Minas Gerais, had pointed this out in the Brazilian Chamber of Deputies.[27] Provided that slave-owning planters in Brazil were powerful enough to resist British pressure, the trade continued. But around 1850 the balance of forces was finally upset, and the *Esclavocrate* government (to use the Brazilian term) had to resign itself and enforce obedience to the prohibition of the trade, so as to stave off British intervention which was threatening the whole economic existence of the country. The 'economic imperatives' of expanding liberal capitalism had finally got the better of those of the slave plantation - an economic structure inherited from the period before industrial capitalism, which had contributed most effectively to the primitive accumulation that was necessary for it to flourish.

Certainly - and here we rejoin Mr Brunschwig - the effects of the slave trade on African development, and the way in which they became apparent, remain to be analysed. This is one of many fields of research open to historians. But the effect of general retardation seems beyond dispute. The productive forces torn away from Africa, and the wealth which they then created, went to build up modern capitalist civilisation and then imperialism. They had been one of the basic sources of primitive accumulation - and here I can only send you back to the classic chapters in Marx's *Das Kapital*. Non-Marxists have not hesitated to recognise the fact. It was Werner Sombart who wrote: 'We have become rich because entire races, entire peoples have died for us. It was for us that continents were depopulated.' No doubt the dead should not be written into the credit side of the ledger, but under general expenses; they have produced nothing. It was the labour of the deportees which produced one of the sources of primitive accumula-

---

see also B. Schnapper, *La politique et le commerce français dans le golfe de Guinée de 1838 à 1877*, Paris: Mouton, 1961, pp. 170–1. It was evidently not by chance that Paul Masson, eulogist of Marseilles business (*Marseille et la colonisation française*, Paris: Barlatier, 1906, new edn Hachette, 1911), passed over the 1857 'contract' in total silence while going into detail concerning all the other activities of the house of Régis!

27. H. Brunschwig, op. cit., p. 79.

tion, along with that of the expropriated peasants of France and England. There is an interesting investigation to be made into the slaver origins of part of the present-day financial oligarchy, even of certain quarters of the 'aristocracy'.

It was by coincidence that while conducting research in the archives of Maine-et-Loire I was able to trace the fortunes of the Walsh family: they were Irish, and notorious slavers.[28] Gaston-Martin, Ducasse and others have written of their activity at St-Malo and Nantes. With the backing of the banker Pâris, Anthony Walsh set up the 'Compagnie de l'Angola' in 1748, and it seems that he cheated his associates. Gaston-Martin relates that 'the man seems to have been an uncouth companion, though in business, proud and intractable, whose attitude in relation to authority was arrogant, not to say insolent. Among those who fitted out expeditions, he was pre-eminent for crossing swords with the tax-farmers and the *Bureau des Classes* [a body concerned with taxation in the pre-1789 regime], and in these disputes the small size of the sums involved, usually a few hundred *livres*, did not modify the arrogant asperity of his tone.' He had 'the reputation of over-working his sailors without a care, recruiting his crews by mere chance, and disciplining them with the cat-o'-nine-tails, and seeking his profit by means of dangerous economies in the quality of equipment and the expense of provisioning.'[30] Gaston Martin also notes: 'Further examination of the way he fitted out his ships can only lead one to conclude that they were usually crammed to the gunwales with negroes, and that the mortality on board was usually above the average, at least as far as the cargo was concerned.'[31]

A Catholic and a Jacobite, Anthony Walsh was affected by Charles Edward's defeat at Culloden in 1745 and the extinction of the Stuart dynasty's last hope of supplanting the house of Hanover on the British throne. In 1753 he retired from business and became 'proprietary colonel' of the so-called 'Royal Irish'; Louis XV accorded him the title of Comte de Serrant, which he had bought along with the *château* of that name in Anjou. With the same roughness that characterised his business affairs at Nantes, he was soon involved in numerous lawsuits with his tenants and neighbours, contesting their rights of usage or passage in his woods, and causing their animals to be seized and slaughtered by his bailiffs. He sued one of his noble tenants who, in his opinion, had

28. J. H. Rodrigues, *Brasil e Africa*, op. cit., ch. VI, par. 3.
29. J. Suret-Canale, 'Un procès relatif aux droits d'usage dans les forêts de l'Anjou à la veille de la Révolution: François Walsh et la réformation des bois du Fouilloux', *Revue historique de droit français et étranger*, 1958, pp. 634–5.
30. Gaston Martin, *Nantes au XVIIIe siècle: L'ère des négriers (1714–1774)*, Paris: Alcan, 1931, p. 242.
31. Gaston Martin, op. cit., pp. 242–3.

failed to accord him the title 'High and Mighty Lord'. The defendant, in a pamphlet, recalled that his suzerain had, only a short time before, not figured in the capitation registers of the nobility. These suits were continued by his descendants, and were not even settled by 1789! Those descendants, on the eve of the Revolution, were at the head of the aristocratic reaction in Anjou, doing battle for the rights of the 'Lords High Justices', and in particular for their rights to 'trees scattered along the highways'. In 1789 the head of the family emigrated, but his brother, 'Citizen Walsh Serrant', obtained a certificate of good citizenship and guarded the family properties. The elder returned under the Consulate (1799–1804) and integrated himself with the new regime, even having the honour of receiving Napoleon in his *château*. Connected to the 'best families in France', he left his heritage to the Dukes de la Tremoïlle, whose descendant still owns the *château*, the product of the sweat and blood of Angevin peasants and African slaves. This is only one example among many which it would be interesting to study, but such study has hitherto been thought inopportune or inconvenient. This discretion is not unconnected with the myths of which we have spoken, myths that would reduce the trade to a historical chance or of minor importance.

In history, Paul Valéry said, 'the selection, classification and expression of the facts conserved for us are not imposed by the nature of things; they must result from analysis and from explicit decisions. They are almost always given over to habit and to traditional ways of thinking and speaking, of which we do not suspect the accidental or arbitrary character.'[32] In fact these prejudices are not always as arbitrary as they appear, and often reflect an all too obvious social pressure. Nothing is more necessary for historians than to guard themselves against second-hand ideas, also when they affect the form of the paradox.

32. Paul Valery, *Regards sur le monde actuel*, 1931, pp. 15–16. Valery (1871–1945) was one of the great French poets and literary figures of his time.

# 4

# SENEGAMBIA AT THE TIME OF THE SLAVE TRADE[1]

In the past twenty years the general history of pre-colonial Africa has become much better known, but this is not true of its economic aspects. To remedy this ignorance, there was a strong temptation either to resort to hasty generalisations about the four centuries preceding the colonial conquest (a period which was anything but one of universal happiness) on the fragile basis of a few scattered surveys, or to apply improperly to past centuries established facts borrowed from those vestiges of the 'traditional' economy that still remain or were observed by the explorers and colonisers of the nineteenth century. This last error was largely the result of that committed by the ethnologists who, by abstracting data from colonial Africa, reconstituted a 'traditional' past which often proved on close examination to be mythical. Such a vision led to an under-estimation of the economic and social changes in pre-colonial Africa, which were no less real than those in Europe during the same centuries merely because they were slower.

For several years an important effort has been made to uncover these changes, despite the insufficiency and often fragmentary nature of the available sources. The work of Philip D. Curtin forms part of this effort. This author has placed himself in an interdisciplinary perspective, going beyond a narrowly 'historical' viewpoint and appealing to a 'historical economic anthropology'.[2] He has chosen a relatively well demarcated territory, Senegambia – the area within the frontiers of the present states of Senegal and the Gambia – from its discovery by the Portuguese till the middle of the nineteenth century.

Besides his own research and personal investigations, Curtin has been able to benefit from an accumulation of many works on this region written in the last few years, notably by his American pupils – on Futa-Toro, Bundu, Gajaaga and the Gambia – but also by a number of other researchers, notably Africans. Although the localisation of his sources results in certain inadequacies concerning the Wolof and Serer kingdoms on the littoral, he thus had the means of sketching a synthesis based as much on the collecting of oral traditions as on the colonial archives. Curtin was obliged to bring into play the

1. Published in the *Revue canadienne des études africaines*, XI, 1 (1977), pp. 125–34.
2. P. D. Curtin, *Economic Change in Precolonial Africa: Senegambia in the Era of the Slave Trade*, Madison: University of Wisconsin Press, 1975, p. xix; and see *Supplementary Evidence*, Madison: University of Wisconsin Press, 1975.

methods of quantitative history – in so far as this was possible with the material available – as he had done earlier in *The Atlantic Slave Trade: A Census*.[3] The supplement to the work provides the basic material which appears in a more elaborated form in the main text. He has adopted a method of transcribing local names used officially in the republic of Senegal – a good method, even if it may puzzle the reader accustomed to 'colonial' transcription. The material Curtin has produced constitutes a major contribution to the history of that region and of that period. Its wealth and diversity are considerable, and there could be no question here of making an incomplete evaluation, as in a review; it will be enough to say that this work now represents an indispensable reference which anyone undertaking new research in the field must consult. We will confine ourselves here to emphasising some particularly important themes among those on which Curtin sheds new light.

### *External commerce and its effects*

Curtin attacks a 'received idea', a cliché, which he summarises as follows (we will discuss its pertinence later): 'The received wisdom about the precolonial trade of West Africa is that Africans exported mainly slaves and received in return worthless goods such as cheap gewgaws, beads, rum, and firearms.'[4]

Detailed examination, as to value, of Senegambia's external trade (with Europe) in the sixteenth century allows Curtin to contest this point of view. Among imports, trade goods and alcohol accounted (approximately) for 54 per cent in 1680, 23 per cent in 1730 and 16 per cent in 1830. But the author shows that, at least in the earlier period, these goods included a fair proportion of items of genuine value, such as amber and coral. Textiles had an important place, and their growth was complementary to the diminution of trade goods: 4 per cent in 1680, 28.2 per cent in 1730 and 58.9 per cent in 1830, when Indian cotton goods made up 33.9 per cent of all imports. This is enough to make Curtin cast doubt on the contribution of Africa, before the nineteenth century, to the development of the European export markets in manufactured goods and the rise of European industry. Raw metals, notably pig-iron, assumed a place in imports of a far from negligible value, the quantity remaining remarkably stable (about 25 per cent in 1680, 21.2 per cent in 1730 and 21.5 per cent in 1830).[5]

By contrast, the import of firearms was not as important as has been claimed; with gunpowder, it represented 2.7 per cent of the value of

3. Madison, University of Wisconsin Press, 1969.
4. Curtin, *Economic Change in Precolonial Africa*, op. cit., p. 309.
5. Curtin, op. cit., table on p. 318.

imports in 1680, 9.6 per cent in 1730 and 9.9 per cent in 1830. It does not appear at all before the end of the seventeenth century, and only developed during the eighteenth. Thus the picture of a trade which exchanged slaves for arms that were later used in slave hunts reflects a false idea. The length of time needed to operate a musket and even a flintlock made firearms of doubtful utility in the forays necessary to capture slaves; a raid by horsemen armed with cold steel, or an attack by archers on foot using poisoned arrows, was far more efficacious in this kind of warfare. The use of firearms did not become general in the coastal kingdoms till the seventeenth century; Mungo Park attests that in 1795 the Bambara kingdoms still used very few firearms, which did not come into general use till the middle of the nineteenth century.

Now let us look at exports. Still reckoning by value, slaves represented 55.3 per cent in 1680, 64.3 per cent in 1730, 86.5 per cent in 1780, and 1.9 per cent in 1830 - if one can trust this last figure, the trade by then being illegal. In interpreting the 1780 figure, one must consider the enormous rise in the price of slaves at the close of the eighteenth century (eleven times the price of 1680). And one must also observe (something long known, though without supporting figures being available) that Senegambia, which furnished a substantial proportion of all the slaves exported across the Atlantic in the early stages of the trade (25 per cent in 1525–50, according to Curtin), was only a very minor exporter in the eighteenth century; and that the actual numbers of slaves being exported, which had previously been increasing, were declining by 1780 in comparison with 1730, this fact being disguised by the raising of their prices and their higher relative value. We need only add that throughout the period of the trade, slaves were by far Africa's dominant export. This was even true of Senegambia which, more than some other African countries, was an exporter of products (notably gum, which accounted for 12 per cent of its exports by value in 1780 and 71.8 per cent in 1830). On this point, Curtin's figures do not contradict received ideas but support them.

## *The commercial network of the interior: the Dioula diaspora*

European commerce on the coast developed largely in close connection with the networks of commerce - partly pre-existing and partly reoriented - in the interior stretching over vast distances. (The best description of it for the period before the arrival of the Portuguese is in the *Tableau géographique de l'Ouest africain au moyen-age* by Raymond Mauny.[6]) This inter-regional commerce was secured mainly by African merchants, who had originally been intermediaries for Arab-

6. Dakar, I.F.A.N., 1962.

Berber merchants from North Africa and had become converted to Islam through contact with them. They were Soninke, or Soninke who had acquired the character of the Malinke, and were known in West Africa by the generic term *Dioula* (*Juula*). This word was at one time a generally accepted synonym for a travelling merchant, and at another time, in the area between the middle Niger and the edges of the forest country of present-day Ivory Coast and Ghana, had an ethnic signification. They were the people who controlled the trade routes between north and south, the routes along which salt and cola were carried and which, well before the fifteenth century, were extended to become trans-Saharan arteries; they also controlled the east-west route, to which the arrival of the Europeans on the coast was to give decisive importance during the period of the slave trade.

They were merchants, and they were Muslims. But how did they implant themselves in societies and in dominant states with a peasant base and a military framework? As Curtin makes clear, there is no easy answer. Their position is ambiguous. From certain points of view, it seems to be a matter of professional caste (a word one should use with care in relation to these societies), which is a characteristic of West African societies influenced by the Soninke or Malinke pattern; in certain cases it seems to be a matter of one's ethnic group. The latter is true of the Diakhanke (Jahaanke), 'Malinkised' Soninke speaking a specific Malinke dialect; according to tradition, they originate from Macina but were later caught up with the routes leading from the upper Niger to the coast. To this group, hitherto little known or studied, Curtin brings a knowledge and a focus which in future will be authoritative.[7] On the other hand, the Soninke of Gajaaga are indistinguishable from the people among whom they have established themselves, except by religion and their professional specialisation. The 'Malinka-Mori' of the Gambia form a third *dioula* group, about whom Curtin gives little precise information.

In the surrounding states and societies, the *dioulas* insert themselves in such a way that they preserve their autonomy. They accept the pre-eminence and overlordship of the established power, and attempt to obtain from it peace and toleration in the midst of a complex system of alliances by publicly renouncing any pretentions to military or political power. Chains of villages or autonomous neighbourhoods throughout the length of the trade routes assure them resting-places and protection, as well as brokerage for their transactions once they have been completed. Curtin also points out parallels, suggested by their functions and status, with 'commercial diasporas' in different parts of the world.

7. Curtin, op. cit., pp. 75-81, map on p. 78.

### *The Islamic revolutions of West Africa*

The Islamisation in depth of the rural populations of West Africa is something of recent origin, which only became a full flood in the nineteenth and twentieth centuries. Although Islam had been penetrating West Africa since the time of the Almoravids in the eleventh century, its action for a long time was limited to the commercial milieu – that of the *dioulas* – and in the royal courts. We know little of its penetration at the popular level, even if one may think that it had made greater advances in the Sahel regions. The kings, even if surrounded by *marabouts* and officially professing Islam, remained chiefs in the setting of the local pagan religions, from which they derived their powers. The medieval monarchy of Mali provides the most striking example of this.

This Islamisation in depth began with the appearance, from the end of the seventeenth century, of revolutionary movements directed against the traditional monarchies. These movements, which acted in the name of Islam and against the institution of the theocratic Muslim state, had their first successes in the eighteenth century and widened out in the nineteenth. Against the economic and social background of these religious revolutions, Curtin produces a number of basic ideas, not all of them new.

We must now be critical. Since we are concerned with a work of synthesis, touching on periods, places and themes about which much has been written, and adding the author's own original research, one would like to be able to recommend this book as a trustworthy clarification, incorporating the present state of knowledge and sparing the non-specialist reader the need to refer to earlier and already outdated works, or at least serving as a guide when this literature is being critically examined. Unfortunately this is not the case.

It is necessary with this book to single out two types of defect, which are often linked. First, there are important gaps in the documentation, a fact which is surprising when one considers the resources which the author had at his disposal and his ambition to elaborate an all-embracing view of history. Some of these gaps were apparently involuntary, whereas others appear to be deliberate. Secondly, sometimes linked to these deliberate omissions, there are some serious faults in the logic and coherence of Curtin's arguments. For example, he seeks to give us new and original views on the ethnic characteristics of the Peuls (Fulbe).[8] Let us take up his thesis. The 'Peuls' and 'Tukulors' of French ethnography constitute one and the same *ethnos*, with the same language and the same culture, their only difference being that the first

8. Curtin, op. cit., pp. 18–22.

group are nomadic pastoralists and the second sedentary agriculturalists. The mistake is attributable to the anti-scientific racialism of the nineteenth century which wanted to see the Peul shepherds as 'Caucasians'. The sedentary Fulbe ('Tukulors') came from the north with the Wolof and Sereres, with whose language theirs is linked. The Fulbe nomads are Berbers who followed the sedentaries in their migrations: '. . . serological evidence . . . suggests a Berber connection.'[9] Apart from Armstrong (1964), cited in connection with the 'serological evidence', and an article by Monteil of 1929, there is no reference. Tauxier, who recorded and presented all that has been so laboriously said on the Peuls' origins, does not figure in the bibliography. Here we see an inconsistency in the argument: first it is critical of the 'racist' vision which made of the Peuls and Tukulors two distinct ethnic groups; then it returns to that vision as it makes out that the Peuls are assimilated 'Berbers'. This defeats understanding.

While conceding nothing to racism, it is necessary to state that, despite having the same language, the Peuls and Tukulors are different in other ways besides their respective qualities as nomadic shepherds (not always nomadic, moreover) and sedentaries. The two have coexisted for several centuries in the Senegal river valley without losing their distinct identities; they do not have the same clan names. If the appellation 'Tukulor' is effectively a colonial invention, the fact remains that they call themselves not 'Fulbe' but '*Halpular*' (Peul-speakers). To go further would be to indulge in unfounded speculation. Curtin could have made a much more solid case in his challenge to traditional conceptions had he invoked the Fulakunda (of Guinea-Bissau and Guinea-Conakry), who are sedentary agriculturalists and shepherds of Peul culture, but he seems to ignore their existence. In fact, all his arguments come back to the colonial authors of the beginning of the twentieth century, with whom he seems to be taking issue: Delafosse, whom he cites in the bibliography but appears not to have read, had called attention to the linguistic relationship between the Peul on the one hand and the Wolof and Serer on the other, and makes the Peul shepherds out to be assimilated 'Caucasians' (he attributes to them a 'Judaeo-Syrian' and not a Berber origin, but otherwise follows the same reasoning); however he quickly renounced these risky views.

In fact we know nothing of the links between the Peuls and the Tukulors, and can only raise questions; however, Curtin's propositions take us back, either unconsciously or tacitly, to the most questionable speculations of the early twentieth century. What is certain, however, despite the 'serological' evidence proposed to us, is that the Peuls are not Berbers. Long ago, Lhote noted the resemblance

9. Curtin, op. cit., p. 21.

between the figures drawn by cattle herdsmen on the walls of Saharan caves and the Peuls nomads; with great precision, Amadou Hampaté Ba has identified in some of these representations scenes drawn from the initiation rites of young Bororo Peuls.[10] Since then, the prevailing opinion among specialists has been that the ancestors of the present-day Peuls are the cattle herdsmen of Saharan archaeology, and that for several millennia they co-existed in the Sahara with the ancestors of the Berbers and the black cultivators. Naturally this opinion can only rest on very strong presumptions and cannot be taken as a certainty; meanwhile, the least that one would have asked of Curtin was that, before advancing his own explanation, he had ventilated this one, which is well known to all Africanists, even novices, and discussed it.

But now we come to more serious matters. As we said at the beginning, Curtin challenges a number of received ideas on the slave trade and its effect on African societies. He summarises these ideas as follows: the trade led Africans to supply a preponderance of slaves (relative to other items) in exchange for valueless merchandise, as the result of which the African economies remained stagnant and static during the whole era of the trade, and even underwent a recession in production and in the standard of living.[11] He maintains that the statistics produced by him demolish these received ideas. (Openness and strict scholarship require that he should name and quote the authors he wishes to challenge, and give precise summaries of their arguments.)

Let us look again at these clichés. As for Africa's 'contributions' to commerce, Curtin's figures confirm what cannot be doubted, anyway, namely that slaves were by far the biggest export item. It has never been claimed that it was the only item; but even in Senegal and Mauritania, gum, which was important from the eighteenth century onwards, did not take first place among exports till the transatlantic slave trade had been outlawed. As for imports, the details provided by Curtin are full of interest, and we have to take account of them; thus imported firearms were probably not on the whole used directly in slave-hunting, but served the purpose of consolidating the power of a certain number of mainly coastal states – states whose economic activity had turned increasingly in the direction of slave-hunting – against their eventual enemies. In any case, the products imported – whether firearms, alcohol or common trade goods – did not seem capable of

10. By Henri Lhote: 'L'extraordinaire aventure des Peuls', *Présence africaine*, XXII (Oct.–Nov. 1958), pp. 48–57; *À la découverte des fresques du Tassili*, Paris: Arthaud, 1958; and 'Le peuplement du Sahara néolithique d'après l'interpretation des gravures et peintures rupestres', *Journal de la Société des Africanistes* (Paris), XL, 2 (1970), pp. 91–102. Also A. Hampaté Ba and G. Dieterlen, 'Les fresques d'époque bovidienne du Tassili-n-Ajjer et les traditions des Peuls. Hypothèses d'interpretation', *Journal de la Société des Africanistes*, XXXVI (1966), pp. 141–57.
11. Curtin, op. cit., p. 309.

contributing anything to Africa's economic development. Whatever their real value may have been, these consumer goods were destined mainly for the ruling echelons, and especially for the direct or indirect beneficiaries of the slave trade.[12] The importing of iron, which was only important in terms of relative value in the seventeenth century, is partly explained - as Curtin himself indicates - by the absence of deposits of ore on the Senegambian littoral; here imported iron replaced that formerly brought from the interior rather than being an indication of some sort of 'development' - as the stability of the quantities imported over three centuries bears witness. The advance of textiles, which was tied to the gum trade for which they provided the means of exchange, did not contribute to the development of the local textile industries whose products, as Curtin shows us, were partly re-exported by the Europeans themselves to other parts of the African coast till the eighteenth century. Thereafter, these industries found themselves being undercut in their own zones of production. In short, Curtin's figures - the size of which we are not discussing here, do not by any means prove what he is suggesting, but rather tend to confirm, by specifying them, the very clichés that are in question.

Did the slave trade have no other consequences for the internal evolution of the societies of Senegambia? The ideas on this subject that I first advanced nearly two decades ago are set out elsewhere in this volume (see above, pp. 62–76): one will recognise there the clichés which are Curtin's target (except for those concerning the stagnation and immobility, of which there is no trace), but ones that he stigmatises are perhaps those of some other author, since neither in his text nor in his bibliography does he refer to my writings - not even my chapter on Senegambia from 1600 to 1800 in Ajayi and Crowder's *History of West Africa*,[14] to which he and I were fellow-contributors. I am the first to admit that what I wrote so long ago needs to be clarified and modified. But I believe that the essential ideas have not been found wanting, but have rather been confirmed by specialised works such as those by Barry and by Becker and Martin.[15] Relying particularly on the texts rediscovered by Carson Ritchie,[16] Barry has revealed the economic signifi-

12. In this connection, see A. van Dantzig, *Effects of the Atlantic Slave Trade on some West African Societies*, and C. Becker and V. Martin, 'Kayor et Baol, royaumes sénégalais et traite des esclaves au XVIIIe siècle', *Revue française d'histoire d'Outre-Mer*, LXII, (pp. 226–71 1st & 2nd term 1975, pp. 252–69 and 270–300.
13. J. Suret-Canale, *Afrique noire*, I, Paris, Editions Sociales, 2nd edn, 1968, pp. 203–5.
14. J. F. Ade Ajayi and Michael Crowder (eds), *History of West Africa*, London: Longman, 1971.
15. B. Barry, *Le Royaume du Waalo* (1659–1859), Paris: Maspero, 1972; C. Becker and V. Martin, see note 12, above.
16. Carson I. A. Ritchie, 'Deux textes sur le Sénégal', *Bull. I.F.A.N.* (Dakar), B, XXX, I (Jan. 1968), pp. 289–353.

cance of the first, abortive attempt at a Muslim revolution, known as the 'war of Toubenan', which occurred in Senegambia in 1673–7. The development of the trade made the traditional aristocracies of the coastal kingdoms more and more oppressive, in response to the demands of the European traders in provisions and slaves. They multiplied their forays (on the pretext of collecting dues), and when the occasion presented itself, did not hesitate to enslave their own subjects on the pretext of their rebellion. No doubt, the Mauritanian reformer Nasir-al-Din was motivated in imposing his authority on Futa-Toro, Walo and Cayor in the name of Islam by the diversion of the flow of trans-Saharan commerce to the benefit of European trade; but he struck a note that would call forth a popular response in recalling that 'God does not allow kings to pillage, kill or enslave their peoples.'[17]

The development of internal tensions and contradictions in the Wolof kingdoms of Cayor and Bayol, and the intervention in internal conflicts of the European authorities who allowed the traditional aristocracies to crush the revolt of 1673–7, are illuminated in a remarkable way by Becker and Martin. But let us leave aside these authors, who wrote after Curtin and criticise his view of history with some force. Curtin has the indisputable right to reject Barry's interpretation provided that he states what it is and sets down his own arguments to counter it. But he contents himself with a disdainful footnote, 'See Barry . . . for another interpretation.'[18] This is neither serious nor intellectually honest.

There are other surprising lacunae. At the beginning of the book he gives a short general summary of the political history of the coastal kingdoms, but this contains no reference to the fundamental source for the country's traditional history, namely the 'Notebooks of Yoro Diao' in which an old court dignitary recorded the historical tradition of these countries; these were published between the world wars by Raymond Rousseau.[19] They testify to an extremely troubled history, and to place them beside the colonial sources makes it possible at one and the same time to clarify their chronology and to examine the extent to which this history is connected with the intervention of the European powers and their warehouses. Curtin shows[20] that most of the slaves sold came from the interior of Senegambia, and pays particular attention to the traffic which brought them, principally from the Bambara country, to Galam and the Gambia. According to his figures, 23.5 per cent of the slaves sold originated from that region. How did the Wolof kingdoms procure

17. Chambonneau: quoted by Ritchie, loc. cit., p. 338.
18. Curtin, op. cit., p. 50, note 3.
19. Rousseau was a teacher at the Lycée Faidherbe at St Louis in Senegal during the 1930s, and wrote a number of works on the history and geography of the country.
20. Curtin, op. cit., p. 188.

slaves from the heart of their own ethnic groups? And what were the political and social consequences of this phenomenon? Curtin does not seem to face up to this question at all.

The history of Senegambia at the time of the slave trade leads to the problem of the 'Muslim revolutions'. We will not return to what we have already said above on this subject. To the extent that the Peul converts often took part in revolutions of this kind (Futa-Jalon, Macina, Sokoto), colonial historiography, using frameworks of reference borrowed from the history of Europe and Asia, has tended to see in them the advent of aristocracies of pastoral or nomadic origin, imposing this tutelage on sedentary agriculturalists. Were not these Peuls, who were relatively light-skinned and thus credited with a possible 'white' origin, pre-destined to dominate the 'inferior races'? This 'explanation', in which racism is implicit or explicit, runs up against serious objections. The revolution of 1776 in Futa-Toro was conducted by sedentary '*Halpular*' against a traditional dynasty of Peul origin; and in the nineteenth century even El Hadj Omar himself was a Toronke and not a Peul. Since the 1950s, D. A. Olderogge and Thomas Hodgkin[21] have revealed the social content of the 'revolution' led by Osman dan Fodio against the Hausa monarchies at the beginning of the nineteenth century from Arabic texts (those contemporary with the *jihad* [holy war], and those of Osman dan Fodio himself). The literate Peuls or Toronke had appealed, against the traditional monarchy and aristocracy, to the oppressed in Hausa society - peasants, women, the young; inversely, groups of Peul vassals had remained 'faithful' to the Hausa kings. I tried, fifteen to twenty years ago, to generalise from this social explanation and to connect it with the aggravation of internal social contradictions in African societies brought about by the slave trade.[22] And, since then, innumerable works have shown that this was a fruitful way of proceeding. In the first place, the discovery of the revolution *manquée* of 1673-7, the first of its kind, in which the Peuls played no part, and its interpretation by Barry (see above, p. 83); to which must be added the works of V. Monteil (also omitted from Curtin's bibliography, which contained some of his articles but not his *Islam noir*), Martin Klein, Yves Person and many others whom I regret not to be able to cite here.[23] It is understood that

21. D.A. Olderogge, *The Western Sudan from the Fifteenth to the Nineteenth Century*, Moscow, 1960; T. Hodgkin, *Nigerian Perspectives*, Oxford University Press, 1960.
22. J. Suret-Canale, *Afrique noire*, I, 1958, and 'Zur historischen und sozialen Bedeutung der Fulbe-Hegemonie (XVII-XIX Jahrhundert)' in *Geschichte Geschichtsbild Afrikas*, Berlin (East): Akademie-Verlag, 1960, pp. 29-59 (French text: 'Essai sur la signification sociale et historique des hégémonies peules', *Cahiers du C.E.R.M.*, Paris, 1964.
23. V. Monteil, *Islam noir*, Paris, Eds du Seuil, 1964; Martin Klein, *Islam and Imperia-*

not all these authors have the same conceptions; Monteil, for example, does not refer to Marxism. However, underlying their different viewpoints are some common traits – of which Curtin seems to have been unaware. It is true that he seems to ignore a number of these authors, but it is difficult to understand why he did not use the analysis of the *dioula* networks on the upper Niger in Yves Person's *Samori*, which would have allowed some highly illuminating comparisons with those he was studying himself.

But despite this inadequacy, Curtin – apparently without knowing it – illustrates this conception excellently through the materials he produces which refer to the revolution of 1776 in Futa-Toro and its consequences (including the 'recuperation' of the movement by the new ruling élites who were responsible for the assassination of Abdul Kader and finally the setting up, under cover of a Muslim theocracy, of an oligarchy no less oppressive than that which the revolution had condemned and overthrown). On the other hand, as we have shown, he discards all interpretation of this kind for the revolution of the 'Tubenan' in Wolof country, which leads to an astonishing error in reference to the country he knows best, the Bundu.

According to tradition, which there is no reason to doubt on this point, the Bundu state was founded at the end of the seventeenth century by a Toronke *marabout*, Malik Si, founder of the Sisibe dynasty and probably a survivor of the failed revolution of that time. Curtin concludes that the Bundu state 'was the first of a series of almamates founded by religious insurrection or conquest',[24] and that 'The Bundu model was thus available when the Torodbe emerged as successful leaders of a similar religious revolution in Futa.'[25] This is completely erroneous. If there was a 'model' for the Torodo revolution of Futa-Toro, it was a similar revolution in Futa-Jalon twenty-five years earlier, which had 'imported' a certain number of its cadres, as well as its 'traditionalists' and *griots*,[26] from Futa-Toro. The territorial and

*lism in Senegal: Sine Saloum, 1847–1914*, Stanford University Press, 1968; and Yves Person, *Samori, une révolution dioula*, Dakar: I.F.A.N., I (1968), II (1970) and III (1975). For our present purposes, Person's vol. I is the essential authority.

24. Curtin, op. cit., p. 42.
25. Ibid., p. 43. The Torodbe referred to were the authors of the Islamic revolution in Futa-Toro in 1776.
26. An endogamous caste, with a status similar to that of other artisan castes – blacksmiths, weavers, jewellers and suchlike; castes peculiar to Soninke-Malinke societies and other societies which came under their influence (mostly in the far west of the savanna zone). There are different categories of *griots*. The humblest are simply musicians and praise-singers to the nobles whom they serve; a prince has his own personal *griot* who, as well as performing these functions, will also be a messenger or adviser, and can acquire great influence until eventually he assumes a place in the prince's intimate entourage. The highest category is that of 'traditionalists' attached to great princely families, whose function is to memorise and recite, in metrical song, the family's historical traditions. This was a way for the family to remind itself of its rights, precedence and so on.

military chiefdom founded in Bundu by the miracle-working *marabout* Malik Si, though of slight importance as reflected in the works of eighteenth-century authors, not only was not a theocratic state despite the title of *eliman* borne by its ruler, but had actually become pagan. (On this process of reversion to paganism, Yves Person's *Samori* offers illuminating points of comparison, notably in the developments which relate to Samori's family origins. The truth was otherwise; it was at the end of the eighteenth century, under Futa-Toro's influence, that the Sisibe monarchy changed into a theocratic state. On this point we have exact and irrefutable evidence from Houghton (1790) and Mungo Park (1795) - whom Curtin cites abundantly elsewhere - and, for the beginning of the nineteenth century, from Gray and Dochard.[27] Houghton shows us that Bundu, like Wuuli and Bambuk, was shared between Muslims and pagans; from Mungo Park, writing a few years later, we learn that Islam had claimed almost the whole population - *with the exception of the king*.[28] According to Gray and Dochard,[29] it was only at a late stage - at the beginning of the nineteenth century - that *almamy* Amadi Aisaata decided for political reasons to be converted to Islam. (Aisaata was the ally of the pagan Bambara, and instigator, with the Toronke oligarchs, of the assassination of Abdul Kader, founder of the Toronke state and chief representative of the revolutionary religious tendency.) I noted all this in an unpublished lecture to the congress of Africanists at Dakar in 1967; this may well have escaped Curtin's attention, but he cannot have failed to read my chapter (12) in volume 1 of the Ajayi/Crowder *History of West Africa*, already mentioned above, - in which he too was a contributor.

This confusion on his part indicates a more general confusion which follows from his refusal to proceed to an analysis of the social content of the Muslim movements. No analysis is offered which highlights the classic distinction between two types of Islamic society. First there is the Islam of the *dioulas*, which is liable to become the Islam of the court among traditional kingships, based on a kind of association and integration with the traditional society, hostile to *jihad* and forced proselytisation (the court *marabouts* are royal counsellors and providers of Koranic amulets, but do not seek to deflect the rulers from their role linked to the local religions); and secondly, there is the military and conquering type of Islam, propagandising for the *jihad*, and not hesitating to mobilise and convert the peasant masses, legitimising their grievances against the traditional hierarchies in the name of the true

27. Mungo Park, *Voyages dans l'intérieur de l'Afrique 1795–1797*, Paris; Gray and Dochard, *Voyages dans l'Afrique occidentale pendant les années 1818, 1819, 1820 et 1821*, Paris, Avril du Gastel, 1826.
28. Mungo Park, op. cit., p. 91.
29. Gray and Dochard, op. cit., p. 178.

faith. Between these two is the faith of relationships – *dioula* Islam often provides the warlike, political Islam with its chiefs or at least its theorists – and of contradictions which, in the case of Samori, Yves Person illuminated in all its ramifications.

Curtin has admirably illuminated the ideology of *dioula* Islam, based on the example of Diakhanke in which this ideology developed in a particularly typical way; but now here does he seek to explain how this pacific Islam, which loftily rejects any political ambition, has in certain circumstances been able to give way to a conquering faith, the inspiration of a theocratic state. This is one of the main problems posed by the history of Senegambia between the seventeenth and the nineteenth century. To make rather severe criticisms of the lacunae and inadequacies of Curtin's book is not to underestimate the contribution to historical knowledge with which he must be credited and of which we emphasised the essential features at the beginning of this essay. One thus regrets all the more that on his chosen territory he has not managed to achieve that solid and reliable clarification which one has the right to expect from him. This failure is less a matter of certain involuntary gaps in his information, which after all can be excused, than of an unadmitted bias, which appears like a watermark throughout his work. The 'received ideas' with which he takes issue in the name of scientific objectivity are not those of colonial historiography, which scarcely anyone dares to defend openly; they are those of the anti-colonialist and African nationalist historiography of the past two decades. It is implied in his critique that the passionate quality of this historiography gives it an unscientific, subjective character. But this somehow leads him to a contrary prejudice: what of the slave trade and its negative effects on African societies? Undoubtedly none of this was very remarkable, and it has all been greatly exaggerated; the number of slaves exported as not as high as has been claimed, and on the whole the effect of the trade on African societies was negligible. Neither Curtin's professions of faith against the 'pseudo-scientific racism' of the nineteenth century (and that of the twentieth perhaps?), nor his praise for the capacity for development possessed by African societies (a capacity apparently unrecognised by critics of the effects of the slave trade), can conceal the fact that, in spite of himself, he is playing the devil's advocate. And we all know which devil this is. As a result, he voluntarily ignores certain facts and sources, and refuses to raise certain problems – which is the very opposite of the scientific objectivity to which he lays claim. One can only regret it.

# 5

# ANTICOLONIALISM IN FRANCE UNDER THE THIRD REPUBLIC: PAUL VIGNÉ D'OCTON[1]

Paul Vigné d'Octon was born at Montpellier in 1859. To most of our contemporaries this name means next to nothing, but there was a time when it had notoriety in both literary and political circles. Vigné d'Octon was the most courageous and most determined spokesman for anti-colonialism in the French Chamber of Deputies during three legislative terms, from 1893 to 1906. He was also the best informed. His books, like his speeches in the Chamber, contributed to the denunciation of the crimes of conquest and those of colonial exploitation. A supporter of all generous causes, he was systematically attacked by the colonial party, and all available tactics were used to silence him. Around his published works - and his name - there was a conspiracy of silence.

Although Vigné d'Octon's career was played out as much in the first half of the twentieth century as in the nineteenth, he was in many ways a man of the nineteenth century. He possessed an eloquence and a love of words which recall Victor Hugo and the French revolutionaries of the nineteenth century: the pamphleteers of the Paris Commune. He also had spiritual energy. Although his profession was medicine, he was more a poet than a man of science; as a rationalist, he respected and made use of scientific knowledge, he was guided more by feeling than by a cold analysis of reality. A man of the south, he loved his native Languedoc and knew how to convey the life of the country in pages that recall Eugene Le Roy.[2]

Vigné d'Octon kept alive the nineteenth-century tradition of individualism and anarchist leanings, to which he added a hostility to all forms of hypocrisy and puritanism, and perhaps a liking for occasionally shocking bourgeois respectability: he was of the generation of Octave Mirbeau.[3] His work, like his actions, testify to a deep love of life

1. Published by *Recherches africaines/Études guinéennes* (new series), 1-4, 1959, Berlin (East), pp. 23-34, but originally broadcast as a talk on Radio Guinea (the centenary of Vigné d'Octon's birth was honoured particularly in Guinea where, as we shall see, he had special links). The author records his thanks to Madame Vigné d'Octon, who gave him much detailed information on her husband's life and work.
2. A 'regionalist' author (1836-1907) who spent his whole life in Périgord and devoted his life's work to it. His best-known novel, the factually-based *Jacquou le croquant* (1899), described a peasant revolt against a local aristocrat, whose *château* was burned down. His work is of republican and socialist inspiration.
3. This novelist and playwright (1848-1917), originally a Catholic and a monarchist, moved over to the extreme left in the aftermath of the Dreyfus case. His best-known

and of his fellow-humans.

We will not delve into his purely literary life, which started in 1886 with contributions to the *Revue bleue* and the *Figaro littéraire*, where he first signed himself 'Vigné d'Octon'. Périvier, who ran the *Figaro littéraire* under the pseudonym 'Gaëtan Kérivel', said to him: ' "Paul Vigné" is too short - where are you from?' 'From Montpellier.' ' "Paul Vigné de Montpellier" is too long.' 'My father came from Octon.' ' "Vigné d'Octon" - that will do nicely. It sounds well and has a sonorous ring. It is a name that will etch itself on the memory. I baptise you Vigné d'Octon, without holy water. That is how you will sign yourself.' His first novel was published by Lemerre in 1888.

We are concerned here with the politician, and in this connection we should look at several of the circumstances of his youth. Paul Vigné was born on 7 September 1859 in the rue de l'Université (formerly rue de la Blanquerie) at the bakery called 'Epis d'Or'. The sign outside showing an ear of corn is still there today. His father, a fervent republican, wanted him to become a lawyer, while his mother, a fervently pious Catholic, sent him to the little Montpellier seminary with the intention of his entering the priesthood. As a child he was torn between the two opposite tendencies, but finally his father's ideas prevailed. He wanted to become a doctor, and began his medical studies in Montpellier, continuing them in Aix-en-Provence. Paul Vigné belonged to the generation of Arthur Rimbaud. From childhood onwards he dreamed of adventure, combined with literary achievement.

As an assistant medical officer in the navy, he sailed for Guadeloupe in the West Indies in April 1881. He returned to France in 1883, having completed his compulsory military service, and took his final examinations in medicine, presenting his doctoral dissertation at Montpellier. He was now twenty-four, a qualified doctor and penniless. He had also fallen in love, during his holidays at Octon, with a rich girl, Madeleine, who lived in the nearby *château*. Her family opposed the match and compelled Madeleine to marry a lawyer from her 'own world'. In despair, Paul asked to be sent again to the colonies, and it was as a naval surgeon that he arrived at Dakar in 1884. Assigned to the French West African fleet, he thus stayed first in Senegal, and later in the 'Rivières du Sud' (today the coast of Guinea, but then also including Casamance) - brought to Africa by disappointment in love, combined with the lure of exotic adventures often felt by the young of those days. The experience was decisive, if not in his political orienta-

---

novels are *Le Jardin des Supplices* and *Le Journal d'une Femme de Chambre* (made into a film by Luis Buñuel). A virulent critic of the army, the Church, the bourgeoisie and social hypocrisy, notably over sex.

tion, then certainly in what was to be his preoccupation: the colonial problem. From now on, this was to be the subject of much of his writing, as of his political activity. Here Vigné d'Octon had his limitations. Like most of his contemporaries, he never had a clear understanding of the nature of African civilisations, in which he could only see horror and barbarism. He never analysed in any depth the economic driving power behind colonial imperialism. His reaction came entirely from the heart. He noted that in Africa both soldiers and administrators, sent there as harbingers of civilisation, became guilty of the worst atrocities. Young Frenchmen were being exposed to the risk of sickness and death, and were led astray by the role assigned to them, while financiers and sharks grew rich from the colonial enterprise. He was to denounce what he had witnessed with all the eloquence and indignation at his command.

On this point his position - though dictated entirely by his emotional response - was considerably clearer and more coherent than that of many socialist leaders. Jean Jaurès was at first seduced by his admiration for Jules Ferry into an attitude towards the colonial party which was more than conciliatory. From the very beginning, on purely humanitarian grounds, Vigné d'Octon displayed a relentless hostility - from which he never wavered. In his first books - *Au pays des fétiches* ('In the land of the fetishes', 1891), *Terre de Mort* ('Land of Death', about Sudan and Dahomey, 1892) and *Journal d'un marin* ('A Sailor's Journal', 1897-8) - he described the demoralisation of small garrisons eaten up by the fever which was allowed to run rampant, and he showed how because of this demoralisation it was possible to use them for inhuman tasks; the soldiers and sailors were ready to venge themselves on the inhabitants for the hardships and the homesickness they were forced to suffer. One knows how, in recent times, this psychological mechanism was activated in Algeria. In *Terre de Mort*, which he dedicated to a fellow naval doctor and to Governor Bayol, he narrowed down the question of the supposed barbarity of Behanzin[4] and his subjects. He exposed the scandal of the Cayor railways (the 'Dakar-St Louis') in which private companies, the most prominent among them being the 'Batignolles' trust, had defrauded the state into making good a deficit which had been created deliberately. He denounced the sending of young Frenchmen to their deaths in defence of sordid commercial interests. But the episode which scarred him most

4. Behanzin (1844-1906) was the last king of independent Abomey (Dahomey). Conquered by the French, he surrendered in 1894 and was deported to Algeria, where he died. The human sacrifices practised in Abomey (as in many other states in this part of Africa), particularly on the occasion of royal funerals, were invoked as a 'humanitarian' justification for the conquest of Dahomey.

deeply was taking part in the 'Nunez column' in 1885. The 'Rivières du Sud' area was then being constantly ravaged by wars between rival chiefs, which were complicated by parallel interventions by the French, British, Germans, Portuguese *et al.*, all seeking to eliminate each other! Since 1870, the chiefdom of Nalous in the Rio Nunez was in dispute between Dinah Salifu - nephew, minister and successor-designate of the old chief Yura Towel - and Bokari, chief of the village of Katinu. For fifteen years the struggle had gone on, with some fearful atrocities being perpetrated. An occasional truce would interrupt the warfare, which was only stopped eventually through the arbitration of the commander of the 'circle' of Boke, where the French had built a fort in 1864 - only to start again in 1884. The European merchants appealed for an intervention to put a final stop to a conflict which was harming their interests. In a panic, Bayol sent the gunboats *L'Ardent* and *Héron* to anchor in the Rio Nunez in March 1885.

Vigné d'Octon described the mentality of the naval officers, pleased to be given some relief from the boredom of lengthy stationing before Goree:

> Bokari and Yura had their enemies and their backers among the officers. . . . Occasionally, a voice could be heard suggesting a peaceful solution, drawing attention to the apparent harmony of the country, and asserting that the crimes committed were not proportionate to the vengeance which it was proposed to exact for them. Anyone who spoke in that way would scarcely be listened to, and there were cries of 'down with the trouble-maker!' And promotion? And decorations for gallantry? And carrying out the order of the day? That was how one amused oneself in this benighted country. The orders from above were there - categorical.[5]

It was decided to use cannon - but against whom? Yura and Bokari were both under French 'protection'; both flew the Tricolor, and each separately had come on a mission to the French high command to demonstrate his loyalty and ask for its intervention on his behalf. The French merchants were on the side of Bokari; it seemed that they resented the high customs dues exacted from them by Dinah. But Bokari was believed to enjoy the support of the English, and the civil administrator of the Boke circle, De Beeckmann, urged that the decision should go against him. Vigné d'Octon gave a thumbnail sketch of De Beeckmann: 'a broken-down man-about-town, whom an influential friend had saved from ruin and sent to the coast of Africa, plastered over with gold braid. He was as terrible as he was diminutive in stature, and could only talk of bursts of gunfire, revenge and exemplary punishment.'[6]

5. Vigné d'Octon, *Journal d'un marin*, Paris: Flammarion, 1887, p. 253.
6. Ibid., p. 254.

The work of repression then began. Several dozen villages were systematically razed to the ground by cannon fire, encircled and burnt along with their inhabitants. Bokari, clutching the French flag which he had hoisted at his own house, was killed by a cannot shot and his head was cut off and sent to his adversary. The so-called 'auxiliaries' (irregular troops belonging to local chiefs who were allied to France) succeeded in 'cleaning up' the village of Katinu:

One of them, with sneering laughter, disembowelled a dying woman and amused himself by smashing her teeth with his heels; another went about, stamping on all the dead bodies with an inexpressible frenzy and plunging the point of his assegai into every eye where one last glint of agonised life flickered. This man wound bloody intestines around the barrel of his rifle, and his companion, with great persistence, used the blunted blade of his sabre to cut off the breasts of an old woman whose tiny carcass still breathed.

I saw the body of a little girl aged six or seven which had been cut into two parts of equal size. Beside the stumps lay a baby (her brother, presumably) with his skull flattened like a cheese, and I noticed stretching towards the two of them the stiff and contorted arms of a dead woman lying, her stomach cut open, in the mess of her entrails.

Then there was the line of prisoners, with lacerated chests and heads, and all their limbs riddled with sabre cuts and their backs grazed by bullets. Many had hands burnt to a cinder, and noses and ears three-quarters torn off, and some had only the vestigial remains of their feet, and dragged themselves along painfully. The faces of several were no longer anything but a great wound, with their eye sockets emptied by the flames; their companions helped these ones to stand upright. There was not a rag of clothing covering them, which made the spectacle of these mutilated bodies all the more frightful.

However, a selection was made, and only those capable of being sold, and whose wounds could be patched up before the next time the caravans passed, were put under restraint. The rest were put - horribly - out of their misery.

All the eye-witness accounts are agreed on the horror of the repression. On this, the administrator Demougeot wrote: 'It is hard to understand such a pitiless repression, as unjust as it was useless.'[7] And in his *Histoire de la Guinée française*,[8] A. Arcin concluded: 'As once in Warsaw, peace reigned at Nunez over smoking rubble and corpses.' This was how, here as in other places, the 'French peace' was established. Thus an episode of Guinean history through which he had actually lived made Vigné d'Octon suddenly aware of the reality of colonialism.

Returning to France in 1887, he came into conflict with his superiors over his articles, and resigned his commission as a naval doctor. He

7. A. Demougeot, 'Histoire de Nunez', *Bulletin du Comité d'Études historiques et scientifiques de l'A.O.F.*, XXI, 2, 1938, p. 263.
8. Paris, Challamel, 1907, p. 402.

was accepted in the literary circle of the publisher Lemerre, to which the poets of the 'Parnassian' school had brought glory. He published his first novels.

In 1893 a cholera epidemic broke out at Clermont l'Hérault, near Vigné's native village, and his self-sacrifice in the battle against the disease won the admiration of the local people. He was then induced to stand as a parliamentary candidate for the administrative district of Lodève, against Paul Leroy-Beaulieu, professor at the Collège de France, a 'distinguished economist' and theorist of colonisation – and won the seat. He wrote to *Aurore*, the newspaper of Georges Clemenceau, then a left-wing radical, and his first contribution took the form of a protest against the banning of Gerhart Hauptmann's play *Einsame Menschen* (Lonely Lives) – the main objection to it being that it had been translated by an anarchist, Alexandre Cohen. His protest was successful, and the play was put on.

A speaker of formidable eloquence, Vigné d'Octon took pleasure in the electoral and parliamentary game, and in his old age used to recall the tricks of the political trade with indulgent self-complacency.[9] The colonial party (whose anti-parliamentarianism was of a kind that was ready to resort to arms if the occasion arose – against the parliamentarians whom they could not corrupt) took the opportunity to denounce him as guilty of fraudulent vote-catching. Being easy-going by nature and ready to give his friendship easily, Vigné d'Octon was tolerant towards the compromises of political life, but his own incorruptibility was never doubted. His whole career is a clear testimony to this, and the conspiracy of silence to which he was subjected was the penalty and the revenge exacted by the colonial party against its implacable and incorruptible foe. It was in effect the colonial party, then under the inspiration of Eugène Etienne and other businessmen-politicians, that he was to attack unstintingly.

In a study entitled *Comment on lance une conquête coloniale* (How to launch a colonial conquest), Francis Delaisi described the methods of this party. At the top of the tree was the *Union coloniale*, and dependent on it were various 'committees', including that of 'Afrique française'. He described a banquet given by the *Union coloniale* in 1903 at which the conquest of Morocco was decided upon:

In the place of honour, fittingly, sat Mr Jules Charles-Roux, director of the *Comptoir d'Escompte* and chairman of the *Compagnie générale Transatlantique*; on his right was Mr Doumer [future president of the Republic]; on his left Mr René Millet, former resident-general in Tunisia, and an ambassador; and opposite, Mr Eugène Etienne, vice-president of the Chamber of Deputies.

9. P. Vigné d'Octon, *Les grands et les petits mystères du Palais-Bourbon*, Paris; Radot, 1928.

Elsewhere were all the big exporters, shipowners, textile mill-owners, bankers and contractors with colonial interests whom Paris, Bordeaux, Nantes, Lyon and Marseilles could muster. Several Deputies and Senators, and former or future ministers, had come to receive their keynote from the financiers. Finally, there were the big press chiefs.

This is one of the practices which gives capitalism its strength. Every month, the businessmen who operate in some part of the public sector meet at a dinner. They discuss together one specific question; arrive at a consensus; not without some lively discussion beforehand; and convey the result to the parliamentarians and the press. Thus the authorities and those who form opinion obey them submissively.

It was these men with whom Vigné d'Octon did battle. In correspondence with numerous colonials, he denounced the crimes of the conquest, the abuse of power, and the thefts committed by 'heroes' - Gallieni,[10] Archinard and others. Among his parliamentary interventions, those in the debate of November 1900 following the Voulet-Chanoine affair have the best claim to be quoted here.

Briefly, the circumstances were as follows. Voulet and Chanoine were two young officers who had already 'distinguished' themselves in the conquest of the Mossi country, and they were selected to lead the 'Central Africa/Chad mission'. Their task was to set out from the Sudan and, in the Chad region, meet the Foureau-Lamy mission which had crossed the Sahara from Algeria, and the Gentil mission which had come from the Congo. Thus effective French sovereignty over Chad was to be affirmed; the British were to be kept out of the area; and uninterrupted French sovereignty over the whole region between Algeria and Senegal in the west and the Congo in the east would be assured.

The choice of these two men - Chanoine, incidentally, was the son of the then minister of war - aroused the jealousy of many older and higher-ranking officers. Neither of them had any experience of the Sahel regions, nor of the semi-desert territories north of Nigeria which the Franco-British accords had reserved to France. Their column, which was much too heavily equipped, came to grief on first setting out, and Voulet and Chanoine wanted to follow a more southerly route through territory reserved to the British, but in the aftermath of the Fashoda incident there was concern to avoid further friction, and ministerial instructions categorically forbade such a course. The two officers then cut off all contact with their superiors and, freed from all restraint, these upholders of strong-arm methods - who had gained

10. Joseph-Simon Gallieni (1849-1916). Sent to Africa in the mid-1870s, and captured by the forces of King Ahmadu in 1881, but within a year had extracted exclusive privileges for France in that area. As governor of the French Sudan, he successfully quelled rebel forces.

their spurs in Mossi country and, at the start of the present expedition, on the banks of the Niger – engaged in numerous massacres. One member of the mission, sent home after a personal quarrel, revealed this to *Le Matin* to exculpate himself.

Before the scandal broke, but primarily because the mission's progress had been delayed, a Sudan veteran, Colonel Klobb, was despatched to take the mission in hand. But when Klobb arrived, rather than give up his command, Voulet shot and killed him; Lieutenant Meynier (a future general), who had accompanied Klobb, was wounded. Voulet and Chanoine decided to break with France and set up an African kingdom, but the riflemen in the party, who had gone to even greater lengths of brutality and were not prepared to give up their chances of returning to base in the Sudan with their plunder, shot the two officers. The scandal had now assumed such a scale that a debate in parliament could not be avoided.[11]

Vigné d'Octon was not satisfied with denouncing the crimes of Voulet and Chanoine; quoting numerous facts and examples, he showed that they were the natural consequences of the methods employed previously in the conquest of the Sudan. He publicly denounced the French methods of warfare: the 'breaking' of villages, the requisitioning of provisions and of labourers and porters without giving them either food or payment, and the sharing out and sale of prisoners as if they were slaves. He drew attention to the state of mind of the officers in the Sudan – unbridled ambition and desire for 'glory' (in the form of decorations and additional gold braid on their uniforms), which led them to increase the frequency of *colonnes* ('columns' = expeditions), leading to victory bulletins and promotion. Not only was Vigné listened to, but men of the colonial party were compelled to acknowledge that his accusations were just. Even Le Myre de Vilers, a former Resident at Madagascar, lent his weight to the overwhelming revelations, and refused to associate himself with the colonials: 'I am completely in agreement with Mr Vigné d'Octon as to principles, but we are absolutely at variance over who is responsible. Our honourable colleague goes for the agents who carried out the deeds; I accuse the governments.'[12] The Comte d'Agoult, the recognised spokesman for the colonial party, also acknowledged part of the facts and saw the necessity to put a stop to the excesses which had been denounced. The minister of the colonies, Albert Decrais, proved incapable of responding to Vigné's particular accusations, and contented himself with describing them as 'exaggerated'.

11. The affair was hushed up, and for thirty years afterwards the general staff forbade all witnesses of the affair to divulge anything of what they had seen. Official histories stated that Voulet and Chanoine had been afflicted with a stroke of madness', and dismissed the affair in a few sentences.
12. Chamber of Deputies – session of 30 November 1900.

Only a few representatives of the Sudan army, like Captain A. Mévil in the *Nouvelle Revue*, protested violently against Vigné d'Octon's intervention. Mévil found it necessary to defend Gallieni, against whom Vigné had brought terrible accusations (which remained unanswered): the 'exemplary' execution of Malagasy ministers; the systematic practice of bribery and of levying taxes, which were then not declared; regular use of forced labour, and so on. He took the minister of the colonies to task for not coming to Gallieni's defence.[13]

Vigné d'Octon's intervention had caused a stir, and he decided to make his accusations known to the public at large in a book denouncing the methods used to conquer the Sudan. This was *La Gloire du Sabre*, published in 1900. Many publishers had been anxious to acquire exclusive rights to his work; then the colonial party intervened. As long as the matter was confined to the National Assembly, the harm was not so great; and after all, it was mainly those serving in the field who had been criticised. But a book giving wide circulation to the accusations (the press had obediently made little of the affair up till now) was a threat to the whole colonial enterprise. Now, with the book written, the very publishers who had previously been so keen refused to touch it. It was Flammarion, his regular publisher since 1895, who finally accepted it. But when the book was printed, the firm refused to put it on sale and had the author officially threatened with legal action if it appeared with the publisher's imprint. The minister intervened. . . .

Vigné d'Octon, who had not asked the publisher for a formal contract beforehand, could do nothing. He had to take over the copies of the book at his own expense, obliterate the publisher's name with stickers, and arrange for their distribution by a small bookseller. The *Comité de l'Afrique française* took upon itself the task of making this dangerous book go out of circulation as quickly as possible, and copies were soon impossible to find. For all that, Vigné d'Octon did not give up the fight. In a new book, *Quelques coins de la IIIe République* (Certain Corners of the Third Republic), he set forth the abuses of which he had knowledge, and the publisher Tallandier, this time in spite of having signed a contract, refused to publish it. In a pamphlet, Vigné

13. We can possibly judge the quality of Capt. Mévil's arguments by quoting some samples: 'It is not true that our rule in the Sudan has been based, and is based, on pillage, arson, theft, murder and traffic in slaves. These assertions are infamous slanders! [. . .] It is possible that occasionally, after the capture of an important village, the soldiers have been guilty of certain abuses – it is impossible to keep a watch over every one of their actions. And besides, the morality of the negresses is often doubtful, and more than one has thrown herself into the arms of the victorious soldiers.' ('Nos officiers coloniaux', *Nouvelle Revue*, 15 Dec. 1900, pp. 595 and 596.)

recounted his experiences in connection with the publication of his books.[14]

Vigné d'Octon did not follow his fellow left-wing radical, Georges Clemenceau, in his evolution towards the right. He remained faithful to the radical tradition, personified by Camille Pelletan.[15] An individualist by nature, he had little or no understanding of socialism; his move to the left took him towards anarchism.

In 1906 he failed to gain re-election to parliament, but the friendly personal relations he had kept up with the radical leaders (including Stephen Pichon,[16] to whom he spoke as his convictions dictated, and whose compromises he did not hesitate to denounce) made it possible for him to be sent on a mission of inquiry to North Africa. From the three missions he undertook (in 1907, 1908 and 1909) he brought back a formidable 'bill of indictment', which he published in 1911 with the title *Les crimes coloniaux de la IIIe République*. The work was to be in three volumes, but only the first, *La Sueur du Burnous* (The sweat of the burnous [an Arab cloak]), dealing with exploitation and extortion in Algeria and Tunisia, actually appeared. The other two volumes, one of which was to be concerned with the Algerian-Moroccan struggles between 1900 and 1910, and the other with the Foreign Legion and the 'Biribi',[17] were never published, for reasons we have not been able to discover.

In *La Sueur du Burnous*, Vigné d'Octon showed the arbitrary nature of the administration in Tunisia, which was recognisable as the model for all French colonial administration. At the bottom level were sheikhs and *caids*, whose main task was the collection of taxes. They obtained their posts for the price of a few 1,000-franc notes, and to hold on to them had to hand out further gifts subsequently. They lived by the exploitation of those they administered, but still could never feel confident that the next day would not bring oblivion if they should succumb to the intrigues of some jealous rival. At the next level above them were

14. *Comment on étouffe un livre*, Paris: Ed. du Progrès, 1905. The forbidden work was published in serialised instalments in *Bataille Syndicaliste* in 1912, with the title *Le roman d'un politicien*.
15. Pelletan (1846–1915), a French politician who was Deputy for Bouches-du-Rhône and Navy Minister in the Combes government (1902). A representative of left-wing radicalism, he favoured an alliance with the socialists and was vigorously anti-clerical.
16. Stephen Pichon (1857–1933), a radical Deputy in the French parliament, 1885–93; Resident-General in Tunisia, 1901–6; Senator, 1906–24, and three times Foreign Minister between 1906 and 1920.
17. *Biribi* was the slang term for the 'African battalions' to which the toughest delinquents and those who would otherwise have been sentenced to prison terms were sent to do military service. Their last station was Fum Tatauine, in Southern Tunisia.

the civil controllers, this job being the 'dumping-ground of ex-officers of tainted reputation and officials who were no longer employable in metropolitan France, dug out of obscurity by influential politicians'.[18] 'To live on the native: not only never to spend a penny of one's salary, but to receive two and often three times as much – that was the ideal of the civil controllers and military commanders in Tunisia.' One can see that these civil controllers and the circle commanders of black Africa were as alike as peas in a pod.

The book shows the crushing fiscal system, which drew a quarter of its revenue from poll tax – then assessed at 25.80 francs a year – 'which affected the miserable up-country Beduin, the Meskine, the very epitome of the "poor devil in his tent", no less than the rich middle-class Tunisians'.[19] Not only that, but the taxpayers in the five richest towns (Tunis, Sous, Monastir, Sfax and Kairouan) were exempt! To this already heavy burden of capitalism were added 'traditional' taxes: *kanoun* on olive and palm trees, *achour* on cereals, *zekkat* on animals. When payments fell into arrears, spahis and auxiliaries were detailed to obtain them by force: those who were insolvent had all their goods confiscated and were thrown into prison. To this were added frauds: for example, false papers presented to illiterates from whom taxes were demanded a second time. The whole system is well known to anyone with some experience of the French colonial empire. With variations in detail, it was applied in Indochina and black Africa as in North Africa – Algeria having served as a test-bed for these methods.

Vigné d'Octon went on to attack the beneficiaries of colonisation. He showed how Jules Ferry had distributed vast areas of land dirt-cheap to his cronies among financiers and newspaper directors. Among these beneficiaries he singled out Boucher, a senator and former chairman of the budget committee in the protectorate (3,000 hectares), Mougeot, a senator (12,000 ha.), Cochery, a deputy and ex-minister (10,000 ha.), Hanotaux (2,000 ha.), Chaumié, a senator, ex-minister and one-time budget chairman (3,000 ha.), Chailley-Bert, a deputy, former budget chairman and a 'theorist' of colonisation (30,000 ha.), Chautemps, a senator (4,000 ha.), and so on. 'One could say that there is not a single parliamentarian who, having chaired the Tunisian budget committee during the Régence (the regime ruled by the Bey during the nineteenth century), did not become a landowner there. I challenge a good proportion of those men to show how much they paid for their property.'[20]

18. P. Vigné d'Octon, *Les crimes coloniaux de la IIIe République*. I. *La Sueur du Burnous*, Paris: Eds de la guerre sociale, 1911, p. 28.
19. P. Vigné d'Octon, ibid., p. 29.
20. P. Vigné d'Octon, ibid., p. 273. Vigné recalled that in 1900, to stifle his inter-

He gave several examples of the methods used. Ferry, with Adrien Hébrard (director of *Le Temps*) and Paul Leroy-Beaulieu (the colonial theorist, compromised in the Panama Canal scandal of the early 1890s), set up a consortium with the task of appropriating the maximum amount of land. To this end Paul Bourde, a journalist with *Le Temps* and agent for Hébrard, was appointed as director of agriculture and commerce in Tunisia and, with his master, set about appropriating 100,000 ha. (Because of the protests of rivals who were equally interested, he had to be content with 10,000 ha.) Vigné went on to cite the case of Mougeot (mentioned above), who arranged for himself to be allocated 5,000 ha. of land which had been the territory of a single tribe for eight centuries. He had the land classified as 'state property' and let at 1,000 francs a year; to make this possible he had the unfortunate inhabitants turned off the land they had occupied for so long.

Vigné d'Octon denounced the swindle practised by the directors of public works, Pavillier and de Fages, who made vast contracts for the construction of the Tunisian railways at the expense of the protectorate, and were to be found soon afterwards, having resigned from the public service, as directors of the companies whose interests they had served so well.[21]

From 1911 to 1913, Vigné d'Octon toured France giving anti-colonial lectures, and indeed in these years leading up to the war, he moved ever further to the left. As an anti-militarist, he contributed to *La Guerre Sociale*, edited by Gustave Hervé[22] who published his last political book. Then came the war, and although Vigné enlisted as a doctor, he refused to recant, as Herve and some others of the same persuasion did. At the end of the war, in *La Nouvelle Gloire du Sabre* (The New Glory of the Sword),[23] he exposed 'the crimes of the health service and the naval staff', and in the *Pages Rouges* (Red Pages) he denounced the murder of Jeanne Labourbe at Odessa and *Les drames de la Mer Noire* (Black Sea Dramas).[24] In a chapter of *La Nouvelle Gloire du Sabre*, entitled

vention in the Voulet-Chanoine affair, he was offered the post of reporter of the Tunisian budget. . . .

21. The details of this affair are to be found in P. Sebag, *La Tunisie*, Paris: Eds Sociales, 1951.
22. Journalist and politician (1871–1944), before 1914 close to the anarchosyndicalist position, and expelled from the university where he was a professor for his anti-militarism. The 1914–18 war converted him to militaristic patriotism, his journal being re-named *La Victoire*. In the 1920s and '30s, he belonged to the extreme right.
23. Marseilles: Petite Bibliothèque du Mutilé, no date.
24. Jeanne Labourbe was a teacher in Russia before 1917 who, with a group of French Communists in Moscow, rallied to the Revolutionary cause. Sent to Odessa in 1919 to organise propaganda aimed at the French occupying troops, she was cap-

'La Terreur en Afrique du Nord', he enumerated the exactions carried out in Algeria during the war for the purpose of recruitment, and described the revolts, the famine and the inhuman treatment meted out to prisoners. He concluded: 'At the moment when I am writing these lines, there is no Arab or Beduin between the southernmost point of Tunisia and the extreme west of Morocco who is not aware of the great Russian Revolution and who, turning towards the east, does not implore his God to make the reign of social justice prevail, along with the Republic of the Soviets, in the lands of Islam and in the world.'[25]

But even if he saluted the Russian Revolution, Vigné d'Octon did not become a marxist or a communist. A fierce individualist, he remained faithful to his radical and anarchistic conceptions. Until his old age he was bursting with activity, and particularly militant in the cause of the Free Thought movement. No doubt the man had his limitations, but on the colonial problem his generous instincts made him clairvoyant in a way that scarcely had an equal. In his time many men of the left, even avowed socialists, bowed before colonialism as before an ineluctable necessity, even while deploring its misdeeds. In 1909, in his book on the crimes committed in the Congo, Félicien Challaye wrote: 'Colonisation is a necessary social fact. . . . But justice demands that domination by whites should not entail the worst consequences for the blacks - slavery, theft, torture, assassination. Justice demands that the natives should desire some advantages from our presence among them.'[26] He realised later that he had been deluded, and that the justice he had called for was incompatible with colonisation. At the same time, Vigné d'Octon himself wrote confidently as follows:

I have had this dream: that finally there was justice on earth for subject races and conquered peoples. Tired of being despoiled, pillaged, suppressed, massacred, the Arabs and Berbers chased their rulers out of North Africa, the blacks did the same for the rest of Africa, and the yellow people for Asia.

Having thus reconquered, by violence and force, the indefeasible and sacred rights which, by violence and force, were torn from them, each of these human families followed its destiny which for a moment had been interrupted.

And forgetting that I am a Frenchman - which is nothing - in order to

---

tured by White army officers, tortured and shot. Vigné d'Octon's pamphlet *Les drames. . . .* was devoted to a mutiny of units of the French fleet in the Black Sea which followed. The mutineers surrendered on condition that they would be returned to France - where in fact they were court-martialled and received heavy prison sentences.

25. *La Nouvelle Gloire du Sabre*, 1st series, p. 136.
26. F. Challaye, *Le Congo français*, Paris: Alcan, 1909.

remember just one thing: that I am a man – which is everything –, I felt in the depth of my being an inexpressible joy.[27]

In spite of illness, Paul Vigné d'Octon continued right into old age to show an extraordinary youthfulness of spirit. To the malaria which he had contracted in Africa, and deafness which had come on during the 1914–18 war, was added partial blindness in his last years. Still alert, he continued to be optimistic and to love life, writing 'I have made the evening of my life into a dawn.' He divided his time between long walks across the stony countryside of his native Languedoc and working at his desk. He died with his pen in his hand, at Octon, on 20 November 1943.

Such was Paul Vigné d'Octon. In his time, the men of the colonial party did their utmost to discredit him, making him appear a fantasist and trying to suppress his work and wipe out all remembrance of him. Now that history has proved his dream to be true, all democrats, and none more than those whose tireless defender he was, will want to honour his memory.

## FURTHER THOUGHTS ON VIGNÉ D'OCTON: DID ANTI-COLONIALISM EXIST BEFORE 1914?[28]

It was in the course of preparing the first volume of my history of black Africa that I re-discovered Paul Vigné d'Octon. Much more recently Henri Brunschwig has examined the question.[29] He has analysed the principal documents: Vigné d'Octon's published works, the parliamentary records and files of archival material. One could, as he says, certainly pursue the research further by working through his many newspaper articles and papers deposited in the archives at Montpellier. In Brunschwig's opinion, the game would not be worth the candle – an opinion which, while not wishing to discourage the adventurous historian, I must admit that I share.

The following discussion will not bear on questions of erudition but only on interpretation. What, then, is its purpose? I saw Vigné as one of the most courageous and most determined spokesmen of anti-colonialism in the French parliament under the Third Republic. I stated that he was the victim of a palpable conspiracy of silence on the part of the colonial party. For Brunschwig, there are two errors here. 1. Vigné d'Octon only denounced the excesses of the conquest, but

27. P. Vigné d'Octon, *Les crimes coloniaux de la IIIe République*, op. cit., p. 8.
28. The remainder of this essay was first published in *Cahiers d'Études africaines*, XVII, 1-2, pp. 233-9. It was written in 1978, some twenty years after the preceding part of the essay.
29. H. Brunschwig, 'Vigné d'Octon et l'anticolonialisme sous la Troisième Republique (1871-1914)', *Cahiers d'Études africaines*, XIV (2), 1974, pp. 265-98.

never questioned the actual principle of colonialism. In these two respects he was no different from most of his contemporaries, including certain spokesmen for the colonial party who, on occasion, denounced 'excesses' and 'abuses' just as he did. Also, since practically nobody questioned the principle of colonialism before 1914, to talk of anti-colonialism is to be guilty of an anachronism: 'In reality, anti-colonialism between 1871 and 1914 should be placed among the myths.'[30]

2. Vigné d'Octon was not the victim of a conspiracy of silence. As someone who indignantly denounced abuses, he never lived up to his principles. 'It is why history, when it it is anxious to elucidate general ideas, ceases to be true to its name.'[31]

3. Beyond the particular problem raised, Brunschwig comes to a much more general and fundamental historical question, already posed by Lucien Febvre,[32] that of the temptation to fall into anachronism. By talking of anti-colonialism before 1914, is one not improperly projecting on to the past conceptions which are appropriate to a later age and which, in that past age, were really unimaginable?

Let us take the first point. The texts produced by Henri Brunschwig ('scientific' articles by Vigné d'Octon[33] and certain extracts from his parliamentary interventions), which had previously escaped me, leave no room for discussion. Up till a date which is difficult to establish, but which in any case did not precede the end of his parliamentary career in 1906, Vigné d'Octon denounced the horror of the conquest, like others but with more vehemence – some would say more pathos. However, this was not in order to challenge the colonial idea itself; it was to make himself the champion of a 'good' colonisation. On this point Brunschwig is right. I had certainly been aware of Vigné's limitations: the purely sentimental nature of his positions, unsupported by any analysis in depth, and his total incomprehension of African civilisations. . . . I had noted his political evolution from 'advanced republicanism' to extreme leftism of an anarchistic character; but I ascribed excessive importance to the continuity of his denunciation of the 'colonial crimes' without seeing the break which separates his positions before and after 1906 (a date given as a first approximation and with fullest reservations). Thus to speak of anti-colonialism in connection with Vigné before 1906, even if his writings of that time could later be used to contest the very principle of colonisation, is questionable; but I do not agree with Brunschwig's proposition that it would be more judi-

30. Ibid., p. 296.
31. Ibid., p. 282.
32. L. Febvre, *Le problème de l'incroyance au XVIe siècle. La religion de Rabelais*, Paris: Albin Michel, 1942.
33. Articles published in 1887 and 1888 in the *Bulletin de la Société de Géographie commerciale de Bordeaux* and the *Revue scientifique*, quoted in Brunschwig, op. cit., pp. 271–2.

cious to talk of anti-militarism[34] because, in a text which Brunschwig quotes, Vigné defended himself against this by saying 'I am not an enemy of the army.'[35] It would also be difficult to apply this label to Paul Déroulède, who vigorously denounced the Dahomey expedition.[36]

How should one designate the current of opinion (which had a left-wing component but also one from the right and even the extreme right) that, from 1871 till the end of the century, fought against the colonial conquest? This current certainly did not question the principle of colonisation; but, for want of any other term, must one deny it the label 'anti-colonialist'? It is a point worthy of discussion. In 1951 Gabriel Esquer published, with the striking title *Anti-colonialism in the eighteenth century*, a selection of the works of Abbé Raynal.[37] And why not? The words 'colonialism' and indeed 'anti-colonialism' were unknown in the eighteenth century, but there had been a colonisation, and from the Abbé's pen a body of doctrine critical of it: by what other name could one describe that doctrine? We have no other word at our disposal, since the eighteenth century did not invent one. But is there any need to emphasise that the eighteenth century's colonialism, and consequently its anti-colonialism, were very different from our own? If on occasion it shed a few tears over the fate of populations which had been enslaved or exterminated, that particular form of anti-colonialism was supremely that of the colonist against the mother-country: it inspired the American Revolution, many of whose heroes were slave-owners and had massacred Indians. Equally, Abbé Raynal, in a posthumous work, the *Histoire d'Afrique septentrionale*, extolled the conquest of North Africa, of which he had already approved the principle in his *Histoire philosophique . . . des deux Indes*, praising the 'generous design' along these lines conceived by the Emperor Charles V, and invoking the 'abominable mentality' of the rulers and peoples of those countries: here, ahead of their time, are to be found almost all the 'received ideas' which were to be the common basis of the colonial ideology in North Africa in the nineteenth and twentieth centuries.[38] So, if in the two cases mentioned one can accept – with the requisite caution – the use of the term 'anti-colonialism', my view is that it should be avoided: the risk, not merely of anachronism but also of confusion, is too great.

34. Brunschwig., op. cit., p. 281.
35. Ibid., p. 285.
36. J. Suret-Canale, *Afrique noire*, I, 3rd edn, 1968, p. 244.
37. Abbé Raynal, *L'anticolonialisme au XVIIIe siècle. Histoire philosophique et politique des établissements et du commerce des Européens dans les deux Indes*. Introduction, choice of texts and notes by Gabriel Esquer, Paris: Presses Universitaires de France, 1951.
38. D. Brahimi, *Voyageurs français du XVIIIe siècle en Barbarie*, II: *L'Abbé Raynal et Venture de Paradis*, Lille: Atelier de reproduction des thèses de l'Université de Lille

Let us return to Vigné: does one judge his post-1906 opinions in the same way as those expressed before that date? It is difficult to say exactly where the turning-point occurs: there is no doubt that it had been passed with the publication in 1911 of *La Sueur du Burnous*. Is it too polemical to be fully convincing, as Henri Brunschwig contends? The facts he cites, and particularly their attribution to unscrupulous businessmen, publicists and politicians in colonial circles in Tunisia, are correct and have been confirmed by later historical studies.[39] But what was most important here was the fact – and the terms – of his challenge to colonialism. To publish the passage from *La Sueur du Burnous* quoted above (p. 18) called for some courage. Can one deny to someone holding such views the description 'anti-colonialist'? In fact – Brunschwig shows this very clearly elsewhere – the true turning-point came not in 1914 but around 1905. That year saw the appearance of the pamphlet by Paul Louis, *Le colonialisme*, which contained the first fundamental challenge to the institution. From this moment on, one has a perfect right to talk of anti-colonialism.

Let us now go to the conspiracy of silence. To me there is no doubt that it occurred. History – with or without a capital 'H' – is made by historians. It is they who, when faced with the facts of a case, judge them and then either retain them or consign them to oblivion according to their merits. And, particularly in relation to contemporary history, their judgment reflects their politics. Thus, with rare exceptions, colonial history was written up till the middle of the twentieth century – at first hand, or supposedly so – by those personally active in colonisation, or by its apostles, and professional historians, when they became involved in it, limited themselves to copying or popularising them. This is why, when I began working in the field myself and had the task of teaching this colonial history, I knew nothing of the name of Vigné d'Octon or of the Voulet-Chanoine affair. On the other hand, I had known since childhood the name of Paul Holle, the hero of the defence of Medina against El Hadj Omar, and that of Brazza's Sergeant Malamine. Were these two any more deserving of the judgment of history than the others? Their names occurred in the colonial hagiography and therefore in the '*Petit Lavisse*'.[40] Yet the voluminous *Histoire des colonies françaises*, edited by G. Hanotaux (whom Vigné d'Octon condemned for having 2,000 ha. of land in Tunisia allocated to himself) did not mention Vigné and said very little about Voulet and

III/Paris: H. Champion, 1976.

39. Cf. P. Sebag, *La Tunisie*, Paris: Eds Sociales, 1951; J. Poncet, *La colonisation et l'agriculture européennes en Tunisie depuis 1881*, Paris–The Hague: Mouton, 1962.
40. Nickname of a patriotically inspired history textbook by the renowned historian Ernest Lavisse (1844–1922), used in state primary schools up till 1940.

Chanoine. It is pointless to expatiate on the causes when they are so obvious.

It is true that before 1914, when no threat of colonisation seemed to exist, certain liberties were taken in the language used of it – as in speaking uninhibitedly about its '*bavures*' (burrs or barbs), or in resorting to a cynical manner of defending it.[41] This was no longer found after the First World War, when the blast of the Russian Revolution and the first tremors felt in the colonial world induced caution. Opponents of the system were more rigorously censured, and doubts on the virtues of colonisation were considered subversive.[42]

However, the colonial party were vigilant to ensure that there was no over-reporting of '*bavures*'; for an example one need look no further than the suppression of the Brazza mission's report in 1906, and we have already referred (p. 97, above) to Vigné's published account of how his regular publisher Flammarion solicited and accepted his book *La gloire du Sabre* and then, under pressure, refused to distribute it. Vigné was obliged to buy back the copies on his own account, and then massive purchases quickly made the book unobtainable. The latter procedure was used again in more recent times to bring about the disappearance from sale, in Madagascar, of a very moderate book on the country's economy, which had made the mistake of bringing out the role of the trading companies!

It was the discovery around 1949, in the files of documents held by the French Communist Party, of many quotations from Vigné d'Octon which started me on my researches. Who was this man, of whom I had never previously heard? From what works had these extracts been taken? At first nobody could tell me, but gradually I picked up his traces, at least as far as the origin of the quotations was concerned. These had been reprinted in the special issue of *Le*

41. Thus Charles Regismanset, a senior official in the ministry of the colonies, and a 'theorist' of colonisation, had no qualms about writing the following: 'Poor black humanity! Let us at least be honest enough to admit that if we take so much care of you, it is because you appear to us to constitute an inexhaustible source of labour. [. . .] It is our intention that the races of Africa should produce the maximum possible. We want ivory and balls of rubber to pile up on the dock-side at Bordeaux and Le Havre, groundnuts to increase, and palm oil to fill the vats to overflowing. What place do science, justice, kindness or, most of all, progress have here? We do not want black education pushed forward too hard. As long as they [the populations] are the weaker, they will recognise the right of the stronger. The day when the "stronger" disarms himself, and when they begin to understand all those admirable false abstractions, they will soon renounce this supposed "contract of association" between us and rise up against European rule and exploitation. The Indo-Chinese are giving us a foretaste of it.' (*Questions coloniales*, Paris: Larose, 1912, p. 183.)

42. J. Suret-Canale, *French Colonialism in Tropical Africa*, London: C. Hurst, 1971, pp. 201–4. (English transl. of *Afrique noire*, II: *L'ère coloniale, 1900–1945*, Paris: Eds Sociales, 1964.)

*Crapouillot*[43] devoted to colonialism which appeared in 1936, and of which, after the war, I was to see some torn and crumpled copies that African officials in 'French West Africa' still passed from hand to hand. That I somewhat over-estimated Vigné's historical importance in the first enthusiasm of having 're-discovered' him I would now agree. But I am persuaded that no future study in any depth of French colonial policy under the Third Republic can refrain from mentioning his name or his proper role as an activist and as a forerunner - the principal authority for this opinion being the article by Henri Brunschwig!

It remains to come back to the most important problem raised by Brunschwig, namely that of anachronism. The danger cannot be doubted, and every historian must guard against its insidious nature. It is only possible to assess it when one has lived long enough to see events which one has witnessed or participated in, described or analysed by others younger than oneself, who know of them only through written sources. Not that the witness or participant is a better historian concerning what he has lived through; experience leads me to the opposite conclusion. Subjectivity, the 'trees which prevent one from seeing the wood', are for him a greater danger. But, whatever the risks of anachronism, he has an irreplaceable contribution to make. Naturally, when we are concerned with more remote history, of which there are no longer living witnesses, this resource is not available to us.

So we must, as far as possible - and using all the evidence and all the sources - try to place ourselves in the context of the period we are considering. In 1914 anti-colonialism was not, and could not be, the same as in our own time; nor can we relate it to the version current as late as the 1920s and '30s. But we must not be led into the opposite excess, of which a caricature is to be found in a 'mechanistic sociology' sometimes attributed to marxism (wrongly so, even if certain authors who claim marxism as their authority have in fact been guilty of it). There are certain institutions and ideas which straddle different ages and different societies and which, despite the ravages of time, do not lose their identity. It is very clear that the Christianity of a believer today, after the Second Vatican Council, is not the same as that of Saint Augustine. But there is a common element which over-rides the differences and makes it possible to speak of Christianity as a reality which has existed for two thousand years. It also causes the words of one of the early Church fathers to have meaning for a Christian today. It is this very continuity which, though not historically measurable, opens the way to anachronism. If the realities and the ideas of each age

43. *Le Crapouillot*, Jan. 1936, special number edited by Francis Delaisi, André Malraux and Galtier-Boissière: 'Expeditions coloniales. Leurs dessous, leurs atrocités'.

were all radically different, there would be no risk of anachronism!

In this connection Lucien Febvre does not strike me as entirely convincing. I would like to recall briefly here the subject of his *Problème de l'incroyance au XVIe siècle* (Problem of unbelief in the 16th century). In an introduction to Rabelais' *Pantraguel* written in 1923, Abel Lefranc was determined to see in the parish priest of Meudon – by way of criticism! – 'the precursor of the atheists and libertines of the eighteenth century'. Febvre went to great lengths, and with great erudition, to show that Rabelais was in all probability a Christian of liberal and humanist tendencies and not an atheist. He demonstrates this quite convincingly, but one cannot follow him when he infers from it that in the sixteenth century unbelief was impossible: 'As for the unbelief of men of the sixteenth century, in so far as it had any reality, it is absurd and childish to suppose that *what little there was* bears any comparison to our own. Absurd and anachronistic.'[44] Even more specifically, he says: 'To speak of rationalism and free-thinking in connection with an era when the most intelligent, learned and brave men were unable to bring any strength to bear against a religion which had a universal hold – either in philosophy or science – is to speak of an idle dream.'[45]

Yet there were atheists in the sixteenth century, and even much earlier; it was not coincidental that the theologians of Rabelais' time attacked the 'emulators of Lucretius and Lucian'! Obviously atheists did not seek notoriety at a time when the slightest heresy could lead one to the stake. But the fact that theologians expounded their ideas (with the intention of refuting them) makes it certain that they existed. Certainly they did not have the same points of reference as the atheists of the eighteenth, nineteenth and twentieth centuries, but one only needs to read Lucian to see that, just as there is continuity between the Christians of the second century and those of today, so there is continuity – perhaps even more pronounced – between the atheists of that period and our own. From Lucian to the anti-clericals of the time of 'little father' Combes, one sees the same rationalist critique and the same arguments (also found between-times in Jean Meslier[46] at the beginning of the eighteenth century), which had no need of the support of modern philosophy or science. If there is a break in continuity, it is with Marx and his atheism based on a sociological critique. Not only that, but for reasons which are easy to understand, some of the evi-

44. L. Febvre, op. cit., p. 497. Emphasis added.
45. Ibid., p. 382.
46. Jean Meslier (1664–1729), was the parish priest of Etrépigny in what is today the *département* of the Ardennes. This priest, who was a contemporary of Louis XIV, left at his death a manuscript 'memoir' (known as the 'Testament of the *Curé* Meslier'), in which he developed a systematic critique of the Christian religion, affirmed his atheist convictions, and advanced a communist conception of society.

dence is missing. Thus it is not certain whether the pamphlet *De Tribus Impostoribus* (concerning the Three Imposters), which two witnesses claim to have seen before 1580,[47] is the same as that of the same name preserved at the Bibliothèque nationale in Paris, which is dated 1598 (it is not certain whether this date is authentic). But one cannot blame the atheists of the sixteenth century for not having had the courage of their convictions, any more than one can blame Meslier for having written down his convictions. The fate of the Chevalier de la Barre[48] at a time when the Enlightenment was in full flood enables one to understand their prudence, which was shared by those theists, rationalists and pantheists with whom they are often confused. Vincent de Paul had to confide his Socinian convictions[49] to a sealed testament with instructions that it should not be opened till a hundred years after his death, and even in the Netherlands Spinoza could not express himself with complete freedom.

We seem to have come a long way from Vigné d'Octon and anti-colonialism. But from what we have been discussing I am able to conclude even more firmly that, even while taking account of the errors and inadequacies of my text of 1959, for which Henri Brunschwig has properly taken me to task, it is possible to speak of anti-colonialism before 1914 and to see Vigné d'Octon as its undisputed champion.

47. In the thirteenth century, the Hohenstaufen Emperor Frederick II was accused by the Pope of having initiated the idea that humanity had been deceived by three impostors - Moses, Jesus and Mohamed.
48. Jean-François Le Fèvre (1747-66), Chevalier de la Barre, a young nobleman of Abbeville who fell victim to a vendetta by a judge who denounced him for blasphemy and sacrilege. Accused of not baring his head at a religious procession, of singing irreverent songs and of mutilating the cross, he was condemned to be burnt alive after first having his right hand cut off and his tongue torn out. On appeal, the Paris *parlement* allowed him to be beheaded before burning. Voltaire tried to obtain his rehabilitation. Eventually the anti-clericals put up a statue to him in Montmartre.
49. M. Emerit, 'Saint Vincent de Paul fut-il chrétien?', *Information historique*, March-April 1970, p. 211, and 'Comment se crée une légende: L'exemple de Saint Vincent de Paul', *Cahiers rationalistes*, 339 (Feb. 1978), pp. 138-51. Socinians or 'unitarians' were rationalists and theists who rejected the dogma of the Trinity and, consequently, the divinity of Christ.

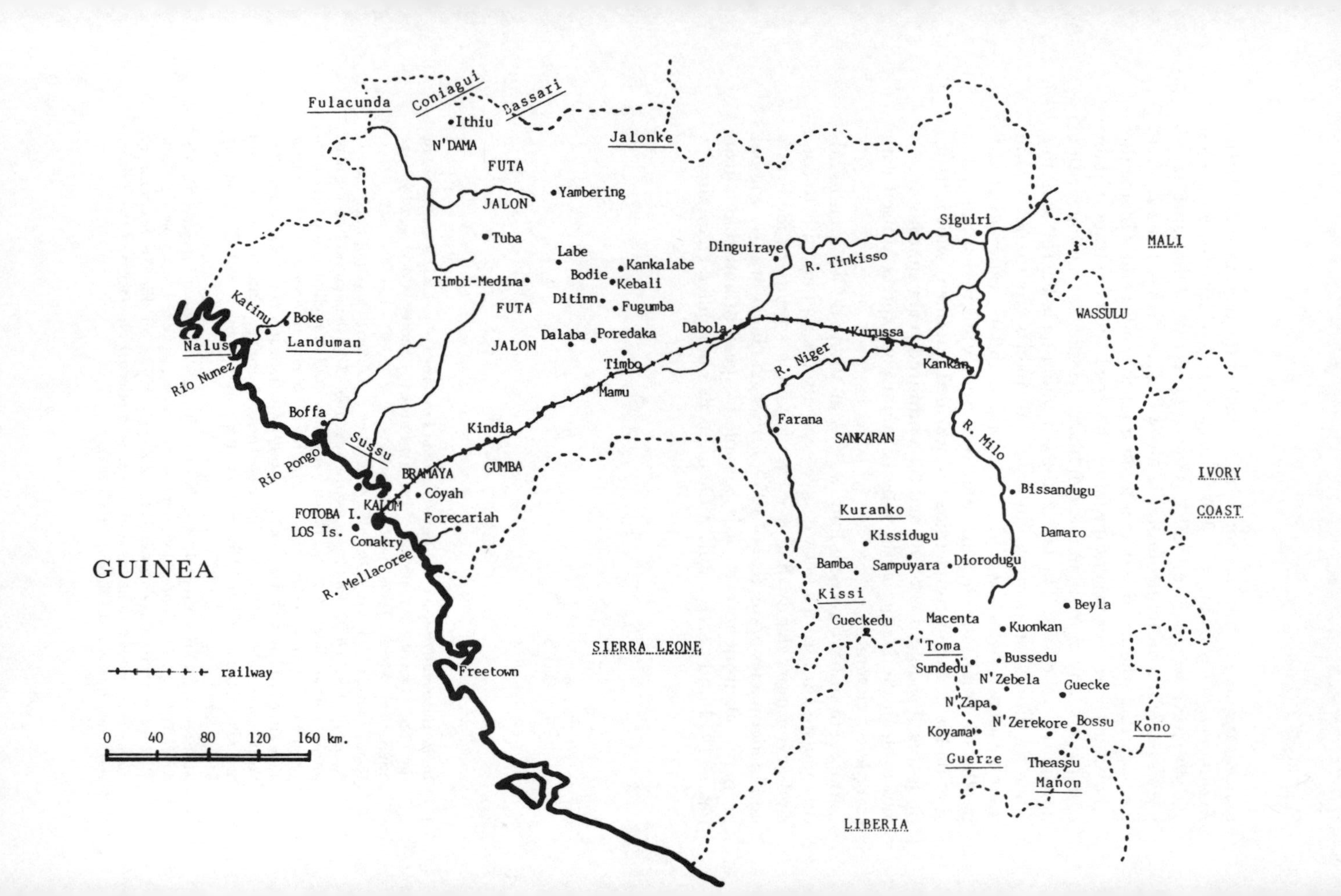
GUINEA
Fulacunda
Coniagui
Dassari
Ithiu
N'DAMA
Jalonke
FUTA
JALON
Yambering
Tuba
Labe
Kankalabe
Bodie
Kebali
Timbi-Medina
Ditinn
Fugumba
FUTA
JALON
Dalaba
Poredaka
Timbo
Mamu
Dabola
Dinguiraye
R. Tinkisso
Siguiri
MALI
WASSULU
Kurussa
Kankan
R. Niger
Farana
SANKARAN
R. Milo
Bissandugu
IVORY
COAST
Damaro
Kuranko
Kissidugu
Bamba
Sampuyara
Diorodugu
Kissi
Beyla
Gueckedu
Macenta
Kuonkan
Toma
Bussedu
Sundedu
N'Zebela
Guecke
N'Zapa
N'Zerekore
Bossu
Kono
Koyama
Guerze
Theassu
Manon
LIBERIA
SIERRA LEONE
Freetown
Katinu
Boke
Nalus
Landuman
Rio Nunez
Boffa
Sussu
Rio Pongo
Kindia
BRAMAYA
GUMBA
Coyah
KALUM
FOTOBA I.
LOS Is.
Conakry
Forecariah
R. Mellacoree
railway
0
40
80
120
160 km.

# 6

# GUINEA IN THE COLONIAL SYSTEM[1]

If one consults official publications, even the most specialised, one will not gather much information on the fate of Guinea during the 'colonial period', at least from the conquest till the end of the Second World War. Undoubtedly one will find details of military operations, the dates of expeditions, and the names of those who covered themselves with glory. One will find the dates and particulars of decrees and decisions modifying the laws and the frontiers of the territory, and its division into 'circles' and 'circumscriptions'. There will be a list of governors, praise for their 'work' and their virtues, and - very important - their portraits, with pince-nez and turned-up moustache, and chest and collar bedecked with gold and silver.

But the ordinary man, the Guinean who worked the fields, bent double over the earth, and weighed down by heavy loads on his back over long journeys on foot - where is he? All one can say is that he hardly ever appears except by accident and in a round-about way, as a statistic that throws some light on his condition. The *Grand Siècle* (Great Century) of Louis XIV of France was not short of authors and chroniclers who give us a wealth of information about the court, on persons of rank, and even on the bourgeoisie. On the other hand, the seventeenth century is one of the least known in terms of economic and social history - even less so, it has been said with deliberate exaggeration, than the Egypt of the Ptolemies. In colonial Africa, the colonisers wrote their own history. The history of the 'natives' had no place there; it did not count, except under the heading of manpower. They only counted after the day in 1946 when they took the initiative in history, occupying the centre of the stage without being invited, and making all the cracks in the decayed colonial edifice become suddenly visible.

In these conditions, it was clear to historians that there was a point beyond which they could go no further along their chosen route. With everything to be done, with a new edifice needing to be built up from the foundations, all one could aspire to was a provisional assessment. Hence, this has to be an essay in the true sense of the word - a few strokes to try and penetrate the chinks in the armour-plate of ignorance forged by colonisation.

Another difficulty is that Guinea, a colonial creation arbitrarily carved out, does not lend itself easily to the kind of study I had in mind. For the time before the end of the conquest, it is necessary to add toge-

1. Published in *Présence africaine*, XXIX, 1959-60, pp. 9-44.

ther the separate histories of regions which were organically linked to other parts of Africa, but once the conquest was completed, Guinea was poured into the mould prepared for it by the ministry of the colonies. Its history thereafter is difficult to separate from that of French West Africa and the 'empire' as a whole.

Not having been able to follow the history at the local level in all its detail, and not wishing to produce, for Guinea, a history of French colonial Africa, I have had to accept the necessity of leaving certain gaps. To the historians of independent Guinea, with the archives in their possession, and above all with the freedom to say what they could not say before, belongs the task of producing definitive contributions.

### *The conquest*

The birth of 'French' Guinea took place by chance. During the time of the slave trade, and up to the beginning of the nineteenth century, it was the Portuguese and the English who 'held' the 'Rivières du Sud' (the Portuguese by arriving first, gave their names to the Rio Pongo and the Rio Nunez). But the prohibition of the trade (despite long-standing relations with Brazil, where slavery still continued), Portugal's weakness, and the abandonment of the forts previously used by the African-Portuguese gave a considerable advantage from 1820 onwards to the English, who were firmly ensconced in Sierra Leone. With them the 'new style' of trade, dealing in merchandise, gained the upper hand. At this stage, the English - confident of their maritime and commercial superiority, and prime advocates of free trade - proposed, of their own free will, the abandonment of the colonies. More precisely, they were willing to renounce theirs, provided that their action was reciprocated; this would give them genuine and total mastery, just as they already had mastery of the seas. On the whole, their prudent 'realism' did not make them slacken in any way, but rather the contrary; but here, for once, they were outsmarted. While commissions of inquiry were considering the evacuation - at some future date - of Sierra Leone, and the English were awaiting developments in Guinea, Bouët-Willaumez, King Louis-Philippe's naval commander in Africa, was making an increasing number of 'treaties' with the littoral chiefs. Thus the navy was assured of a strong position at sea, and business in Marseilles would have favourable conditions for obtaining palm oil, which was increasingly used after 1840 for soap manufacture, lighting and lubrication.

Competition with England continued for a long time. The fort at Boke, built in 1865 in the hinterland of the Rio Nunez which had been ceded to France, was insignificant compared to the settlements at Freetown. And Bayol only signed a treaty for a 'protectorate' with Futa-Jalon some months after the English Gouldsberry had done the same thing. In short, it was the consolidation of the French positions on the upper Niger which gave France an assured position of advantage. In 1882, the British 'recognised' French rights over the 'Rivières du Sud', not without pursuing their own intrigues in the interior under cover of the difficulties with Samori (see above, page 000). This was one of the rules of the game; the French did as much at the same time on the lower Niger and at Benue. The Germans, for their part, gave up alleged 'rights' on the Rio Pongo in 1885 in exchange for France giving up her 'rights' to Porto-Seguro and Petit Popo (Anecho) on the Togolese littoral. In 1886 the frontier on the Rio Cassini was corrected in favour of Portugal, in exchange for the latter giving up Ziguinchor. An agreement in 1904, consecrating the British renunciation of the Los islands in exchange for that of the Gambia by France was the last such re-touching of the map.

At first a mere dependency of Senegal, the 'Rivières du Sud' did not attain administrative autonomy till 1890. Under their new style of 'French Guinea and Dependencies' (decree of 17 December 1891), they still included the settlements of the Ivory Coast and Benin, which were only detached in 1893. The lieutenant-governor installed at Conakry from the same date, wielded authority over several enclaves of French sovereignty and innumerable 'protectorates' on the coast, just as he did over Futa-Jalon. When the interior (the Dinguiraye region – the empire of Samori) fell into French hands, it first came under the military administration of the Sudan. In 1895, at the same time as the government-general of French West Africa was created, the Farana sector, which controlled the frontier with Sierra Leone, was transferred from the Sudan to Guinea. Only when the decree of 17 October 1899 attached the Ivory Coast and Dahomey to the government-general did Guinea acquire its present frontiers. The fall of Samori put an end to wide-ranging military operations, and the '*Grand Soudan*' military area was divided up among the other colonies of the group, Guinea receiving its share.

The annexation of the littoral – the 'Rivières du Sud', to use its correct title – had not presented major problems. Its disintegration into numerous rival chiefdoms made European expropriation easier – which is not to say that it was achieved without fighting. Incessant intrigues with the object of supporting this chief against that rival, the rivalries between European powers (Britain, Germany and Belgium had a policy of intervention aimed, if not at installing themselves, then at least at obtaining pledges of concessions), the disagreements between the military and the traders, the demoralisation among the little fever-ridden garrisons in the forts – all encouraged an increase in bloody incidents. One of the most notorious of these 'affairs', the Rio Nunez 'incident', is described in the previous essay.

*The conquest of Futa-Jalon.* Futa-Jalon presented scarcely any more obstacles to its conquest by France than the littoral, and here one has to ask why this state, one of the oldest and most developed in black Africa, offered no serious resistance to the conquest, while others equally ancient (if not more so, like Dahomey) or much more recent (the empires of Ahmadu and Samori) put up a famous resistance? It is not our claim that we can provide an answer, but we will put forward some hypotheses.

The weakness of the state of Futa-Jalon is probably explained by its feudal character, which made the organisation of a national resistance difficult, and at the same time the persistence of its ethnic institutions which prevented any genuine central authority from developing. In each small locality and each province, just as at the apex of the confederation, order resulted less from the exercise of genuine authority than through the unstable balance between the forces of rival families. The double-headed constitution - whereby power was held for alternate two-year terms by the *almamy* of the 'Soria' branch and the *almamy* of the 'Alfaya' branch (a source of incessant civil wars) and the inadequacy of the power maintained by the oligarchy of great electors - deprived Futa of any capacity for self-defence. The conqueror had a fine time stirring up the rivalry between the pretenders, only to relieve them of their power in the end without effort. In our view, the state of Futa-Jalon was weak because it had practically failed to evolve since the eighteenth century, while for example the state of Dahomey showed a remarkable evolution right up to the end of the nineteenth century, adapting itself at least partly to its new environment.

It was as part of a so-called 'peaceful negotiation' that Dr Bayol, entrusted with preventing the British from establishing themselves by signing 'treaties of protection', concluded the agreement of 5 July 1881 with *almamy* Ibrahima Sori. This may have been a protectorate agreement in European eyes (it was necessary then, before the Berlin agreements, to extract the maximum security), but it certainly was not so in the eyes of the *almamy*, since the tributary, in this treaty, was the French government. The latter, in exchange for commercial advantages (and the guarantee that European traders would only be obliged to pay fixed dues), agreed to pay an annual rent of 3,000 francs to the two *almamys* and a rent of 1,500 francs to two *diwal* (province) chiefs. In the preamble to the agreement, the *almamy* proclaimed with sublime confidence: 'Futa-Jalon, united with France in a long and old friendship, knowing that the French people desire no extension of their possessions in Africa but amicable relations destined to provide commercial exchanges; knowing for a long time that the French never involve themselves in the private affairs of their allies. . . .' and so on.[2] A megalomaniac adventurer, Aimé Olivier, calling himself Count of Sanderval,[3] lured by the vision of setting up an African kingdom for himself (he turned some land which the *almamy* had granted to him into the 'kingdom of Kahel', and struck his own coinage), had contributed to the success of the transaction, thanks to his good relations with the *almamy*.

While the war continued in the Sudan, the 'protectorate' was exercised within prudent limits. But after the treaties of Bissandugu (with Samori) and Guri (with Ahmadu), and the building of the fort at Siguiri (1887–8), Gallieni believed himself to be strong enough to re-tighten the purse-strings (which was very much his normal practice). The Audéoud mission had linked up the Sudan with Conakry and the littoral, via Timbo, and from that moment one could regard Futa as isolated. The Gallieni Convention of 30 March 1888, while it renewed the French 'undertaking not to become involved in the internal affairs' of Futa, abolished the rents payable to the *almamys* and the dues imposed on traders. . . . As the result, war with Ahmadu and Samori flared up again, and it was then thought politic to cancel the Convention and continue the payment of rents. A war of succession, which began when the *almamy* of the 'Soria' branch died in 1889, enabled the French to reinforce their authority, which had as its local representative, from 1890 onwards, a lieutenant-governor residing at Conakry. The 'pacification' of the Sudan was still awaited so that a new stage could be begun (Ahmadu had been pressed back towards the north and Samori to the edge of the forest region in the east). When *almamy* Bokar Biro refused to give up his post at the end of his two-year term and re-took Timbo, the pretext was at hand for an intervention with the support of the Alfaya clan chiefs (later accused – in order to get rid of them – of having 'conspired' with Samori) and of Olivier de Sanderval (he too was eliminated once he was no longer useful and had become an embarrassment, and spent the rest of his days complaining of the French administration's ingratitude to him). The French columns moved into Timbo in November 1896. Bokar Biro was defeated at Poredaka and killed by his adversaries a few weeks later. A new 'treaty of protection', signed on 6 February 1897, stipulated:

2. E. Rouard de Card, *Les traités de protectorat conclus par la France en Afrique (1870–1895)*, Paris: Pedone, 1897.
3. The Portuguese title was his reward for ceding some rights which he had acquired in the region to Portuguese Guinea. He had begun his African career as agent in Bolama for the Marseilles firm of Pastré. (Archives nationales de la République de Guinée, 1 E 27.)

*Article 2.* France undertakes to respect the present constitution of Futa-Djallon. This constitution will function under the authority of the government of Guinea [*sic*!] and under the direct control of a French official, who will take the title of Resident of Futa-Djallon.
*Article 3.* The *almamys* at present commissioned and recognised will exercise power alternately and in conformity with the constitution of Futa-Djallon.

This, in fact, was annexation. This 'scrap of paper'[4] was respected for a shorter time than its predecessor. From 1897, *almamy* Umaron Bademba, who had been elected in place of Bokar Biro, was deposed and replaced. His successor Baba Alimu was given an area that had been reduced to three *diwe* (provinces), the others, like Labe already, being proclaimed 'independent' – which meant that they were placed under the direct control of the French administration. On his death in 1906, Futa-Jalon was shared between two *almamys*, under the pretext of substituting the joint rule of the Alfaya and Soria families over different territories simultaneously for their alternation in power. At that point, the *almamys* were reduced, in political terms, to the rank of 'provincial chiefs', only retaining their 'religious powers'. The official report of 1906 did not beat about the bush in its ratification of the political system adopted by the colonial administration – 'the progressive suppression of the important chiefs and the parcelling out of their authority'.[5] Finally, in 1912, the old provinces of Ditinn and Timbo were deliberately dismembered and the *almamys* reduced to the rank of cantonal chiefs. Bokar Biro, the *almamy* of Timbo, was removed to the periphery of his former domain, with the style of cantonal chief of Dabola.

The 'traditional' or imposed chiefs could no longer cause any serious concern to the colonial administration. Official historiography mentions the 'two emergencies of 1905 and 1911 due to the agitation of Alfa Yaya and some xenophobic *marabouts*'.[6] This agitation belongs to mythology. That there was discontent and bitterness among the feudal chiefs of Futa-Jalon as the result of the French administration's actions is certain; but as for genuine attempts at resistance, there seem never to have been any. Caught between their subjects and the conqueror, they had neither the means nor the desire to go in that direction. According

4. This term was used in the Chamber of Deputies by Etienne, the secretary of state for the colonies, concerning the treaty concluded between Gallieni and Ahmadu several years before being borrowed (without acknowledgment) by the German chancellor Bethmann-Hollweg in his more famous reference to Germany's treaty with Belgium.
5. *Rapport d'ensemble sur la situation générale de la Guinée française en 1906*, Conakry: Imprimerie Ternaux, 1907; also P. Marty, *L'Islam en Guinée*, Paris: E. Leroux, 1921.
6. J. Richard-Molard, *Afrique Occidentale Française*, Paris: Berger-Levrault, 1948, p. 144.

to Demougeot,[7] Alfa Yaya, chief of the *diwal* of Labe, was disgruntled over the Franco-Portuguese frontier agreement, which removed part of his territory and transferred it to Portuguese Guinea, and threatened a revolt – as the result of which an order of Governor-General Roume dated 23 November 1905 dismissed him from office and caused him to be shut up in Dahomey for five years.

The version of André Arcin,[8] confirmed by the archives, is quite different. Immediately after the conquest, Alfa Yaya was one of France's most reliable allies; he had been at the heart of the conspiracy hatched against Bokar Biro. It was the administrator Noirot who was responsible for his fortunate position: in a letter to Governor Bellay written on 6 April 1898,[9] Yaya recalled that he had always been friendly to the French, and had promised to obey all the Governor's orders and ensure that all taxes collected would be handed over intact. As a *quid pro quo*, he asked to be accorded seniority over the other Futa chiefs who were making war against the French. Up till 1904, Yaya was indeed one of the government's most loyal supporters, but in that year the governor, Cousturier, was dismissed and replaced by Frézouls, an appointment which arose purely out of French domestic political rivalries. For Frézouls it was important to demonstrate the 'faults' of his predecessor. By a 'clever manoeuvre' (the very words of the journal *A.O.F.* of 11 February 1911) he enticed Alfa Yaya to Conakry. The chief came with his retinue, completely unsuspecting, and attended an official reception – at which he was arrested before being deported. One result of this action, according to Arcin, was that in future the Futa chiefs prudently refrained from visiting Conakry. Demougeot notes that Yaya's arrest provoked considerable popular anger. A European observer wrote of the episode as follows:

Among those acts which excite universal condemnation, and which disgrace those who commit them – to borrow the very phrases used by the minister of the colonies in his recent instructions to the commissioner-general of the Congo – one has to include failure to abide by promises one has given, and a want of loyalty on the part of certain representatives of government in their relations with the natives whom they administer. . . . To an impartial public no other description can be given to the ambush which put an end to the power of the former king of the Labe, Alfa Yaya, who had earlier faithfully helped the French government to take possession of Futa-Djallon, almost without a blow being struck. It is known that Alfa Yaya was summoned to Conakry some months ago for a discussion: calmly and confidently, as befits a man with

7. A Demougeot, *Notes sur l'organisation politique et administrative du Labé*, Dakar: I.F.A.N., 1944.
8. *La Guinée française*, Paris: Challamel, 1907.
9. The original is in the national archives of the Republic of Guinea, 1.E.7, 1.

nothing on his conscience, he took a costly journey of several weeks accompanied by a guard of honour in response to the French representative's invitation – and that as he left the government buildings he was seized, placed on board a ship bound for Dakar, and then deported to Dahomey.[10]

Yaya's son Modi-Aguibu was soon arrested too. 'On 1 November 1905, he dared to draw his sword against an officer in the Native Affairs department called Proust. He was immediately arrested, tried and sentenced to two years' imprisonment. It is not impossible that this incident was blown up for reasons of state.'[11] On consulting the archives one finds that not only was it not impossible, but that the incident was a put-up in every detail. Having been notified of his father's arrest, Aguibu was afraid and thought of fleeing to Portuguese Guinea. The governor had the clever idea of sending him a telegram, signed Alfa Yaya, asking him to go to Conakry – but the deputy administrator of Labe, Tallerie, considered this manoeuvre dangerous: Aguibu might pretend to leave for Conakry but actually flee – with his people and his herds of animals, and at least a part of his father's property. It was therefore necessary, on some pretext or other, to arrest him before his departure. So Tallerie invited him to his office, as he said, to discuss the journey to Conakry, and was so insistent at the meeting in requesting his visitor to lay down his sword that Aguibou sensed he was about to be arrested; scared, he fled with his sword drawn. He was then surrounded, seized and charged with 'armed rebellion against the agents of authority' (article 212 of the Penal Code). In a report of December 1905, Louis Giraut, the administrator of Timbo, wrote that according to the statements made by witnesses, 'Aguibu had not at any time drawn his sword with the intention of attacking the circle commander or any European,' and he concluded: 'What therefore remains of the accusation brought against Aguibu? Nothing.' This did not prevent him a month later, acting in his capacity as 'judge of the peace with extended jurisdiction', from sentencing Aguibu to two years' imprisonment for a crime which he himself had recognised as being non-existent.[12] Colonial reasons of state had prevailed.

Returning to Guinea with Aguibu in 1910, Alfa Yaya and his supporters 'held mysterious secret meetings' and 'sought to provoke disturbances' (Demougeot); here again the archives show that these supposed plots were fictitious. Trusting in promises made by the Governor-General, Alfa Yaya believed that the possession of his property had been restored to him, and that he had been invested once

10. M. Crespin, 'Alpha Yaya et M. Frézouls', *Revue Indigène*, 1906 (2), pp. 45–6.
11. A. Demougeot, op. cit., p. 51.
12. National archives of the Republic of Guinea, 1. E. 2.

again with his former power. The contacts he made on his arrival at Conakry could have had no other purpose than as a preparation for his re-installation at Labe, and his intentions were so lacking in secrecy that he expressed them in a letter to the governor, asking that he should be allowed to replace the chiefs then in office in the province with his own men. He and Aguibu were again arrested at Conakry on 11 February 1911, and this time held at Port-Etienne, known as an efficacious place of solitary confinement for African chiefs. Yaya died there the following year, the victim of rivalries between cliques of colonial officials, and above all of the application – thereafter systematic – of direct political administration. Considering the lessons to be learned from the affair, the *Revue indigène* noted: 'This was not a mere isolated occurrence; the condemnation of Alfa Yaya and his supporters is of profound political significance. . . . One must not hesitate to make a break with the high command, which is acting immorally if the appointed chief is not held in the country itself, and dangerously if on the other hand he has deep roots in the country with whose administration he is entrusted.'[13]

The 'Wali of Gumba' affair (to which our earlier allusion to 'xenophobic *marabouts*' referred) was of a similar kind. Tierno Aliu, known as the Wali of Gumba, was an aged *marabout*, more than eighty years old. His learning and piety had earned him great authority, although he was not a member of any of the reigning dynasties. He proved himself a loyal helper of the French administration, down to the exact payment of his taxes. Because of the commotion caused by the Muslims announcing that the advent of the Mahdi would put an end to taxation by the French, and despite reports indicating that he had calmed the excitement by urging that the advent of the Mahdi – while it should not be forgotten – should be regarded as an event in the remote future, it was decided to arrest the Wali. But, as it turned out, the operation was a failure: the population mobilised to prevent the arrest, and two French officers and fourteen infantrymen were killed (30 March 1911). The result was the sending of an expedition, which achieved the following: the burning of all the houses passed en route, together with the provisions found there; the capture of important herds of bulls, cows and heifers; and the freeing of numerous captives.[14] The Wali had taken refuge in Sierra Leone, but he was condemned to death, extradited from there, and died in the prison at Fotoba on 3 April 1912.

13. G. Teullière, 'Alfa Yaya et la politique indigène', *Revue Indigène*, 1911, pp. 615–20.
14. Report of the head administrator of the circle of Kindia, 15 May 1911 (National archives of the Republic of Guinea, 1.E.3). The affair was extensively studied by Mlle Verdat (*Etudes guinéennes*, 3, 1949, pp. 3–66), but her approach owes as much to the traditional viewpoint as to academic objectivity, with contradictory results.

*The struggle against Samori*

In the former Sudanic regions it is impossible, as we have already said, to dissociate the territory incorporated into Guinea from the whole of which it used to form a part. First there was Dinguiraye, the old stronghold of the Tukulors, and El Hadj Omar's point of departure; it had been given by Ahmadu to his brother Aguibu. The latter did not emulate Ahmadu's defiant attitude; instead he thought it smart to play the French card against him, for which he was poorly rewarded: after the fall of Nioro in 1891, he saw himself 'transferred' from the authority of Dinguiraye to Bandiagara, which was still unconquered. He followed Archinard's forces in the conquest of the Sudanic lands on the Niger, and made vain efforts to prevent the sack of Djenne. Enthroned as 'king' of Macina by the French army, he did not retain his new crown for long: in 1902 he was pensioned off, and his kingdom came under direct administration.

Beyond Tinkisso, with the Wassulu empire,[15] we come to another area and another man: Samori. This was a new state, set up between 1870 and 1875 by the newly emergent Samori Toure, whom Peroz calls the 'Bonaparte of the Sudan'. With small, formerly independent states gathered together under his rule, the Wassulu empire was bordered by the Tukulor empire to the north-west, Futa-Jalon to the west, the kingdoms of Kenedugu (Sikasso) to the east, and the forest-covered frontier regions of Sierra Leone and Liberia to the south. Except for a few extensions - into the Sudan and the Ivory Coast - Samori's empire fell within the part of the Sudan transferred to Guinea in 1899.

No one has been subjected to greater calumnies that Samori. French colonial historiography named him 'Samori the bloody', a monster and a new Attila. School textbooks have always repeated this stereotyped image, grotesquely magnified; thus one author - whom, out of charity we refrain from naming - describes him as grinding little pieces of wood with his teeth while in a violent rage and regards this as unequivocal evidence of his 'ferocity'. On the other hand, Samori does not need to be idealised; he was a man of his time and of the society into which he was born. He was a warrior, and the kind of war which he waged was not of the 'humane' variety. That said, his moral worth was equal to that of a hundred Gallienis, Archinards and Voulets. Compared with men ready to resort to any lie and any crime, and motivated by unscrupulous ambition and the passion for glory and decorations, he remained to the end a man of honour, respecting the moral rules which belonged to his time and his people. From 1889 onwards,

15. So-called by Péroz, but incorrectly so because Samori's possession did not correspond to any historical territorial entity.

Colonel Péroz has written, 'it is not immaterial to note that in the whole western Sudan we [the French] - from this point of view [keeping our promises] - had an odious reputation, in no way superior to that we attributed to *almamy* Samori. It should rather be said that, according to the testimony of Samori's most dedicated enemies, he was never once known to break his word.'[16] And Delafosse acknowledged that 'treachery was not his custom.'[17] But after 1889 a slanted myth was created; for the benefit of French public opinion, Samori had to be depicted as a barbarian and a cheat, to justify in advance all the cruelty and deception that was to be practised against him! It was the same with all the heroes of the resistance to colonial conquest. By his attitude of resistance alone, Samori would have deserved a place of honour among the fighters for African independence. One of the paradoxes of his fate is that the most resounding tributes to his character and his ability as a statesman and as a strategist came from his enemies - Péroz, Baratier and Gallieni. But popular history designed for public consumption and for use in schools systematically willed this evidence into oblivion.

Péroz sketches this portrait of Samori the man: 'His general appearance was ascetic, with a look in his eyes that was sometimes sharp but more often veiled, and a subtle, gentle air. His strong, square chin suggested that he had unusual willpower.'[18] Again: 'He was very simply attired, with Moorish boots, a black turban and a dark caftan covering a white *bubu*. His head-dress - a kind of diadem of fine fretted gold - and a necklet, also of gold, were the only visible insignia of his rank.'[19] According to one tradition, he was a simple pedlar who took up the profession of arms out of filial love to obtain the freedom of his mother, who had been reduced to slavery. It is unlikely that, as has often been alleged, this was mere propaganda. If Samori had wanted a mythology to arise around him, he would not have chosen an episode that recalled his humble origins; and at the time when Péroz was in Bissandugu there were too many people still alive who had personal knowledge of Samori's beginning for the truth to have undergone much of a change.

16. E. Péroz, *Au Soudan français*, Paris: Calmann-Lévy, 1889, p. 348. Lieut-Col. E. Péroz was born at Vesoul in 1858. He joined the Carlist army in Spain at the age of 17, and after its defeat, joined the French marine infantry, in which he made his career. After taking part in the war against Samori, he became officer commanding troops in French Guiana. He published several books on the French campaigns in Africa and an autobiography *Par vocation. Vie et ventures d'un soldat de fortune*, Paris: Calmann-Lévy, 1905.
17. *Histoire des Colonies françaises*, under the direction of Gabriel Hanotaux and Alfred Martineau, vol. IV: *A.O.F.* by Maurice Delafosse.
18. Péroz, *Le Tour du Monde*, 1890, p. 360.
19. Péroz, *Au Soudan français*, op. cit., p. 357.

This same Péroz emphasised the positive aspects of Samori's work. He had collected under his authority many states or chiefdoms which were 'continually in arms against eachother due to the irresistible passion for taking a few captives from eachother, sometimes beaten and decimated, at other times victorious but weakened by fighting. [. . .] [These states] were threatened with total depopulation when the strong arm of the *almamy*, grouping them together in one kingdom and giving them a community of interests, stopped these everlasting wars and opened up for the states an age of relative prosperity.'[20]

Although he was the master of a large town, Kankan, Samori preferred to set up his capital near his native country, at Bissandugu. Péroz admired his 'air of wellbeing', and how 'even outside the strict limits of his palace, there was a great effort to achieve relative comfort and an exquisite neatness.'[21] He goes on to describe the shaded place where 'every Friday, after leaving the mosque, the *almamy-emir* came to hear the complaints and grievances of his subjects, who come for this purpose from the farthest parts of his empire.' And he concluded: 'In a word, Bissandugu, seen from a distance, has more the cool and pleasant appearance of a great agricultural settlement than the residence of the feared chief of a large empire.'[22] The empire of Wassulu, divided into 162 cantons which themselves were grouped into ten governments, was administered in a very precise fashion: apart from the administration of justice, which was carried on after the manner of St Louis, king of France,[23] each of the governments had as its head a relative or comrade of Samori, assisted by a war chief (*keletigui*) and a religious leader. As far as possible, the cantons and governments united ethnic groups and families which had previously been opposed to eachother, in order to wipe away the memory of former quarrels. The responsibilities which he placed on his people were mild. On this subject Colonel Baratier wrote: 'In financial terms, he exacted little from his people. He required each village to till one field for his profit, and levied a tithe on gold.'[24]

20. E. Péroz, *L'Empire de l'Almamy-Emir Samory ou Empire de Ouassoulou*, Besançon: Imprimerie Dodivers, 1888 (Extraits des Mémoires de la Société d'émulation du Doubs).
21. Ibid.
22. Ibid.
23. I am well aware that some will regard this comparison as either absurd or outrageous. However, St Louis was a saint in the manner of his time, for whom 'the laity, when they heard ill spoken of the law of Christ, could defend it in no other way than with the point of a sword, which they would drive into the belly of the slanderer as far as it would go' (Joinville, *Histoire de Saint Louis*, Wailly's edn, p 53).
24. A. Baratier, 'Samory', *Revue indigène*, 53 (1910), p. 513. General Albert Baratier (1864–1917) took part in the Samori campaign under Humbert, the Monteil

The country was scarcely Islamised; Samori wanted to impose Islam generally, and so took the religious title of *almamy*. He had not the learning of Ahmadu, but nor was he the ignoramus of colonial mythology. His piety was sincere; wherever he travelled, he caused fetishes to be destroyed and mosques to be built. 'He required that the greatest possible number of people, and all chiefs without exception, should send their sons to school. Those who did not comply with his orders were reminded of the need for obedience by heavy penalties.'[25] When occasion arose, he questioned pupils himself to test their knowledge. Thus Samori added the style of Charlemagne to that of St Louis!

The army was highly organised. It included seven and later ten corps (corresponding to the ten governments) stationed on the frontiers, and an élite mobile reserve based at Bissandugu. Each corps comprised a permanent nucleus of professional soldiers (of slave origin, as in all the African states), *sofas* and *bilakoros* (cadets). In war, popular militias - the reserves - were added. The troops wore uniform (cap, short jacket and yellow trousers tightened at the ankle),[26] and the military workshops were capable not only of repairing but of manufacturing, evidently to a high standard of craftsmanship, all the parts of the rapid-firing Gras rifle (in service in the French army 1874–86).

Samori had showed his administrative talent before 1891; but his military ability, which had only been put to the test against the small chiefdoms of the Mande plateau, was not yet proved conclusively. He had succeeded in establishing his empire as much through the incompetence of his adversaries as by his own courage, 'almost without firing a shot'. The only wide-ranging military campaign he had ever undertaken - against Tiéba, during the siege of Sikasso - resulted in defeat, which could have raised doubts about his capability in the field. On this Baratier noted: '[In 1891] no one in the Sudan knew what Samori was capable of. All were agreed that a surprise attack would succeed; the Sultan would be unprepared and everything would be over in a few weeks, almost without resistance.'[27] Archinard, who had just beaten Ahmadu, believed that Samori could be 'liquidated' in one or at most two campaigns. But Samori's resistance held out not for a few weeks but for seven years (1891–8).

'It is no exaggeration', wrote Baratier, 'to say that Samori proved himself the superior of all the black leaders who fought against us in

---

'column' against Kong and the Marchand expedition to Fashoda in 1896–8. He published several books on his military exploits.

25. Baratier, *À travers l'Afrique*, Paris: Perrin, 1912, p. 65.
26. Inaccurate, according to Yves Person (1978).
27. Baratier, *À travers l'Afrique*, p. 71.

Africa. He was the only one who gave proof that he had true chiefly qualities, and that he was a strategist and even a politician. He was in any case a leader of men possessing the boldness, the energy, the ability to follow up his actions and to look ahead, and above all an indomitable tenacity, immune against discouragement.'[28]

His talent was to adapt his methods to the means he was able to deploy. He had the advantage over Ahmadu of possessing a number of rapid-firing rifles, provided by the French traders in Senegal or the British ones in Sierra Leone. But he had not enough to equip his whole army and, like Ahmadu, he had no artillery whatever. He knew by experience that *tatas* (the traditional forts of the savannas, built of dried earth) could not withstand artillery fire, so to be penned into a fort was to ensure that one would be crushed. He therefore decided to use the tactic of scorched earth: opening up the ground ahead of the French advance while harrying them uninterruptedly, and reoccupying the ground once the columns had moved on. In the words of Baratier:

> It was here that Samori showed his foresight at the same time as his strategic genius. While all the warriors armed with quick-firing rifles fought with us and retreated a step at a time, the troops armed only with 'piston' (percussion) or Chassepot rifles were split up in two groups, each with its allotted task. The first of these groups had the care of the populations and escorted them on the move, and the second conquered territories to the east which brought the Sultan [Samori] an empire to which the exodus could go. This organisation of his forces into three groups – for defence of the territory, for the evacuation, and for external conquest – allowed him to achieve something unique in history: for seven years his people changed their country every year, and dug themselves into new regions to eastward, already obedient and well-organised, without leaving behind one old man or one grain of millet for the conqueror.

Even if the enemy's physical superiority made the final outcome of the conflict a certainty, one cannot but acknowledge the extraordinary intelligence with which Samori deployed all the means at his disposal to prolong resistance till the last possible moment.

In an earlier work I have expressed the view that Samori's main weakness lay in his politics. He would not have understood – or at least would only have understood too late – the need for a common front of African resistance. From this point of view his campaign against Tieba, in which he failed to make effective use of his forces, was undoubtedly a mistake. But after 1891 he seems to have understood the danger. I have never previously thought it possible to affirm – but do so now – that from that date he offered an alliance and aid to Ahmadu – who rejected the offer out of feelings of pride. Samori showed undoubted diplomatic talent; he played on the opposition

28. Ibid.

between French and British imperialism, and negotiated alliances right as far as the coastal regions of Guinea, which had long been occupied by France.

After this, how much remains of the contemptuous portrait (the only one, as we have said, which is retained in schoolbook historiography) which Binger left of the African monarch?[29] According to Binger, Péroz deliberately embellished the true facts. But when one examines his account in detail, the author's racism and his incomprehension of African realities emerge at every point. One is reminded irresistibly of the question of Montesquieu, author of the classic *Persian Letters* (1720): 'How can one be a Persian?' Binger, in spite of himself, wonders 'How can one be an African?' But the basic explanation of Binger's version is simply his desire to discredit his 'rival' Péroz, whom he could not forgive for having seen and described Samori before him. Moreover, Sudanese policy in Binger's time was no longer what it had been in the time of Péroz. When the latter signed the treaty of Bissandugu, the favoured policy was that of Gallieni, which envisaged that the great African states should be left in being, under French protection. Hence it was quite normal to give a flattering portrait of France's ally. But when Binger came to Bissandugu, the break was imminent, and from that time on, the prevailing policy was Archinard's: the Sudanic empires had to be 'liquidated'. The enemy who was now marked down for destruction was therefore given the most unprepossessing features!

To dispose finally of Samori the 'mass-killer', one has to say that by this criterion he cuts a paltry figure compared with the French expeditions of Archinard and Combes. These expeditions were the ones which turned the country between Kankan and Beyla into a desert; Péroz had described that country as being 'meticulously cultivated' and thus reminiscent of his native Burgundy! And what of Samori the 'slave-trader'? There is no doubt that since the sixteenth century African wars had had no other purpose than to make captives; these were the only 'goods' he could offer to the Moors in exchange for their horses, which he needed to mount his cavalry, and to British and French traders to obtain quick-firing rifles. What the official histories omit to mention is that French arms contributed in the same way, but on an incomparably larger scale, to French military superiority. And after Archinard's conquest of the Sudan and the capture of Sikasso, the French army sold or distributed as 'captives' thousands of their defeated enemies.

We will not discuss in detail here the campaigns waged against

29. L.G. Binger, *Du Niger au Golfe de Guinée*, Paris: Hachette, 1892. Louis-Gustave Binger (1856–1936) was first an explorer, then Governor of the Colonies (1893) and from 1897 director of African affairs at the Colonial Ministry.

Samori, which extended well outside the frontiers of Guinea. When the capture of Bobo-Diulasso by Major Caudrelier closed the way to any further retreat to the east, Samori was without means of escape. The populations he had taken with him in his exodus during seven years were exhausted, and to look after them in a shrinking area of territory presented insuperable problems. He then offered peace, and was encouraged to believe that he would be allowed a peaceful withdrawal if he gave up his arms. It is these negotiations which explain the circumstances of his capture at Guelemu on 29 September 1898. That same morning, he had sent negotiators to the French post at Tuba, and when Gouraud's small party of riflemen crossed his camp, they were not resisted since everyone supposed that they too were negotiators.

Samori never accepted the 'sentence' of exile communicated to him at Kayes: he saw in it a new example of French treachery. He died in Gabon two years later in 1900, and Baratier concluded that 'this conqueror whom the blacks, if they had known history, would have compared to Napoleon, found his St Helena in the island of Ogowe where he had been confined.'[30]

### *The 'pacification' of the borders*

The forest peoples on the Liberian frontier and the Koniagui and Bassari on the frontier with Senegal had never accepted any overlordship. Accustomed to living free, they resisted the colonisers with a fierce energy.

In the Koniagui country, for as long as the station commander at Bussurah did not try to levy taxes, there was no conflict, but in 1902 Lieutenant Moncorgé, backed by a column of troops, came to conduct the levies. In an unprecedented step, Yallu-Tene, the war chief of the Koniagui village of Ithiu,[31] answered that he was ready to pay tax in millet or groundnuts, but that he had no knowledge of money.[32] Moncorgé, ambitious to gain glory for himself, demanded money and persisted in an imperious and provocative way. On 16 April 1902, he formed up his riflemen and Peul auxiliaries (provided by Alfa Yaya, the deadly enemy of the Koniagui) 150 metres from the village of Ithiu, and ordered the chief to present himself. Three times the chief refused, and indeed he had every reason to be prudent: not long before, this same Moncorgé had lured to his side the chief of the N'Dama, Thierno Ibrahima, who was then attacked while asleep, sent in chains to Conakry, and deported from there to the Congo where he died six

30. Baratier, op. cit., p. 76.
31. Or possibly Ityo: but the spelling used in the administrative reports was 'Ithiou'.
32. National archives of the Republic of Guinea, l.D.18.

months later.[33] Moncorgé now shot with his revolver one of the Malinke whom the chief sent to him with his message. The Koniagui took up arms, and after two hours of fighting Moncorgé and his column were wiped out. Two years later, in April 1904, a punitive expedition of 500 men, including a section of artillery, came to avenge Moncorgé. Villages were burned, women and children sheltering in the forest were massacred by artillery fire, and Yallu-Tene and his warriors were killed, to the last man, in the fortified village of Ithiu.[34]

In the forest regions of Guinea, the Guerze, Manon, Toma and Kissi peoples had always held out against the Sudanic conquerors, and most recently against Samori and his underlings. The frontier fixed by an agreement of 8 December 1892 gave Liberia the whole forest region, including Beyla, but their operations against Samori soon led the French troops to over-step this theoretical line. Uncertainty over the exact location of the frontier and the lack of effective occupation by the Liberians made it easier for the forest people to resist. In 1894 Lieutenant Lecerf, who had come to N'Zapu in Toma country to intercept a convoy of arms being brought from Monrovia to Samori, was killed.[35] And in 1898 the Bailly Pauly mission was annihilated by the Toma. No reaction followed from the French side.

However, when this sector was allocated to Guinea in 1899, it was organised as a 'military region' with Kissidugu, Sampuyara, Diorodugu and Beyla as the advance posts.[36] An expedition - the Conrart column - was given the task of relieving the Diorodugu post, which was being constantly harassed by the Toma. It succeeded on 28 February 1900 in taking the fortified village of Bafobakoro, the capital of the hostile war chief Koko Tolino, but the latter took refuge at N'Zapa, inside Liberian territory, and the French troops, who had suffered heavy casualties, withdrew. A little later, operations were undertaken against Chief Digo, self-proclaimed king of Kissi, and Niadu, the centre of resistance, was burned by Lieutenant Crébessac.[37] The annual report for 1903 on the general situation in French Guinea observed: 'The independent spirit of the natives is very great. They live in villages which are independent of each other. The

33. M. Crespin, 'La question du Coniagui', *Revue indigène*, 1906, pp. 88-93.
34. National archives of the Republic of Guinea, 1.D.18. Part of these documents have been reproduced in B. Maupoil, 'Notes concernant l'histoire des Coniagui-Bassari et en particulier l'occupation de leur pays par les Français', *Bulletin de l'I.F.A.N.*, XVI, 3-4 (1954), series B, pp.378-89.
35. The Toma village of N'Zapu had allied itself with Samori, and was obliged to function as a staging post for his communications with Monrovia (to replace those he had had with Sierra Leone, which were no longer safe.).
36. The posts of Sampuyara and Diorodugu were only created in 1899.
37. *Histoire Militaire de l'A.O.F.*, Paris: Imprimerie Nationale, 1931.

authority of the village chiefs is weak, and that of the canton chiefs, whom we wanted to install in the military sectors, is non-existent.'[38]

In 1903, Franco-Liberian negotiations to fix the frontier came to grief, but were resumed in 1904 and 1905. At the same time, the Liberian commissioners Cummings and Loomax occupied the hinterland, and there was now a race between the French and the Liberians for the possession of the best positions. In 1905, part of the troops garrisoning Kissidugu, Sampuyara, Diorodugu and Beyla were moved further south and respectively created new outposts at Bamba, Bofosso, Kwonkan and Gwecke. At once new operations were started to give them some breathing-space and to join them together by means of a road running roughly parallel to the frontier.

Many operations followed in 1905–7 - at Bamba, in the part of Kissi country where the Millimono clan were dominant; at Bofosso, against the war chief Kokogu; in the Kwonkan sector with the object of clearing the road linking Kwonkan, Singenu and Bofosso; and to storm the Toma villages of M'Balema and M'Balasso. In the Gwecke sector, Lieutenant Guingard destroyed the fortified village of M'Pale. But the most famous episode of the resistance took place at the fortified village of Bussedu, east of Kwonkan. Colonel Loomax, the commander of the Liberian frontier force, sent some riflemen to the village where they raised the Liberian flag, an action which put the French on the defensive. At the beginning of 1907, the French commander of the Guinea military region arrived at Kwonkan and authorised an attack on Bussedu. This was an abysmal failure. After a day of fighting (16 February) the French troops, who had taken the first three palisaded entrenchments surrounding the village, were halted by the wall of the fortification and had to fall back with heavy losses. Two months later, the attack was resumed, this time with artillery. After four hours of firing, the assault came to a stop; Lieutenant Guignard was killed and the order was given to retreat. Two demoralised lieutenants even abandoned the position and returned to Kwonkwan. The besieged defenders, knowing that they could not hold out indefinitely against artillery, took advantage of this break in the line of attack, evacuated Bussedu during the night, and reached Liberia. When the French infantry threw themselves into the attack on Bussedu next day, they found the village empty. A Swiss explorer, Dr Volz, who had been careless enough to remain in it alone, was killed by the Senegalese. The French command stated that neither the Liberian flag flying over the village nor the Swiss flag outside the lodging of Dr Volz had been noticed. . . .

38. *Rapport d'ensemble sur la situation générale de la Guinée française en 1903*, Conakry: Imprimerie Ternaux, p. 66.

Resistance continued through 1908; and the mission to define the frontier was forced to abandon its operations east of Gweckedu, where it suffered a reverse at the hands of Koko Tolino. The village of N'Zapa, formerly allied to Samori, was burned in reprisal for the killing of Lieutenant Lecerf (fourteen years earlier!). Dr Mariotte, who was accompanying the mission, fell mortally wounded in an encounter at Koyama. In 1909 the outpost at Bamba was moved to Gweckedu, and a systematic attack was launched against the recalcitrant region of Kamara, where Koko Tolino was still holding out. The centre of resistance in Daorassu was captured on 5 May 1909.

The last major operations took place in 1911-12. In August 1911, French exactions caused a general revolt in the country of the Guerze and the Manon. Samoe and N'Zerekore - 'lairs' (*sic*) of the Manon - were taken, and French troops set fire to the villages of Theassu, Bossu and Thuo. But Captain Héquet, the expedition commander, and Barthié, the agent of the trading post who had provoked the military intervention at N'Zerekore, were killed in the action.[39]

## *Colonisation*

*Establishing the system.* We have followed the stages by which the French installed themselves physically in the country, and the administrative entity of the 'colony of French Guinea' was set up. We must now take up the thread of the enterprise considered from the point of view of economic exploitation and political organisation (of these two, the second was created for the benefit of the first; they are inseparable).

The first forts built in the 'Rivières du Sud' were intended to protect the warehouses of the traders established nearby. The French flag protected free enterprise, including the slave trade which still flourished in the local market if not for export. The French merchants explained their actions on this score without equivocation: their business interests made it impossible for them to refuse the most widely accepted means of exchange in the country. In August 1888, the administrator Guilhon testified in a report that he was certain 'all the merchants in the Nunez, with perhaps two exceptions, deal in slaves.'[40] In 1890 the situation was the same, and in 1902 the administration

39. See *Histoire Militaire de l'A.O.F.*, op. cit.; Baratier, *Époques africaines*, Paris: Perrin, 1913, pp.15-34; A. Terrier, 'La frontière franco-libérienne', *Bulletin du Comité de l'Afrique Française*, 4 (Aug. 1910), pp.127-32; Lt. Bouet, 'Les Tomas', *Bull. du Comité de l'Afrique Française, Renseignements Coloniaux*, 1911, no. 8, pp. 185-99, and no. 9, pp. 220-46.

40. A. Demougeot, 'Histoire du Nunez', *Bulletin du Comité d'Études historiques et scientifiques de l'A.O.F.*, XXI, 2 (1938), pp. 274 ff.

boasted of an 'attempt to suppress the slave traffic', while guarding against measures that were too precipitous.

Altogether, trading remained poor, being confined to the export of certain primary products in exchange for ironmongery, arms and 'trade' gunpowder, i.e. of the lowest quality. Already rubber had a leading position among exports, before oilseeds (groundnuts, sesame, palm-kernels and palm oil). The creation of the port of Conakry in 1890 and its elevation to the rank of a colonial capital brought about a qualitative change in the situation. With its better geographical situation and with better equipment, Conakry outclassed the old ports of call on the 'Rivières', which thenceforward settled into a long slumber; numerous trading houses at Boke, Dubreka, Boffa and elsewhere closed their doors. Between 1891 and 1902, the annual volume of business of the establishments at Boffa fell from 1,600,000 to 23,000 francs. At the same time, the concentration of traffic brought benefits to the big specialised companies, especially those based in Marseilles. From 1890 to 1896 the situation in the political sphere remained somewhat stagnant, and the overall volume of business did not rise from its level of 8–10 million francs a year.

There were several reasons for this. First, the status of the hinterland was not settled. The war in the Sudan did not allow of too brutal an intervention in Futa-Jalon, and Britain took advantage by consolidating its foothold there politically and commercially. African traders – Guineans and above all Sierra Leoneans who were British subjects – had an important share of the traffic, and most commercial exchange was routed through Freetown which was better equipped and had an advantageous location. As well as these internal political-commercial rivalries, there were external ones. In the Sudan the military government had instituted an 'energetic' financial system – with a poll-tax and *ussuru* (market tax) of 10 per cent *ad valorem* – and a customs duty of 5 per cent *ad valorem* was levied on exports of rubber, ivory and gold at the Sudan-Guinea frontier. Dr Ballay, the first governor of Guinea, protested strongly against this system which diverted a large part of the traffic to Senegal at Freetown's expense without benefiting Conakry. Behind Dr Bellay in his protest was the big business established in Guinea – while behind the military in the Sudan were the old business houses in Senegal (mainly of Bordeaux origin) and small traders, both European and Senegalese from St Louis, who had become reduced merely to the role of middlemen.

The final subordination of Futa and the elimination of Samori changed the face of things between 1896 and 1900. Commercial activity quickly increased, reaching 10,400,000 francs in 1896 and nearly 25 million in 1899. A decree of 1897 placing a surtax on goods routed via Freetown dealt a death-blow to Sierra Leonean competition, and the Sudan-Guinea customs barrier was removed on 12 August 1898. The carving up of the military entity of the Sudan and the transfer to Guinea of its own 'piece' of that entity sealed the victory of 'Guinean' big business - principally that of the C.F.A.O. (French West Africa Company) of Marseilles - over its rivals from Bordeaux in Senegal. At the same time, the administrative and financial system was effectively established. Before 1896, no one had dared to introduce a poll-tax and general forced labour,[41] but in 1897 they were officially imposed. (A local order fixed the poll-tax at 2 francs for all natives of either sex over the age of eight.)

At first this led to some difficulties with the *almamys*, but the latter were told bluntly of the role they were now expected to play. Noirot, the administrator, proclaimed: 'The chief [almamy] will be obliged to collect taxes and provide labour for public works. . . . If he does not, he will be smashed like glass.'[42] The difficulties were thus short-lived. In 1898 there was self-congratulation in high places, because the revenue from the poll-tax had exceeded all expectation. From 1896 to 1899 it increased from 13,900 to 861,000 francs, while revenue from customs and indirect taxation increased from 628,000 to 1,136,000 francs. In 1900 revenue from the poll-tax was higher than other income allowed for in the budget.

Those from whom tax payments were expected did not yield without a struggle. When he tried to extract payment of the tax, 'Milanini, the administrator of Nunez, had to spend the night in an open boat to escape being killed by Baga women armed with the pestles they used for husking rice.'[43] But from this time onwards, armed force was available to impose 'respect for the law'.

Even before 'budgetary autonomy' had become a legal obligation for the colonies (i.e. to provide for all expenses, including the salaries of European administrators and officers of the armed forces, from their own resources), Guinea was in a position to comply with such a rule. Its budget showed a surplus from 1891 onwards, and there was no hesitation about drawing on it for extraneous needs (Dr Ballay had to protest against the subventions to the 'Colonial Museum at Marseilles' which he had generously imposed on him). On 30 June 1900, reserves amounted to 743,000 francs, and André Arcin shows that it 'grew from

41. After 1896 the circle of Farana, which controlled the Sierra Leone frontier, was detached from the Sudan and incorporated into Guinea, and this introduced into the budget of Guinea the resources of the poll-tax which was imposed there, as in the whole of the Sudan.
42. A. Arcin, *Histoire de la Guinée française*, p. 592.
43. Ibid.

year to year, the different budgets correcting each other by means of significant surpluses'.[44]

Thus it was possible – at the expense of the colony (that is to say, of the African masses) – to undertake the only important 'investment' in the territory: the building of the Conakry railway, which remains to this day the sole route that goes into the interior, and is thus the axis of commercial traffic. Work on it began in 1900. The bed of the first 120 km. of track was laid down under state supervision with a loan of 12 million francs, and the permanent way was contracted out to a private concern employing the usual methods – to the point of provoking protests from the business sector. In December 1900 the colony's commission for commerce and agriculture complained that caravans were being attacked and robbed on the road to Conakry, and that the navvies working on the railway were stripping fields and villages bare and so reducing them to famine. 'The ration of 500 grams which [the workers] are supposed to receive is reduced by embezzlement, but in any case it is utterly inadequate and should be raised to 750 grams.'[45] Those workers who were exhausted or sick did not touch their rations and had to be fed by their comrades. Mutinies broke out on some of the sites, and the contractors asked for soldiers to be sent. . . .

The method of carrying out the work prompted some polemics. Ballay, the former governor – against the wish of his one-time secretary-general, by now his successor – supported a concession request emanating from a 'Franco-Belgian' group inspired by Colonel Thys, the notorious 'strong man' of King Leopold of the Belgians. This group, hoping to widen the scope of its activities by the same methods which had served it so well in the Congo, French Equatorial Africa and the German colony of Kamerun, demanded – on top of the concession – the mere trifle of 120,000 hectares of land. However, Cousturier ensured that good administration prevailed. The insufficiency of the loans for the work was made good from the colonial treasury's reserves, and – helped by numerous requisitions of labour – the track reached Kankan. It is permissible to ask what was the cost in human lives.

The defeat of this last attempt to introduce into Guinea the system of 'big concessions' (which triumphed in the Belgian Congo and in French Equatorial Africa) requires us to retrace our steps a little. French West Africa, as is well known, did not experience this system. No doubt, some concessions for 'plantations' and for forest and mining rights were given out with a liberal hand, but the attempts to bring in

44. Ibid., p. 622.
45. Ibid., pp. 701–2.

great monopolistic concessions with sovereign rights failed. The business houses, whether from Bordeaux or Marseilles, killed them off at birth. They were powerful enough to do this, and could not tolerate a system which would remove a part of the territory from their sphere of activity. They preferred 'free trade' to continue, thus assuring them of a *de facto* monopoly of external and internal commerce which they never ceased to consolidate.[46]

### *The era of rubber*

With only one port of mediocre quality, and a railway of limited range and difficult gradients, Guinea had to remain like most of French-ruled black Africa - but even more so than many other territories - at the rudimentary stage of simple trading. Entrenched in their routine, and making considerable profits with negligible investment from the import and export of goods which were nugatory in both quantity and quality, the big commercial houses obstructed all development and all productive investment. From 1890 till 1914, the basic export commodity was not a product of cultivation, but one that was non-renewable, and could only be gathered up once and for all. The term *Raubwirtschaft* (a robber's economy - of pillage and devastation), invented by German economists, here came into its own.

At the end of the century the progress of the bicycle and the motorcar, together with the multiplication of other uses for rubber, increased the demand for this primary substance. In the Amazon basin of South America and the Belgian Congo, exploitation was concentrated mainly on tree rubber. In French Equatorial Africa and Guinea, rubber was extracted from lianas which were widely distributed in the savannas, belonging to the *landolphia* group. Production was poor, but because it was obtained by administrative compulsion or in the form of a tax, the trading companies could obtain it cheaply. With 1,500 tonnes of rubber in 1904, and 2,000 tonnes in 1914, Guinea provided the bulk of production in West Africa. (More than 4,000 tonnes were produced in 1906, 1909 and 1910, constituting more than 60 per cent of the value of exports.)

This was a form of exploitation that devastated and exhausted the country, making the savannas sterile. Once the plants nearest to the villages had been used up, the populations were forced to look for

46. In French Equatorial Africa and the Belgian Congo, on the other hand, it was the British trading houses which were ousted by the Franco-Belgian concessionaires. In those territories they did not have political authority behind them, and were thus reduced to revealing to the world the crimes of their competitors, in a not wholly disinterested spirit. E. D. Morel, the author of *Red Rubber*, which denounced the crimes of Leopold II and his agents in the Congo, represented the commercial interests of Liverpool.

rubber farther and farther away. The African peasant could not escape from this process: to administrative compulsion (each circle had to contribute its quota to the 'production') was added compulsion of an indirect kind. On the eve of the First World War, an author was still able to write: 'The exploitation of rubber is still, for many territories . . . the only means the native has of procuring the money he needs.'[47] The primary reason why he needed the money was to pay taxes. He fended for himself as best he could, when necessary putting stones in the middle of balls of rubber to increase the weight. Furthermore, Guinean rubber had a bad reputation: here, as elsewhere, the representatives of the trading houses falsified the weights they used for their own benefit, and it was perhaps they, above all, who were responsible for the 'adulteration' of rubber which the authorities complained of. An order of 1 February 1905 forbade trading in adulterated rubber and specified that it should be produced in sheets, but it was not put into operation because the warehouse managers opposed verification, 'even threatening armed resistance'.[48] Rubber reached its peak in 1909–10, when the price paid per kilo was 14–20 francs in Conakry and 12 francs in the interior. But when there were crises – and speculation on the world market and the weakness of the sources of supply made these occur frequently – the back-breaking toil of the Guinean peasant had been (for the peasant himself!) totally in vain. This is how it was in 1900–1; after 1910 came the collapse. When plantations started producing – and their share of world production rose from 12 per cent in 1910 to 50 per cent in 1913 – prices fell. In Guinea, purchases fell by 60 per cent between those years; the growing of food crops was abandoned, and the result was famine. By 1915 the average purchase price of rubber had fallen to 2.50 francs per kilo.

The oil palm, which was second in the order of exports and which provided the 'Rivières du Sud' with the source of their wealth, was neglected. Guinea scarcely possessed a tenth of the palm groves of French West Africa, and only a quarter of the trees were exploited (against a third on the Ivory Coast and half in Dahomey).

We can throw some light on the drama of 'red rubber' – blood-stained rubber – in the Belgian Congo and French Equatorial Africa. The conflict of interests and the scandal of the brokerage companies contributed to it. Probably the rubber produced in Guinea was no less stained with blood than that of the Congo, but on that the record is silent: the 'good understanding' between the administration and the companies let nothing leak out. The few visitors who left written records only give a few allusions to justify the saying of Albert Londres:

47. H. Cosnier, *L'Ouest africain français*, Paris: Larose, 1921, p. 7.
48. Ibid., p. 11.

'The rulers of our colonies are glad to show "their" country to a few French citizens, but by the beams of a very faint lantern.'[49]

Rubber was not Guinea's only open sore. Like the other colonies, it had a taste of many kinds of forced cultivation, at the whim of administrative fantasies. An investigator (albeit an official one) will take up the story:

The administrator, on his own initiative or on instructions from his provincial centre, will assemble the native chiefs, speak highly of the benefits of this or that type of cultivation, and call on them to put it into practice. He hands out the seeds and sends his guards to mark out the fields, and to see that his orders are carried out, both in the growing and in the harvesting. Those who will not or cannot obey are punished with fines and imprisonment.

Governors and administrators change frequently - and the agricultural programme changes with them. Continuously, a new form of cultivation is demanded of the agriculturalist without preliminary study, without preparation, and sometimes with no chance of success. Every year thousands of hectares constitute what the native calls 'the commandant's fields' - a heavy tax which costs the budget nothing, but which discourages the native or makes him resolutely hostile to our influence. . . . In the Kurussa circle in Guinea, in 1914-15, 800 hectares of land chosen by the circle guards were planted under compulsion with cotton plants from Dahomey of an unsuitable type. No consideration had been given to the subsequent ginning and sale. . . . Throughout French West Africa there was forced cultivation, imposed according to this circumstance or that opinion. . . . During the war, the system reached its height.[50]

On the pretext of aiding the 'war effort' and provisioning the invaded French homeland, an 'extravagant programme' was activated. The systematic pillaging of produce led to famine, and 'the only result was that a few thousand tons of sorghum, which could not be preserved, and rice were exported.'[51] The initiator of this programme was the Governor-General Joost van Vollenhoven, whose departure for the war and glorious death in 1918 have served to make him a hero. The man's courage cannot be doubted; but what was less certain was his humanity, which was given as the reason for his dismissal, since he had opposed the intensive recruitment for the army begun at the end of 1917. Intelligent and industrious, but with a boundless ambition and authoritarianism, this French-naturalised Dutchman, brought up in the milieu of colonists in Algeria, had served in Indo-China as a protégé of Albert Sarraut, to whom he owed his speedy promotion.[52] He was appointed Governor-General of French West Africa in 1917

49. Albert Londres, *Terre d'ébène*, Paris: Albin Michel, 1929, p. 260.
50. H. Cosnier, op. cit., pp. 146-7.
51. Ibid., p. 148.
52. See A. Prévaudeau, *Joost van Vollenhoven*, Paris: Larose, 1953.

with the mission of 're-victualling France' - which he carried out using methods at which one can only guess, and with the derisory results we have mentioned. Intensive recruitment for the armed forces was clearly not compatible with his economic programme, but the actual cause of his resignation was the sending out of the Diagne mission[53] at the beginning of 1918 with the task of stepping up military recruitment in West Africa: he lost his job not because of the purpose of the mission (which was only a secondary reason, and in the end merely a pretext) but because the Deputy for Senegal, in order to put his sad task into effect, had been given the title of Commissioner of the Republic in West Africa, with the rank of governor-general! This was too much for the authoritarian proconsul, who announced his refusal to countenance the 'fragmentation of the command', above all for the benefit of a 'native', and asked to be relieved of his responsibilities. He then left for the front.

Thus to the evils of forced labour were added those of military recruitment. The result, in certain places, was rebellion and the exodus of populations into neighbouring foreign territories.

*Persistence of slavery.* Forced cultivation, forced labour, military recruitment (for a three-year term), taxes - these were the benefits which the 'French peace' brought to the people, and especially to the lowest orders of society, the former slaves, who were more crushed than ever in spite of numerous declarations of the 'humanitarian' intentions of European public opinion. At this point we must return to the problem of slavery.

The decree of 27 April 1848 issued by the provisional government of the Second Republic, abolishing slavery in the French colonies, was never put into effect in Africa. At the beginning of the Second Empire, Faidherbe expressly stated that it did not apply to Senegal. It was necessary to wait till the decree of 12 December 1905, which did not strike at slavery itself but at actions connected with the trade (from two to five years in prison for the parties to any agreement having as its object the removal of a third person's freedom).

In practice, the policy of the French government appeared highly contradictory. Now, and even before 1905, there were indignant denunciations of slavery, and measures for freeing captives: it was a matter of self-justification for French opinion, to which the abolition of slavery had never ceased to be cited as one of the objectives of colonisation. But anti-slavery was equally in accord with the wishes of certain 'large economic interests', which had assessed the profits to be made

53. Blaise Diagne, an African, was the Deputy for the four communes in Senegal.

from colonisation. In their eyes, domestic slavery (i.e. the only form of slavery which survived the abolition of the trade) was a 'barbaric' custom because it was unproductive. . . . 'As practised in West Africa, [domestic slavery] results in an easy and idle life for men who, if they were skillfully stimulated by the spur of self-interest [*sic*!], would have been able to become active workers desirous of enriching themselves by their labour. . . .'[54] . . . . And, we should add, capable above all of enriching with their labour the promoters of the colonial enterprise. Thus, the issue is clear: the suppression of slavery was a matter, not of improving the lot of former captives but of keeping their former masters at work!

Meanwhile, the freeing of former captives was utilised in a way that had not been foreseen. The creation by Gallieni, from 1887 onwards, of 'freedom villages' which subsequently multiplied in the Sudan (although there was also one in Conakry) gave rise to an idea. Their object in fact was to place at the disposal of government outposts, in the neighbourhoods where they had been set up, a fresh workforce to replace that which had been driven to take flight by repeated forced labour requisitions. 'It is quite certain that the motive which led to "freedom villages" being set up everywhere was that it provided an excellent solution to the problem of finding porters and labour gangs; in any case, it was greatly superior to the system of going out armed looking for people every time they were needed, only to have them escape the first moment they were not being watched. It was a slow, hazardous and complicated system. Because of political requirements and the scruples of public opinion, what in Africa was a demographic question was portrayed in Europe as a humanitarian undertaking.'[55]

It was no coincidence that in the Sudan the 'freedom villages' were much more straightforwardly described as 'villages of the commandant's captives'. Escape was punished by imprisonment, and one of the most effective methods of exacting payment of taxes was to take a hostage from the village concerned and detain him in a 'freedom village' until the tax was paid in full.[56] As for those captives held by the 'friends' of the French, woe to those who took the official anti-slavery declarations literally, as happened at Siguiri in 1895 following a circular from the governor, Grodet, forbidding trading caravans. The captives rebelled, the circle commander sentenced the 'leaders' to

54. R. Cuvillier-Fleury, *La main-d'oeuvre dans les colonies françaises de l'Afrique Occidentale et du Congo*, Paris: Sirey, 1907, p. 31.
55. Denise Bouche, 'Les villages de liberté en A.O.F.', *Bulletin de l'I.F.A.N.*, 3–4 (1949), p. 529.
56. We should add that the 'freedom villages' were freely drawn on to provide labour and domestic servants (the local people spoke simply of 'slaves') for Europeans and the Catholic missions, and women for the amusement of soldiers.

several years in prison, and the 'liberal' governor demanded that they should be given the hardest work in the station. The 'freedom villages' were disbanded progressively between 1905 and 1910, by which time administrative distraints had allowed for all future taxes, forced labour and requisitions to be exacted.

The policy of 'freedom villages' mostly affected the southern part of the Sudan which had been joined to Guinea. In Futa-Jalon a rather different policy was followed. Because the prospects of 'utilisation' were minimal there, and the administration had decided to give its support to the local aristocracy, slavery was maintained and protected, at least for the benefit of 'friends' of the French. The right to pursue escaped slaves was continually exercised with the co-operation of the administration, in spite of the Ponty circular of 1 February 1901 which expressly forbade it. Unless he purchased his freedom (for 150 francs), every escaped captive was returned to his master, even one from whom he had suffered ill-treatment. None of this prevented the laws forbidding the slave trade being invoked when it was a question of bringing down a political opponent. The method was all the more effective since slaves, together with herds of animals, constituted practically the entire wealth of the aristocracy of Futa-Jalon.

Such action was taken against Alfa Yaya, who was accused of the crime of trying to recapture his captives when he returned to Conakry in 1911. A little earlier (in 1909), the inspector of administrative affairs, Bobichon, had ordered Alfa Alimu, who had been nominated chief of Labe province after Alfa Yaya's first disgrace, to be arrested and condemned to three years' imprisonment for 'slave trading acts'. Since Alfa Alimu had been chosen to carry out the functions of Alfa Yaya specifically in his capacity as the latter's personal enemy, the governor, Liotard, judged this action of his former friend Bobichon to be 'disastrous', especially on the very eve of Alfa Yaya's return. Again in 1911, to punish the 'revolt' of the Peuls of Gumba (in the Kindia circle), 1,500 captives were freed (we saw above what this supposed revolt actually was).

For staunch members of the administration, nothing had changed. Even the 'suppression' of slavery had some surprising effects. A report of 1911 noted: 'In Futa-Jalon it had the paradoxical effect that domestic captives of the Fulas were transformed into free sharecroppers, paying dues four or five times higher than before, to the great joy of their dispossessed "masters".'[57] In fact, on the eve of the Second World War domestic slavery remained a reality – at least in Futa-Jalon – and was discreetly protected by the administration. Even if the services rendered by the captives were negligible, and as the result of

57. Denise Bouche, op. cit., p. 524.

this their exchange value was considerably lowered (their value in 1936 was 150 francs or half a cow, as against three cows in earlier times and eight cows for a blacksmith), they remained an important element in heritable property, and it was on them that the main burden of tax, requisitions and military recruitment fell.[58]

Understandably, the League of Nations condemned in 1925 the slave practices tolerated in French Africa. And in this connection the virtuous people who in 1948–50 heaped coals of fire on Saudi Arabia, where 'French citizens' of French West Africa were sold as slaves, forgot to explain that if there had been trading, it was because the said 'citizens' were still captives in the eyes of the administration, which in Mauritania for example still exercised the right of pursuit against fugitive slaves, for the benefit of pro-French notables.

*Direct administration and the chiefdom.* Between 1890 and 1914, the system known as 'direct administration' was gradually installed. The old rulers – including those who had given most assistance to French penetration – were eliminated and the old political framework was turned completely upside-down: ethnic boundaries, the traditional boundaries of the *diwe* of Futa-Jalon, were cut up and reshaped according to administrative necessity or fantasy. The political reality thenceforward was the 'circle', and eventually the 'sub-division', commanded by a European administrator, and below that the canton and the village commanded by African chiefs styled 'traditional' or 'customary'.

In reality there was nothing traditional or customary about these chiefs, either in their role or in the powers devolved on them. Their assignment was to ensure that many administrative tasks (taxation, forced labour, military recruitment etc.) were carried out at the lowest possible cost and on their own responsibility, and were thus the exact counterparts of the *caids* in Algeria (a sub-order of administrators). The system of direct administration was quite simply modelled on the one tested in Algeria, that test-bed for French colonisation, but without the slightest concern to take account of 'traditions' or even the actual conditions prevailing in black Africa.

The fiction which had hitherto made a distinction between a 'country under French sovereignty' and a 'protectorate' was suppressed by a simple decree, that of 23 October 1904, whereby in effect all the territory of Guinea (like that of French West Africa generally) passed into the ownership of the French state. Unilaterally the French government turned into 'scraps of paper' the thousands of

58. See G. Vieillard, 'Notes sur les Peuls du Fouta-Djalon', *Bulletin de l'I.F.A.N.*, 1 (Jan.–Apr. 1940), pp. 87–210.

treaties of protection it had signed and thanks to which it had implanted itself successfully in Africa. It is true that out of concern for efficiency, the chiefs were usually chosen (above all in Futa-Jalon) from among the old ruling families. But traditional rules of investiture and succession were no more respected than the boundaries of the old provinces. For most of the time, the role of the traditional assemblies – when they met – was merely to rubber-stamp the decisions of the administration.

Not only were earlier abuses not suppressed, but they were aggravated. For its own ends, colonisation had systematically cultivated and developed all the negative, retrograde aspects of the old chieftaincy and feudalism, and suppressed or obscured the limits imposed by true custom: in short, everything that was at all positive or democratic in the traditional institutions. The 'despotism' of chiefs is an innovation of colonisation. It was simply the reflection of the despotic basis of the colonial command, which was totally alien to the African tradition whereby the chief was, before all else, the servant of custom and the law, and was genuinely controlled by democratic or oligarchic assemblies. This is how it was in Futa-Jalon, where the assemblies, at one time numerous (in each *misîde* or parish and each *diwal* or province, and at the level of the confederation), were suppressed, and the councils of elders reduced almost entirely to a consultative role. 'The present canton chiefs', Gilbert Vieillard noted, 'have more power than the former *diwal* chiefs because they are no longer restrained by those bodies consisting of the powerful families whose rival strengths counterbalanced each other in the *misîde*.'[59]

The exactions which had formerly been blamed on the chiefs not only did not disappear; they became worse. In former times, the victims of raids carried out by chiefs at least had the recourse of defending themselves with hand-arms. But from this point on, raids were made under cover of the imposition of taxes and with the assistance of the circle guards, and resistance was no longer possible – or it exposed one to the full severity of the law. Relatives and courtiers of the chiefs (*batulabe* – men of the 'bag' and the 'cord', so called in reference to their administrative functions), in the course of their official 'rounds', vied with one another to carry off grain and oxen in addition to the taxes. In the famine of 1936 they even went so far as to help themselves to basic necessities. In the words of the administrator Gilbert Vieillard,

> The young people who had left to earn [the wherewithal to pay taxes] and had not returned; taxpayers who had emigrated, gone into hiding or were actually fleeing; and dead persons included in the census weighted the tally of those

59. Ibid., p. 133.

enumerated. Too bad – money had to be found; and so they were reduced to selling the property of those whose affairs were not in order and even of those whose affairs *were* in order but who did not dare to complain too much. First they sold the animals – cows, sheep, chickens – then grain, cooking pots, Korans, anything that would fetch a price. The prices were low and the chiefs' men and the Syrian traders fished in troubled waters. The taxpayer seldom saw the difference between the sale price of his goods and the total tax due. When there were no goods to sell, they obtained pledges on the next harvest and the children.[60]

When Vieillard blamed his 'notables' for surrounding themselves with obvious riff-raff, the latter replied, with reason: 'Do you want us to collect taxes and provide men liable for forced labour and conscription? We will not be able to obtain them for you with gentleness and persuasion. If the people are not scared of being trussed up or beaten, they will merely laugh at us.'[61] And the administrator had no answer because the tax had to be brought in; it was well understood that for the chiefs who did the dirty work, the key phrase was 'I don't want to know about it.' If the tax did not come in, or if there was a public scandal, the chief would foot the bill for the operation. His despotism had as its limit that of the circle commander who, at the slightest dissatisfaction, could destroy the lesser despot.

The system of forced labour, requisitions etc. began in the rubber era, and continued until quite recent times, after reaching a new climax during the Second World War. So that time, in the name of the 'war effort', the peasants were hit once again by the most extravagant exactions, being forced to buy at high prices products they had not cultivated, and then let them go to European traders for a tenth of the prices they had paid. There were times when this was too much for the circle commander. One administrator, called on to provide an impressive number of kilos of honey in a circle which did not produce it, answered by telegram: 'All right for the honey. Send the bees.' He was punished for this insolence. Ray Autra recalled in his poem *L'effort de guerre* the calvary suffered by the Guinean peoples during this grim period. The end of the war and then, in 1946, democratic pressure and the abolition of the *indigénat* and of forced labour still did not put an end to the traditional practices, least of all in remote regions. Even in 1949, the counsellor-general Camara Caman revealed that all the taxpayers of the Macenta circle had to make a forced contribution of almost 20 kilos of rice, which was then carried on men's heads over distances of dozens of kilometres to the appointed centres, where it was resold for 11 francs per kilo to European traders who resold it for 16 francs. The market at Macenta was guarded to prevent the producers from coming

60. Ibid., p. 171.
61. Ibid., p. 129.

to sell directly to consumers.[62] And he added: 'Anyone who passed the administrator and did not salute him had his head-dress confiscated and deposited in the circle office.'[63]

### *A balance-sheet*

It is too easy, in order to give a good account of what the French achieved, to invoke the very modest achievements of the last ten or twelve years of colonisation, forced upon them by pressure from the mass of the people, who had by now organised themselves. It is more advisable to examine the balance-sheet of the first forty or fifty years of colonisation, such as one might have drawn up on the eve of the Second World War. For some of the data we will make use of figures produced later and hence all the more significant. In 1939, Guinea had much the same infrastructure as in 1914: 662 km. of metre-gauge railway and a poorly-equipped port – all obtained from the country's own resources (forced labour, taxes and loans). The trade economy, with all its parasitic characteristics, still prevailed, though showing signs of stagnation even more pronounced than those in the other territories of French West Africa.

Only commerce – exporting and importing – represented a considerable volume of turnover. Concentration was more and more in evidence. Indeed, the quasimonopoly of several houses was already established by 1900. In first place was the C.F.A.O. (French West Africa Company) of Marseilles; then some large British concerns; and finally the Swiss company Ryff and Roth, which was still in a relatively modest position. In all there were scarcely twenty companies of any consequence in Conakry, and with warehouses in the interior. The other merchants were merely their intermediaries.

Customs legislation had got rid of the Sierra Leonean traders in 1897, the same time as saw the appearance of the first 'Syrians' (in fact Lebanese) who were soon to have a monopoly of the direct purchase of rubber, for they paid in cash while the old trading houses continued to insist on giving in exchange trade goods from their warehouses. But the Lebanese were never able to rise above the level of intermediate retailers, having to be content with a slender profit margin, and thus eliminating the competition of the trading posts, where overheads were too high.

62. *Réveil*, Dakar, 4 April 1949.
63. The administrator in question was a man of relatively mild disposition. Some of his colleagues resorted on similar occasions to the whip, or to giving the offender a spell in gaol for 'insulting a magistrate while in the performance of his duty' or expressing 'contempt for French authority'.

The 1914–18 war made it possible to eliminate the German houses, which had been of some importance; and several old Manchester-based British houses disappeared or were absorbed by the branches of Unilever. In future the Big Three – the C.F.A.O., the Société commerciale de l'Ouest africain (S.C.O.A. – formerly Ryff and Roth) and 'Niger français' (in other words, the Anglo-Dutch Unilever company) – controlled the market, keeping a tight hold over houses of the second rank like Rouchard (which had become Unicomer), Chavanel, the Comptoir commercial franco-africain etc.

With the administrative stranglehold, commerce had managed to penetrate deeply, but much more through administrative constraints (forced deliveries to European firms at controlled prices) than by the working of supply and demand. At the same time the economy of Guinea vegetated, uncertain of its direction and second-rate in every area. The absence of a dominant commodity, like groundnuts in Senegal, resulted not so much in stability as in a lack of development, in the most 'colonial' sense of that term. And meanwhile Lower Guinea, Futa-Jalon, the Manding plateau and the forest regions offered the most varied resources.

Since the decline of rubber (production had fallen to 190 tonnes in 1934), no cultivated product had really replaced it. There was just one partial success, the development of banana production in the hinterland of Conakry, and alongside the railway as far as Kindia. With the introduction of the Chinese banana tree, production rose from 7 tonnes in 1903 to 260 tonnes in 1920, 26,000 in 1934 and 52,000 in 1938. Guinea had thus become the leading of producer bananas in French Africa. But the inadequate means of transporting and marketing the production limited its development, as did the competition from producers in the Americas. In short, banana production (which took place only on European plantations – African plantations did not become important till after the war) remained somewhat peripheral in the country's economy. Everything else was insignificant. The orange groves of Futa-Jalon produced a few dozen tonnes of orange essence (144 in 1934,[64] the highest pre-war total being 298), which it was difficult to place on the market. The coffee-tree, which could have been successful, gave only an insignificant production. It had been introduced at Dalaba in central Guinea by Professor Auguste Chevalier in 1914, and the authorities ordered its cultivation over a wide area between 1920 and 1930; then the world economic crisis made its exploitation unprofitable just when the plants were becoming productive. Nine-tenths of the trees were abandoned in 1939, and

64. This figure is close to production at the present day.

production was never more than about 20 tonnes. By contrast, on the eve of the war coffee production was reaching its peak in Guinea's forest regions, having climbed from 11 tonnes in 1932 to 956 in 1940 – but even the latter figure was not significant.

As for other traditional food production, which forming part of the subsistence economy of the peasant population (palm oil, palm kernels, groundnuts, sesame, rice and livestock), the trading firms were only able to obtain a small surplus of indifferent quality. More than elsewhere in French West Africa, agriculture remained the only productive sector. The only industries – and those on a very small scale – were extractive. The mining companies (Mines d'or de la Falémé-Gambie at Siguiri and Soguinex for diamonds in upper Guinea) were content to use their mining rights to carry off the production of the alluvial deposits, obtained by traditional African skilled methods and without any significant investment: this was the equivalent, in mining terms, of what had been done in the sphere of agriculture by the gathering of rubber. We need not discuss these mining 'companies' whose most obvious activity was shady speculation, for which Guinea was merely the pretext. The iron deposits of Kalum had been known since 1904, and there had been prospecting for bauxite. But their exploitation was of no interest either to French industry, itself an exporter of these minerals, or to commerce which had little desire to invest in hazardous speculations. Processing industries were almost non-existent, and in no instance had passed the stage of hand-craft. Even in 1947, by which time the war had stimulated some of these industries, there was no oil plant in Guinea capable of processing more than 500 tonnes a year. The few plants for canning and for production of fruit juices were already in financial trouble.

As we have seen, the government and the administration were no more than the agents of the consortium of large trading houses. The latter had enough direct representatives in the departments of the ministry of the colonies and the colonial inspectorate to keep a firm hold over governors and administrators who were not sufficiently compliant. But most of these fulfilled with spontaneous zeal their mission to 'open up these backward regions to our commerce and hence to civilisation [*sic*]'. But where there were no benefits to the populations, the general costs of the enterprise were firmly placed to their charge. We will leave aside forced labour and forced cultivation in order to concentrate on the tax burden. In 1934 direct taxes were shared out as follows: (*a*) Europeans paid 100 francs per head, plus a contribution of 5 per cent on the rentable value of property and (*b*) natives paid a personal tax of between 11 and 20 francs, plus circle tax, plus a tax on their animals (45 centimes for a sheep, 2.25 francs for each head of cattle, and 13.50 francs for a horse). Contemporary data are lacking, but to measure the relationship between a person's taxes and his income, we should note that in 1951, according to the statistics of INSEE (the National Institute of Statistics and Economic Studies), the average annual income of an African in French West Africa was 10,000 CFA francs (in Guinea it was only 7,000), and that of a European was 315,000 francs.[65]

Now we will look at the budgetary structure, as far as receipts were concerned. In 1940,[66] out of receipts totalling 81.4 million francs, *personal taxes* alone yielded 35.9 million. By contrast, tax on income (paid by the Africans too) produced only 1.3 million, patents and licences 4.1 million, and land tax 700,000. The balance came from indirect taxes, which had their ultimate effect upon the mass of consumers. In short, the European population enjoyed a privileged fiscal status, and the big commercial houses had genuine immunity. On the other hand, the personal tax and its supplements, to say nothing of 'contributions' and 'interest' which had to be paid to provident societies, and to say nothing either about the supplementary dues payable to the chiefs and their hangers-on, frequently accounted for three-quarters of the peasant's money income.[67] To obtain this indispensable cash, the poor regions of Futa-Jalon had no other resource besides the export of their labour, notably as seasonal agricultural labourers ('*navétanes*') in Senegal.

What, on the other side, were the 'benefits' which accrued to the Guinean population? Were there not some famous schools? In 1935, forty-five years after the establishment of 'French Guinea', education was provided in the territory for a total of 6,558 pupils, out of a total population of 2 million; 111 French and African teachers taught in thirty-four elementary and preparatory schools, nine regional schools, two orphanages, one apprentices' school and two vocational agricultural sections at Labe and Kankan. Secondary education did not exist. The one and only 'upper primary school' had the staff and the standard of a 'secondary modern' school. But, it will be asked, did not this modest educational achievement have a positive character compared to the void which it filled? It is this idea of a void that one has to dispute. Early in the nineteenth century, the explorer Gaspard-Théodore Mollien, following Mungo Park, testified that in every village in Futa, at least, there were Koranic schools where the

65. See M. Capet and J. Fabre, 'L'économie de l'A.O.F. depuis la guerre', *Annales africaines*, 1957, pp. 135-94.
66. Colonie de la Guinée française, *Compte définitif des recettes et des dépenses. Exercise 1940*, Conakry: Imprimerie du Gouvernement, 1942.
67. Capet and Fabre (see note 65) estimate that in 1951 the average minimum proportion of an African peasant's money income absorbed by taxation, for West Africa as a whole, was 32 per cent.

instruction was not limited to reciting the holy book – as has so often been said as a salve to the conscience. Mariani, the inspector of Muslim education who visited Guinea in 1911, informed an astonished administration that, not in Futa alone but in Lower Guinea as well, he had found in modest-sized villages *karamokos* capable both of writing and of conversing in literary Arabic. He proposed that *medersas* (Muslim colleges) be instituted. The Mariani report was consigned to the archives, and traditional education, which was suspected of being a vehicle for dangerous influences, continued to languish.

Among the forest populations there were courses of initiation for young people. However archaic they may have been, rites had an educational content which was better than nothing. Here again, the colonial system, always ready to invoke 'custom' to disguise oppression of the people, cared little for these authentic traditions. On this subject Captain Duffner noted: 'The course of training was carried out in the forest, the men and the women being separated, and used to last for between five and seven years for the men and between four and five years for the women. Since the economic conditions of life have changed, and since recruitment has taken away the young people, the course has become shorter in order to allow the villages to build up their workforce.'[68]

We now turn to the subject of hospitals. The same source[69] tells us that in 1935 the whole of Guinea had a hospital in Conakry (built in 1901), two ambulances, twenty dispensaries or medical posts, fifteen maternity units or posts with midwives. . . . The work from which this information is taken states that the department of the Pasteur Institute at Kindia was established in that place to be able to procure the anthropoid apes necessary for its work. . . . Nothing had been done at that time to counter-act sleeping sickness. It was necessary to wait till 1938 for Dr Jamot, who had been dismissed from his post in Cameroon, to set up a specialist service parallel to the one he had created in the latter colony – not without meeting dogged resistance. One can conclude with Gilbert Vieillard that the activity of the medical officers 'was taken up with attending to the little clusters of white people and their employees'[70] – which is to say that they gave almost nothing to the peasant masses, who were the majority of the population.

Thus on the eve of the Second World War the balance-sheet of colonisation appeared to the mass of the population of Guinea – the peasants – as being totally negative. Where, for them, was this famous

68. Captain Duffner, 'Croyances et coutumes religieuses chez les Guerzé et Manon de la Guinée française', *Bulletin du Comité d'Études Historiques et Scientifiques de l'A.O.F.*, 4 (1934), p. 545.
69. *La Guinée française*, Agence économique de l'A.O.F., 1935.
70. G. Vieillard, op. cit.

'civilisation' of which the benefits were to compensate them for their accumulated outpouring in labour and taxes, to say nothing of the tax in blood during the two world wars? The infrastructure which colonisation provided - the railway, posts and telegraph, roads, the port etc. - only had the effect of handing the country over a little more to the usurers of big business, and of intensifying its exploitation. Schools, hospitals - access to these was only available to a privileged few. The peasant continued to live and work like his forebears, except that he worked harder and ate less; undernourishment became chronic in lean periods, the periods when work was hardest. The peasant's average daily diet contained less than 1,000 calories (a normal diet was estimated to contain 3,000). 'The food ration has been known to fall to 208 calories a day - in lean periods certainly, but beyond any typical degree of shortage.'[71] It is not difficult to imagine what famines were like in such conditions; they occurred, whatever the colonial literature may say, in 1913-14, 1931-6 and 1944-5, and they were infinitely more terrible than those recorded from the times before colonisation. We know the appalling rate of infant mortality, the ravages wrought by endemic tropical diseases and epidemics on malnourished and weakened constitutions; and we know that the population level stagnated around the 2 million mark throughout the fifty years of colonial rule.

Meanwhile, by its own contradictions, the colonial system was involuntarily preparing the conditions which would cause its downfall. European education was being spread among a minority, albeit a narrow one, and abridged and depersonalised though this education was, colonialism gave to some Africans at least the possibility of analysing the causes of their own condition and of finding the means to free themselves from it. That the colonial regime would have been glad to dispense with education was shown on many occasions. But it could not slough off this 'necessary evil' which made it possible for it to procure the minimum of subordinate staff needed to ensure that the administrative and economic machine would run smoothly. The progress of the market economy, even in the rudimentary form of trading, encouraged the circulation of men and ideas. And the sending of soldiers to France opened a window on the world outside Africa.

The political awakening of 1945, advances in the organisation of the masses, and the emergence of African solidarity, enabling ancient ethnic and tribal antagonisms to be overcome - all these factors came together immediately after the war, and shook the old structure to its very foundations, causing it ultimately to collapse. But that is another story.

71. Médecin-général Peltier, *Marchés coloniaux*, 242 (1 July 1950), p. 1460.

# 7

# THE END OF CHIEFTAINCY IN GUINEA[1]

On 31 December 1957, a decree appeared in the *Journal Official* of French Guinea signed by Keïta Fodéba, minister of the interior of the *'loi-cadre'* government, announcing the abolition of the 'so-called' traditional chieftaincy'. It is indisputable that there would not have been a 'no' vote in the constitutional referendum of 28 September 1958 without the elimination of chieftaincy. A few weeks after the referendum, in a preface to the report of the Conference of the circle commanders held in Conakry in July 1957,[2] Jacques Rabemananjara (subsequently a minister in the Malagasy Republic) wrote:

> One of the bastions of the [colonial] regime, its heavy artillery, used only in serious circumstances, is the African feudal system. That is a paradox: is it not true that France, 'faithful to her traditional mission, intends to guide the peoples it rules to self-government, to the democratic management of their own affairs';[3] she pretends to teach the worship of democracy everywhere, but, in spite of the most eloquent preambles to her constitutions, she has consistently favoured, secretly or openly, since her penetration of Africa a century ago, an anachronistic institution, the most anti-democratic imaginable: the support, the multiplication, and the protection of the likes of Glaoui.'[4]

Rabemananjara continued, quoting a correspondent of the weekly *France Observateur*: 'Let us pay homage to Sekou Toure who, in eliminating chieftaincy, has seen the light. The elimination of this feudal vestige allowed him to gain his country's independence on September 28.'[5] And he concluded: 'Nothing is more true. Sekou Toure might have shared the fate of Bakary Djibo if he had not known how to dismantle and crush that decrepit structure of unpopular and retrograde dignitaries.'[6]

1. The article orginally appeared, in French, in the *Journal of African History*, VII (1966), pp. 459–93. A slightly abridged English version, in a translation by Susan Sherwin, appeared in M.A. Klein and G.W. Johnson (eds), *Perspectives on the African Past,* Boston: Little, Brown, 1972. This is substantially the version used here. Notes not by the Author but supplied by the editor of the 1972 volume are distinguished by the sign [†].
2. *Guinée. Prélude à l'Indépendence*, Paris: Présence Africaine, 1958. The Conference ratified the Guinean colonial administration's decision to abolish chieftaincy.
3. Text taken from the preamble to the French Constitution of 1946.
4. Op cit., Preface, ii. Glaoui was the Pasha of Marrakech, who supported the French in Morocco during their struggle against Mohammed V.
5. *France-Observateur*, 440 (9 Oct. 1958), p. 23.
6. Op. cit., p. 12. Bakary Djibo was the leader of the *loi-cadre* government in Niger,

Rabemananjara's opinion is now widely shared. Whether or not the abolition of chieftaincy and the 'no' vote of 28 September are regarded favourably (as they are by this writer), there is a clear link between the two. The circumstances and the significance of the abolition of chieftaincy are not always clearly grasped. In giving credit for this measure to Sekou Toure and his friends of the Parti Démocratique de Guinée (P.D.G.), we usually consider it the result of a decision freely taken in 1957, which other leaders in other territories could have taken if they had been more clear-sighted. This viewpoint was implicit in Rabemananjara's preface: '[Toure's] real talent was his ability to recognise what tasks had to be accomplished without delay. Wasn't the *loi-cadre Defferre* in the hands of all African leaders? Not one except Toure knew how to use it or to transform it into an efficient instrument of government'.[7]

Some leftist writers who no longer share the earlier enthusiasm for Toure's regime now question the democratic significance of this measure, if not its very existence. A contributor to the journal *Révolution*, who signed 'Africanus'[8] but seemed not to have direct knowledge of Guinea, doubted that a simple statute could have abolished chieftaincy there, and questions whether it really did so. Ameillon - who seems to have had an administrative post in Guinea during 1957-8 - sees the abolition as the result of a 'judicial battle', a response from on high with political objectives: 'It [chieftaincy] was the only restriction to the absolute power of the Party, and to the interests of large industry, for whom the existence of forced labor was an obstacle to labor mobility.'[9]

I propose to show - using documents from the Guinean archives - that these interpretations cannot be supported. The documents show that the downfall of Guinean chieftaincy was the result of a deep-seated popular movement, beginning before 1957-8. Undoubtedly, Toure and the P.D.G. contributed to the development and orientation of this movement; but their initiative dates back earlier. In 1957-8 the downfall of chieftaincy was an established fact. Its legal abolition was the outcome of a social movement, and it is doubtful whether Toure and his friends could have maintained or revived chieftaincy in 1957, even if they had wanted to. On the contrary, we can ask whether the leaders of other territories could have

---

who called for a 'no' vote, but was neutralised by the administration, and then dismissed. He subsequently lived in exile.

7. Ibid.
8. *Révolution*, 3 (1963).
9. B. Ameillon, *La Guinée, bilan d'une indépendance,* Paris: Maspéro, 1964. At the Conference of the circle Commanders, Sekou Toure developed the argument that traditional structures were incompatible with industrial development.

eliminated chieftaincy in 1957–8 if they had so desired. Only the examination of the facts and the gathering of testimony will give us a valid answer. Before coming to grips with the question, we must examine the social position of chieftaincy in French West Africa before the Second World War, particularly in French Guinea.

### *Chieftaincy in the French colonial system*[10]

It is traditional to contrast the French system of 'direct administration' with the British system of 'indirect administration'. In fact, the differences between the two systems are much less than the terminology implies. Nowhere in Africa did French colonisation actually put a system of 'direct' administration into practice. It always resorted to the intermediary of chieftaincy. However, in tropical Africa it did not use the 'protectorate', which in principle left sovereignty to the former chiefs. Legally, there was no authority other than the colonial authority.

This originated with the advent of the radicals to power in France at the beginning of the century. The land decree of 23 October 1904 ended the fiction of 'protectorates' in West Africa by abolishing the chief's control over land and transferring it to the French state. The policy of 'direct rule', which was official doctrine from 1904 to 1914, tended to 'suppress the great native polities which are nearly always a barrier between us and our subjects'.[11] This policy was rigorously applied, especially in Senegal and Guinea. It eliminated these large states even when they were under men who had been faithful servants of the French cause, such as Alfa Yaya, the 'king' of Labe! Nonetheless, the lack of adequate personnel and the impossibility of doing without native middlemen resulted in the *de facto* support of chieftaincy at the village and 'canton' level (the traditional political unit in Malinke country, more artificial elsewhere). In the eyes of the law, these chiefs, more or less conserving their titles and their past functions, were no more than agents – and unofficial ones at that – of the colonial administration. They lacked any *statut* and consequently any rights. (*Statut* refers to a set of regulations pertaining to the status, behaviour and advancement of a body of civil servants; its absence meant that the chiefs' rights and privileges were not regulated in any way.) They were subject to dismissal by the higher administration, and were liable to penalties applicable to other native subjects. Their

10. See R. Cornevin, 'Evolution des chefferies dans l'Afrique noire d'expression française', *Recueil Penant* (1961), nos 686–8, and J. Suret-Canale, *French Colonialism in Tropical Africa*, London: Hurst, 1971, pp. 77, 79–83, 322–7.
11. Governor-General W. Ponty, in a report to the Government Council of French West Africa of 20 June 1910, *Afrique française*, 7 (July 1910).

primary role was to collect taxes (poll and supplementary taxes) from which they were granted a portion - their only official income - and to provide labour for the various requirements of the administration (transport, construction and upkeep of roads, public buildings, etc.). The chiefs took advantage of this to exact money and labour for themselves, if necessary in the guise of custom. These exactions were tolerated or even enforced by the administration (which would fine or imprison recalcitrants as guilty of resistance to authority), but had no legal basis and could be used against chiefs it wanted to get rid of.

It was not possible for chiefs to avoid using these methods. The rebates they received on taxes and, later, the meagre allowance which was added, were simply not enough to support their style of living and their many responsibilities. The chief had to lodge and entertain in royal style the circle commander and other representatives of the administration on tour. He had to support a secretary, messengers and representatives at the administrative headquarters of the circle. Furthermore, he had to support a court to establish his prestige and to affirm his authority, by force when necessary. 'When the chiefs are reproached for surrounding themselves with questionable people, they rightly answer: do you want us to collect the tax to furnish labourers and conscripts? We will not succeed with sweetness and persuasion; if people are not afraid of being beaten and chained, they may not take us seriously.'[12]

The absence of a *statut* on chieftaincy, as well as its subordinate position, eroded its prestige and its moral authority. If representatives of the traditional hierarchies were not submissive enough, the administration did not hesitate to substitute upstarts or strangers whom they trusted - former soldiers or circle guards, or even houseboys or cooks who enjoyed the governor's favour. The advent of the First World War and the reduction of European personnel enhanced the importance of the chiefs. In response, Governor-General van Vollenhoven tried to re-enforce their authority: respect for customary rules in the designation of chiefs, allocation of decorations, restoration of pensions, and condemnation of the abuse of administrative sanctions against them. However, he vigorously maintained the principle of a single source of authority: 'There are not two authorities in the circle, the French authority and the native authority; there is only one. The circle commander alone commands; he alone is responsible. The native chief is only an auxiliary.'[13] So what was the social position of the chiefs? In fact they were a privileged social group, as in pre-colonial times, but

12. Gilbert Viellard, 'Notes sur les Peuls du Fouta-Djallon', *Bulletin de l'I.F.A.N.*, 1 (1940), p. 129.
13. Circular of 15 August 1917, *Afrique française,* 12 (Dec. 1917), p. 270.

instead of exploiting the peasant masses for their own benefit, they were reduced to being the instrument of this exploitation, with the right to pick up a few crumbs in passing. This explains their integration into the colonial system. But the methods of exploitation remained the same.

This is not the place to debate the term 'African feudalism'. Let us simply note that although on the level of political structure there is a striking analogy between traditional African aristocracies and the medieval feudal system of Europe, there is a major difference on the economic and social level. In Europe, the relations of the feudal lord with his vassals and subjects, and the resulting obligations on the latter, (especially in matters of rent and services), were relations between possessors of individual rights. Individuals had obligations, either as a result of their social status or as private property owners. Private property was the norm, and the Church, which was the prime beneficiary of gifts and land bequests, helped to enforce it. The relation of the African chief to his subjects was more to collectivities than to individuals. Private ownership of land was unknown; there was only inalienable collective property. The chief, whether the heir or usurper of the established rights of 'territorial chiefs', could arrange it as he wished. He could, within certain limits, have it cultivated for himself and decide its use, but in the pre-colonial era this right never took the form of an actual property law entailing the possibility of transferring the land permanently. Rents or labour obligations, even if 'taxed' on an individual basis, were always owed by the community and levied collectively, with the village chiefs and the patriarchal family heads serving as intermediaries.

Colonisation used these convenient traditional methods of raising money; first the canton, and then the village were asked to pay taxes, or provide men for forced labour or conscription under the personal responsibility of the chief. The 'traditional' obligations which had acquired if not a private character then at least a dynastic one, became purely functional – even more than before – under the colonial regime. They were attached to the chief's functions. An individual vested with chiefly authority could dispose of men and land; within limits set by custom (and, when required, somewhat beyond that, if he had the means to impose his authority), he could allocate extensive fields to himself and have them cultivated by labourers. But when dismissed, he lost everything to his successor: the right to take fields on village land as well as the right to 'customary services' without which these fields could not be developed. He retained only his family land.

In short, chieftaincy could not be transformed into a landed aristocracy based on hereditary rights to land. However, there were some variations. In the savanna regions, where annual tillage based on long-term crop rotation and fallow land predominated, the agricultural system itself was an obstacle to the emergence of private property. Hence, the dismissed chief generally lost everything except his personal goods. However, he could procure a relatively privileged position by allocating to himself (or usurping) fairly extensive family land which he could retain subject to challenge by the villagers or by his successor. He could also register lots in the urban centres (in the capital of the circle, or sometimes in the capital of the colony), either by invoking 'customary' rights (often debatable) or by the allocation or purchase of a parcel of land. In the plantation regions, the chieftaincy to some degree transformed itself into a landlord class by using traditional services to get necessary manpower and by creating extensive plantations which were soon regarded as private property, either according to a customary entitlement, or with registration guaranteed. The latter case was geographically limited, and its importance should not be exaggerated. The number of beneficiaries - canton chiefs, and some chiefs of very important villages - was restricted. These plantations only covered a fraction of all cultivated land, and do not appear to have given rise anywhere to a 'land question'.

### *Chieftaincy in Futa-Jalon*

A careful analysis of chieftaincy in Guinea would demand a canton-by-canton study which I have not had the means to undertake. But without risk of error, it is possible to offer the general view that follows, looking at individual regions. Unquestionably, the chief's position was strongest in Futa-Jalon. Chiefs were recruited here from a ruling aristocracy whose economic and social position was not seriously affected by colonisation. The aristocracy of the great Fulbe families continued to live off the labour of their subjects: Fulbe Bororo vassals or clients entrusted with herds of cattle and Matyube slaves, as well as farmers of Sussu or Jalonke origin,[14] who had been reduced to serfdom and progressively assimilated. Up till the Second World War, the position of 'captives' (euphemistically called 'servants' in administrative reports) had not really changed.

In certain regions of the Sudan there was a large-scale emancipation of slaves, as much to force their former masters to productive work as to destroy their political power.[15] There were no economic reasons for

14. This traditional view needs to be corrected. The 'slaves' were of more diverse and distant origins than we suggested above (see J. Suret-Canale, 'Les origines ethniques des anciens captifs du Fouta-Djalon', *Notes Africaines* (Dakar), 123 (July 1969), pp. 91–2).

such a measure in Futa-Jalon. Rubber was the only trading product in which there was then an interest, and it could easily be gathered within the traditional social framework. The aristocracy had accepted French tutelage without resistance, and it seemed logical to the colonial administration to rely on them.[16]

Struggles between aristocratic factions facilitated the occupation by French troops in 1896. The 'Soriya' *almamy* Bokar Biro, conquered and killed in the battle of Poredaka, was unpopular even in his own party because of his severity and avarice, and a number of his vassals, mainly Alfa Yaya of Labe, had continually called for French intervention against him.[17]

The beginning of French occupation - which at first was incomplete - enabled certain allies, such as Alfa Yaya, to strengthen their position.[18] But this short-lived tolerance did not mean that the French Administration decided to allow similar latitude to the chiefs for long. The protectorate 'Treaty', set up with Futa on 6 February 1897 (in which the *almamys* Umaru Bademba and Sori Eli replaced Bokar Biro) stated in its second article: 'France pledges to respect the existing constitutions of Futa-Jalon. This constitution will operate under the

15. Cf. Paul Marty, *La Politique indigène du Gouverneur général Ponty,* Paris: E. Leroux, 1915, p. 14.
16. A single exception: the 'political' liberation of the Fulbe captives of Goumba (a region located on the Futa border), after some incidents in which the Wali of Gumba opposed the colonial authorities. C.F.M. Verdat, 'Le Ouali de Goumba', *Études guinéennes*, no. 3 (1949), pp. 2–66.
17. In the beginning of 1896, Alfa Yaya wrote to the circle commander of Satadugu (Sudan) and the chief of Diulafundu, Bintu Mady, to ask their help. As the circle commander, Lt. Le Brun, wrote on 17 April: '[He] asked for our protection . . . against the Almamy Bokari Biru de Timbo who had just taken away his authority and given it to Mamady Salif, the chief of Gatawundu.' This chief [Alfa Yaya] . . . was the friend of *Almamy* Abdulaye Diallo, who was killed with his family by Bokari.' Archives Nationales du Mali, Satadougou.
18. 'During the last year [1897] Modi Yaya Alfa of Labe informed the Guinean government that his brother Mahmadu Salif was a plunderer. . . . The roles could have been reversed without harm to the truth. The government of Guinea thought, however, that it had to give Modi Yaya Alfa carte blanche in order to have the things stolen by Mahmadu Salif . . . forcibly restored. In 1895, when I commanded the Hamdallahi post (Upper Casamance), I pointed out the high intellectual but not moral, level of Modi Yaya and his disturbing ambition. Since then, this chief has become considerably more powerful by eliminating some members of his family and chiefs around him. Last March, armed with an authorisation, he attacked Gataundu, took possession of it, and simply had his brother, who bothered him, killed.' (Archives Nationales, Mali, Satadugu, Special Report, (1 Feb. 1898). Alfa Yaya also expanded towards the north, at the expense of the independent Fulbe chief of N'dama, whom the French administration deported to the Congo in 1901.

authority of the Governor of Guinea [*sic*] and under the direct control of a French official, who will assume the title of Resident of Futa-Jalon.' The authority of the *almamys* and their alternation in power was maintained by Article 3 of the Treaty. But Alfa Yaya was acknowledged as the 'permanent chief' of Labe, Kade and Gabu. He was dependent on the reigning *almamy*, but could address himself directly to the Resident of Futa-Jalon. 'Ordinance no. 1' of the Resident, approved by an Assembly of chiefs in July 1897, set up a poll tax of 2 francs, or 10 francs per hut, 'each hut supposedly sheltering a minimum of five people'.[18] A Governor's decree confirmed this decision, adding services in labour. Resident Noirot removed any ambiguity by specifying: 'The chief will attend to the tax and furnish manpower for public works, or he will be smashed like a glass.'[20] The 1897 Treaty lasted no more than a year. Almamy Eli Sori was assassinated by a brother of Bokar Biro, and a December 1898 proclamation by Resident Noirot named his son Alimu as *almamy*, and limited the *almamy's* authority to three *diwe* (out of nine): Timbo, Buriya, Kolen. The others became independent, notably Labe, where Alfa Yaya took the title of 'king of Labe'.[21] 'Divide and rule, that is the only policy to follow in Futa-Jalon,' concluded the report on the Guinean situation in 1898.[22]

A new stage was reached some years later with the appointment of Governor Frezouls, a man of the radicals. He brought about the arrest of Alfa Yaya in 1905, and ordered his internment in Dahomey for five years.[23] At the same time, when *almamy* Baba Alimou died early in 1906, his already reduced domain was divided between representatives

19. National Archives, Guinea, 1E6.
20. André Arcin, *Histoire de la Guinée française*, Paris: Challamel, 1911, p. 592. Regarding the methods for tax collection: 'All the chiefs . . . are duly warned that the calculations that they give us are accepted with their assurances; but if someone visits them, counts the dwellings and finds inaccuracies, the additional dwellings will be obliged to pay the tax, and a fine of one ox each, without prejudice to the responsibility of the chiefs and their revocation' (*Journal de poste*, Timbo, 4 Aug. 1898, written by Administrator Noirot; Regional Archives of Mamou, Guinea).
21. National Archives, Guinea, I.E.6.
22. *Rapport d'ensemble sur la situation générale de la Guinée française en 1898*, p. 81.
23. This affair was described in 'La Guinée dans le système colonial', *Présence Africaine*, XXIX (Dec. 1959–Jan. 1960), pp. 16–18. See also A. Demongeot, 'Notes sur l'organisation politique et administrative du Labé, *I.F.A.N.* (1944), and M. Crespin, 'Alpha Yaya and M. Frézouls', *Revue indigéne* (1906), no. 2, pp. 45–6. (A harsh critique of the new policy set up by Frézouls; the same view is found in *L'Histoire de la Guinée française* by Arein, and seems to have been shared by most of the administrators working with the Noirot-Cousturier team.)

of the two families, who had hitherto governed alternately. The annual report of 1906 noted that this was another step towards 'the progressive suppression of the great chiefs and the breaking up of their authority, until the village becomes the basic administrative entity'.[24]

In 1909 Alfa Alimu, a personal enemy of Alfa Yaya, who for this reason had been designated chief of the province of Labe – with less territory than the former 'kingdom' of Alfa Yaya – was condemned to three years in prison and dismissed; provincial chieftaincy was abolished. In 1910, when Alfa Yaya's administrative punishment ended, Governor Guy didn't allow him to get further than Conakry. He was re-arrested there, and this time was sent to Mauritania where he died the following year.

At the same time measures were taken against certain *marabouts*, whose influence could have replaced that of the traditional aristocracy. *Marabouts* Karamoko Sankun and Ba Gassama of Tuba were arrested on 30 March 1911. But the attempt to arrest the Wali of Gumba, planned for the same day, failed; the detachment sent to seize him was wiped out. In retaliation, the Gumba region was sacked, and the goods of the Fulbe were confiscated and their slaves freed. The Wali, who fled to Sierra Leone, was extradited, condemned to death and placed in the Fotoba prison, where he died in 1912 before the date fixed for his execution.[25]

Finally in 1912, Administrator Thoreau-Lévaré, Noirot's companion and one of the colonial officials who knew the Futa best,[26] initiated an ingenious carving-up of the traditional provinces, in order to dismember the ancient historical units. The functions of the *almamy* – 'a useless, indeed bothersome appendage'[27] – were abolished, and the *almamys* of the two branches were transferred to residences along the recently constructed railway line, at Mamu and Dalaba, with the reduced status of canton chiefs. From then on, the situation was stabilised. In this subordinate position, the ex-*almamys* (who continued to bear that title) received awards and pensions which elevated them above their fellow-chiefs.[28]

24. *Rapport d'ensemble sur la situation générale de la Guinée française en 1906*, Conakry: Imprimerie Ternaux, 1907.
25. Cf. M. Verdat, op. cit.; National Archives of Guinea, 1, E. 7; and the *Journal l'A.O.F.* (Conakry), nos. from September 1911.
26. He was the author of a copious volume 'Notes sur les personnalités réligieuses et influentes de Fouta' (deposited in the regional archives in Mamu, Guinea), and probably used by Paul Marty as a source for *L'Islam en Guinée*.
27. 'Gouvernement général de l'A.O.F.', *Rapport annuel d'ensemble, 1912*, Paris: Larose, 1915.
28. A decree of 21 Dec. 1934, fixing the annual emolument of 'canton' chiefs, alloted 11,200 fr. to the *almamy* of Dabola (a descendant of the Soriya branch), compared with 2,000 to 4,000 for the average 'canton' chief (250 fr. for the chief from the Isle of Kassa, the lowest in the hierarchy).

However, the political operations of 1910–12 brought certain reversals of fortune. For example, the family of the former chiefs of the Dalaba region, who had been implicated in the Wali of Gumba affair, gave way to an obscure village chief, Ba Tierno Umar, who succeeded in making the Dalaba canton 'a great fief', ceaselessly expanding at the expense of neighbouring cantons. Thanks to his connections he was able to get rid of the less intelligent circle commanders. He did not neglect any opportunity of strengthening his influence with demonstrations of loyalty.

## *Chieftaincy in other Guinean regions*

The authority of chieftaincy was considerably less in the other regions, where it did not rest on social structures similar to those in Futa.

In Lower Guinea, many chieftaincies, while perpetually at war with each other and torn by internal dissensions, had been friendly with French traders since the seventeenth century. These states were of similar size to the future cantons. Thus the Fernandezes, kings of Bramaya (Dubreka river), or the Cattys, kings of the Rio Pongo, were descendants of traders who had become progressively africanised. They were the signatories of the first treaties, and from the 80's onwards were strictly subject to the authority of a French circle commander. Only one person created an important state under the French protectorate by using French aid to eliminate his rivals:[29] Dinah Salifu, 'king of the Nalus'. His state extended into the Rio Nunez (Boke) region from 1870. He was a minister and majordomo to his uncle Yura Towel, whom he succeeded in 1887. He was honoured by an exhibition at the Paris World Fair of 1889, but in 1900 he was sent to St Louis, his chiefdom was abolished, and he died in exile.[30]

Although the authority of chiefs in this region, which had long been subject to European influences, did not equal that of the Futa chiefs, their power was not negligible. They set up areas of authority that assured them of a certain level of wealth. This was especially true between Dubreka and Forecariah, where the development of banana plantations from the 1930s enabled them to consolidate their traditional authority and create a profitable enterprise.

In Upper Guinea (Malinke country), the situation was clearly less favourable. This zone had been ravaged by the wars against Samori, and French authority had been established without the mediation of

29. Regarding one of these episodes, the 'Nunez column' (1885), see above, pp. 92–3.
30. ANG, I.15 and 1.E.22. Also see Dr Mée, 'Études sur le Rio Nunez', *Bulletin du Comité d'Études historiques et scientifiques de l'A.O.F.* (1919), 3 and 4, and Kake Ibrahima Baba, 'À propos de l'exil de Dinah Salifou', *Présence Africaine*, LI (1964), pp. 146–58.

the great chieftaincies, except for a short period of transition. The most important was Dinguiraye where Aguibu Tall, a French ally, was 'transferred' to Bandiagara as king of Macina, but was able to leave the local chieftaincy to members of his family. It was immediately cut up into cantons. In Kankan the Kaba family, one of whose chiefs Daye Kaba returned with French troops after the defeat of Samori, retained great influence. However, they were somewhat eclipsed by the religious prestige of the '*Grand Marabout*', who was allegedly descended from the Prophet. Indeed, there were other noted families in the region, such as the Keitas of Kangaba, heirs of the Mali emperors. But Samori's destruction of old political units left a kind of vacuum, which made the establishment of French authority easier, reduced the authority of the chiefs to that of strictly controlled subordinates, and cut their territorial jurisdiction down to 'canton' size. The divisions into 'cantons' reflected traditional realities in Malinke country. Beginning with the Sudan, this administrative system was extended to all French colonies of tropical Africa.[31] Economic conditions did not allow the Malinke chiefs to strengthen their limited authority. A grain area, the method of cultivation did not lend itself to the development of private property. The resources of the chief stayed within customary limits.

In the forest regions, chieftaincy was unknown. The only political units were the patriarchal family or alliances between families (in Kissi country),[32] and the village (in Toma or Guerze country). At most, there were chieftaincies on the Northern borders where Malinke conquerors had driven out or reduced the natives to bondage. Other conquerors had introduced Sudanese political structures while more or less assimilating with the country. Here and there, some war chiefs of the country had also succeeded in setting up spheres of influence – which, however, were extremely unstable.

At the time of the conquest, French officers in the Sudan sought to use these 'marginal' chiefs to extend their authority towards the south, but they failed completely. From 1898 on, they substituted a policy of suppression of the great chieftaincies, a step toward direct administration. Thus, the Kissidugu circle was divided into 99 cantons. This solution was scarcely better.

31. Until 1899, Upper Guinea was connected to Sudan. [Samori was the most effective resistance leader the French faced. The bureaucratic state he had created in the 1880s displaced many traditional rulers, who then allied themselves to France.]

32. Cf. D. Paulme, 'La société Kissi. Son organisation politique', *Cahiers d'Études Africaines*, I, 1 (1960), pp. 73–85, and Y. Person, 'Soixante ans d'evolution en pays Kissi', ibid., pp. 86–112.

> . . . The first administrators determined boundaries between cantons, and for each one named a chief who was to transmit their order and exercise local authority. The power of the chief varied greatly, according to place and individual . . . Many of the cantons seem to be artificial creations of the European administration: their make-up could easily change, one village connected first to one canton, then to another. Very small cantons were even known to disappear when their chiefs died, and were combined with a neighbour without provoking serious trouble. In fact, sixty years ago almost the entire country was only a sprinkling of agglomerations juxtaposed without any real unity.[33]

What Paulme says about Kissi is valid, with some differences, for Toma, Guerze, Manon and Kono. The official report for 1903 stated: 'The native spirit of independence is very great. They live in villages separate from each other. The authority of these village chiefs is very weak and that of the canton chiefs, whom we wanted to set up in military circles, absolutely non-existent'.[34]

Resistance to colonial rule, aided by border disputes with Liberia and 'pacification' operations, continued till 1912.[35] In 1914, the necessity of reducing European personnel, and consequently of limiting the number of intermediaries who had to be controlled, led to a policy of combination in Kissi country. In the Kissidugu circle, the number of cantons was reduced to 60 in 1918, 44 in 1938 and 36 in 1957. The chiefs, who were mostly imposed on their subjects, had only the authority given them by the colonial administration. The opposition of social structures traditionally hostile to chiefly authority, and based on initiation societies, made their position dangerous at times, caught between the prison of the 'commander' and the poison of the juju priest.

## *Guinean Chieftaincy during the 'War Effort'*

Guinean chieftaincy scarcely changed between the two World Wars. Its functions and its resources remained the same, as did the ambiguity of the situation. On the one hand, colonial doctrine emphasised the need to reevaluate the institution and respect 'tradition' (e.g. the circulars of Van Vollenhoven); but elsewhere it insisted that authority belonged to the coloniser alone, and that the chief was an instrument

33. Paulme, 'La Société Kissi', p. 77.
34. *Rapport d'ensemble sur la situation générale de la Guinée française en 1903,* Conakry: Imprimerie Ternaux, p. 66. Up till the Second World War the circles of the forest region located on the border were under military administration.
35. J. Suret-Canale, 'La Guinée dans le système colonial', *Présence Africaine*, XXIX (Dec. 1959-Jan. 1960), pp. 25-7, and *French Colonialism in Tropical Africa,* London: Hurst, 1971, pp. 103-7. (Paris: Editions Sociales, 1964), pp. 138-142.

subject to dismissal at any time it judged to be unequal to his duties. A decree of 1934 determined – for the first time – its regulations and a salary scale, but without getting rid of the ambiguity. The chief remained an agent of the administration, without actually being an official. Tradition served here as a pretext for convenience and economy. The Second World War put the institution to a test from which it never recovered. Like 1914–18, the period 1939–45 produced an increase in the burdens which weighed on the population. However, there were some differences: the defeat of 1940 reduced military recruiting, to which they had become accustomed, but from 1943 they were subjected to unprecedented economic demands. In the First World War there had been shortages and often excessive demands for production, but during the Second these difficulties were greater. From 1940 to 1942 French West Africa, isolated by the administration's loyalty to Vichy, had to subsist without imported products, which had become widespread over twenty years. It thus had to feed the cities and food-deficit territories, especially Senegal, with rice and millet.

When French West Africa went over to the Allied camp, the situation of Guinea was not much improved. On the contrary, the Allied supplies were alloted to them less for the improvement of conditions than to stimulate the war effort (e.g. trucks and petrol to speed up the collection and movement of local products). The Committee of the French Empire (in 1942–3), and then the French Committee for National Liberation were convinced that the honour of France depended on the size of its material effort in the war. 'The colonies must thus supply the needs of the metropolis with an unprecedented *war effort*. The war effort demanded by the Federation was evaluated for each circle, canton or village, on the basis of pre-war statistics, generally over-estimated. Now, these idealistic statistics of an earlier time were not concerned with the real material conditions of the country. Under harsh threats, followed when necessary with immediate enforcement, they made insane demands.'[36] Caught between the devil and the deep blue sea, the chiefs had to satisfy these 'insane demands' at their people's expense and sometimes they found a way to plunder their subjects even more than in the past. The scanty quotas of food rations allotted to the 'bush' – especially sugar and textiles – were distributed by the chiefs. They took care of themselves and their entourages first, and the balance generally went to the black market.

However, it was not easy for the chiefs to satisfy their superiors.

36. J. Richard-Molard, *L'Afrique occidentale française,* 'Paris: Berger-Levrault (new edn. 1956), p. 168.

More than ever, they had to provide export products, and especially those needed by the Allied war machine. In Guinea, the supply of products depended solely on the African farmers, and on the coast and in the forest region, tonnes of palm kernels were demanded. Because there were no mechanical crushers, men, women and children had to spend many days crushing the kernels one by one between stones:

> Imagine an edict from the Ministry for National Defence calling French peasants to crush the plum stones of rural orchards one by one, or suffer serious penalties for endangering the security of the state, calling upon them to cease all other occupations and bring these items to their respective prefects, to be paid for at the rate of 10 centimes a kilo: those were the general orders. . . . To begin with, nothing could have been easier: the palm kernels harvested in preceding years were close by, but unfortunately, the inefficient administrator based his statistics on the earlier date, without considering the fact that they would not find the same reserves the following season. The paper of the agricultural monitor thus contained figures which neither the circle commander nor the Governor himself could do anything about.[37]

In the Futa-Jalon and Malinke country, the gathering of rubber was revived after nearly twenty years; a 'rubber service' was created. 'One such circle was accountable for tons of rubber, but had none on its territory. The native was therefore forced to go on foot, sometimes a very long distance, to buy rubber elsewhere, no matter what the price, in order to escape the 'law'. He then sold it to the 'commandant at the taxed price, which was several times less than the purchase price'.[38] Rubber trading had ceased in Kissidugu after 1920, yet in 1941 the circle supplied 9 tonnes, 'most of which was bought outside of the circle.' In the canton of Dialakoro, 476 kilos out of 566 were bought in the neighbouring circles of Kankan and Kurussa at 40 and 50 francs a kilo. In the canton of Tinki, 345 kilos out of 360 were bought outside the circle at prices of up to 80 francs a kilo. Because of the work required to find the rubber, the sowing of rice was delayed and the harvest put at risk.[39]

But food products were also necessary to feed the cities and food-deficit Senegal. Commerce previously had little interest in food, and the farmer produced only a little more than he needed for himself and the local market. Now, tonnes of millet rice and fonio were demanded. But the means of transport were inadequate. In Guerze country, noted Father Lelong (1943), 'the rice campaign defied all means of transport. American trucks arrived just in time to prevent accumulated stocks of rice from spoiling on the spot. People were starving, yet these reserves

37. M.H. Lelong, *Ces hommes qu'on appelle anthropophages*, Paris: Alsatia, 1946, p. 52.
38. Richard-Molard, op. cit., p. 168.
39. Archives of Kissidugu, Report of Circle Commander, 8 Feb. 1943.

could not be withdrawn.'[40] By default, they used porters: 'To transport a tonne of rice to the nearest station – 300 km. away – 660 men were requisitioned who, for ten days, carried 15 kilos each on their heads. Then in ten days they returned, always on foot – a total of more than three weeks, eating who knows what along the way. . . .'[41]

Men were also needed to cultivate peanuts in Senegal (thousands were dispatched from Futa) and for the banana plantations of coastal Guinea. From Guerze country they were sent on foot to Kankan, the terminus of the railroad. They had to prepare themselves for the trip with 25–30 measures of rice. Each canton chief was 'taxed' for a certain number of 'volunteers'.[42] Father Lelong noted:

> A Guerzé man sent to work in the Conakry region was like a Dutch farmer exiled to the Ukraine. 'Local' tasks were also added: maintenance or construction of roads and bridges, the public works of the circle where there were always bricks to be made, trees to be cut down, transported and sawn into planks, whites to be served . . ., not to speak of a thousand unforseen things like mats, seal-skin or pantherskin, charcoal, sheep and oil, Europeans to be carried about[43] and served, rounds of 'trypano' to the hefty fellows who lived off the inhabitants, who needed meat and women, . . . all that and their fees, too, for the profit of native chiefs who had great fields under cultivation and lacked for nothing.[44]

Below is the list of items demanded from the subdivision of Dalaba (*c.* 60,000 inhabitants) for one of the war years, 1943: construction of a large rest camp (for Europeans): 24 large oval huts, 22 large round dwellings and 17 kitchens, 'work on the approaches to the camp, 37 tonnes of rice, 60 tonnes of rubber (collected mainly outside the circle), 70 tonnes of potatoes, 1,300 oxen. Transport for the rubber, grain, straw and bamboo needed for the camp, and brought in from the Kebali plain on men's heads (110,000 days). Farm labour for Senegal: 1,300 men. Tax and assessments from the native Savings Society: 2,800,000 frs. 'Voluntary contributions': 'National Aid', 102,000 frs.; African loan, 658,000 frs.; national contribution for the Resistance, 390,000 frs. (during 1943, the Resistance took over from the *Secours National* of Marshal Pétain). It would be interesting to know to whom and by what means these funds were transmitted.

In 1945 the 'war effort' continued, but the subdivision chiefs took note of the resultant lassitude, and the growing scarcity of money due to tax burdens, low commodity prices and the black market in textiles

40. Lelong, op. cit., p. 261.
41. Richard-Molard, op. cit., p. 168.
42. Ibid., pp. 188–9.
43. In the forest region of Guinea, the civil servants were carried about in litters up till at least 1946.
44. Lelong, op. cit., p. 189.

and other imports.[45] Analogous balance-sheets could be drawn up for other circles or regions. The 'zeal' of the chiefs in achieving these results was not wholly spontaneous: even in 1945, the circle commander of Kissidugu addressed this circular to his canton chiefs:

*Order of service for the canton chiefs of* [a complete list follows]. I give you till May 31 *at the very latest* to complete your supply of millet to the S.C.O.A.[46] for the current campaign. On 15 May, you must deliver *x* kilos more. If you fail to execute this order within the required time, you will be placed in residence in Kissidugu, and subjected to the necessary penalties until your canton quotas are complete.[47]

From the Archives of N'zerekore, Father Lelong extracted this 'Note to the Canton Chiefs' dated 23 February 1944, which is also significant:

I remind you that you must till the Commander's field, the *corvée* [forced labour] field and the individual field. Release the rubber crews so that these men can farm. A canton is worth what its chief is worth: there are very good chiefs in the circle, and, therefore, very good cantons. Unfortunately there are also bad cantons, and therefore mediocre chiefs who must improve their service if they wish to avoid the penalties I shall impose if necessary: dismissal or merely elimination of the canton, which will be attached to a good canton.[48]

Immediately after the end of the war, the newspaper of the Rassemblement Democratique Africain (R.D.A.), *Réveil*, wrote:

Until recently, the African chief was the servant of the circle commander. Able to communicate with the latter only through the intermediary of the circle guard, he also submitted to the authority of the implacable chicote . . . The chief was the man who supplied chickens for the commander, labourers for the commander, etc. etc. In a word, he was the unrelenting steward of the administration. He was rated according to his aptitude and speed in satisfying the innumerable administrative demands. Fiercely oppressed himself, he oppressed others in his turn.[49]

Despite the rule protecting him from the same punishments as the natives, the canton chief was at the commander's mercy. Even more vulnerable was the village chief, who paid for his community's failure to meet its quota. Few had not been in prison. If a chief lacked 'guts' or was too compassionate towards his subjects, he risked the worst, while the ruthless ones were noticed and indeed well off. The war legislation enabled him to do this: 'opposition to the Chief's authority', normally

45. Archives of Dalaba, Annual Political Reports, 1942–45.
46. The large trading firm, Société Commerciale de l'Ouest Africain.
47. Archives of Kissidugu.
48. Lelong, op. cit., p. 264.
49. *Le Réveil* (Dakar), 10 Oct. 1949.

punished under the *indigénat* by 1–5 days in prison, henceforth provided for prison terms of up to six months.[50] The administrators were aware of this situation, but they tolerated it. In 1942, the dismissed chief of Sankaran canton was sentenced to three years in prison (later reduced to six months) for being 'against French authority'. Translated into ordinary language, that meant that 'for more than ten years, the people of this canton displayed a marked lack of discipline in the execution of their duties.'[51] On the other hand, the administration found no fault with the canton chief of Ulada, although it was reported in his confidential file: 'Named in 1926. A sinister scoundrel . . . A former Diula, who thrived on monstrous extortions and graft and has caused terror to prevail in his canton.'[52]

### *The postwar period, 1946–1954*

The end of the war opened up a crisis which seriously threatened chieftaincy in certain territories. This period saw the first election campaigns, the disappointment of the élite and ex-servicemen confronted by an administration determined to maintain the colonial regime, and then the vote by the French Constituent Assembly granting citizenship to former subjects and abolishing forced labour. This trend was apparent in Guinea too, but did not provoke serious or long-lasting problems.

In the election for the first Constituent Assembly, the chiefs of Futa met to endorse Yacine Diallo, a schoolteacher, as their candidate. The electoral body, reduced to civil servants and notables, was sufficiently limited for the chiefs to prevail.[53] In 1946, when Guinea was granted a second seat in the National Assembly, another schoolteacher, Mamba Sano from Kissi, was elected, along with Yacine Diallo. Diallo belonged to the S.F.I.O. while his colleague joined the ranks of the R.D.A.

The basis of political life was the 'ethnic' associations: Association Gilbert Vieillard (the Fulbe), Union du Mandé, Union Forestière, Union Insulaire (people from the Isles of Los) and the Committee of Lower Guinea. They regrouped themselves into 'native associations' of various circles, which at Conakry acted as mutual aid societies and as mouthpieces for local interests. Ethnic and personal rivalries became more important than political ideology since these associations

50. R. Cornevin, 'L'évolution des chefferies . . .', p. 388.
51. Archives of Kurussa, Political Report, 1942.
52. Ibid., 1945.
53. In Dalaba, for the elections of 21 Oct. and 18 Nov. 1945, there were 27 enrolled on the citizens' roll, and 616 enrolled on the non-citizens' roll (Archives of Dalaba, 'Political Report, 1945').

were made up of notables, rather than of representatives of the people.[54] Representatives of these ethnic groupings took part in the Constitutional Congress of the R.D.A. at Bamako in October 1946, despite the absence of Yacine Diallo, who had actually signed the call to the Congress.

In Malinke country, the return of war veterans caused quite a stir. Early in 1947, a former Koranic teacher and member of the chiefly family of Kankan, Lamine Kaba, incited the ex-soldiers against the colonial regime. An immensely vain and muddled demagogue,[55] he was rapidly by-passed by his own troops. 3,000 to 5,000 armed men installed him in the Kankan circle offices. After a time of considerable tension, the movement collapsed, and Lamine Kaba was arrested and deported to Mauritania. It is noteworthy that in his speeches he had attacked the chieftaincy, and his supporters, before heading for Kankan, destroyed the huts of several canton chiefs.[56] However, administrative reports seem to indicate that they blamed individuals rather than the chieftaincy principle.

It was not till May 1947 that the Guinean section of the R.D.A. was formed, after a country-wide tour by Secretary-General Gabriel d'Arboussier, who had conversations with the Futa chiefs, notably the infamous Thierno Umar Ba, and thought he had won their support. But the new section, merely a coordinating committee joining the delegates of ethnic groupings, rapidly splintered after the French government dropped its communist ministers and thus highlighted the antagonisms between it and the R.D.A., the government faithful to colonial methods, the latter connected with the Communist Party at the parliamentary level.[57]

Chieftaincy appeared at first to be moving in a democratic direction, but then it resumed its previous position. 'The Guinean section of the R.D.A. broke up, leaving a small minority of democrats to speak on behalf of their programme'.[58] The political report of 1947 in Dalaba mentioned the formation of a sub-section 'which groups about 15

54. Sekou Toure, *L'action politique du Parti Démocratique de Guinée*, I, Conakry: 1958, pp. 7–12.
55. At that time, the R.D.A. denounced him as a *provocateur*, and recalled that he had been a police informer in Dakar. After his release from prison, the PDG admitted him to their ranks. He died in 1960, a Deputy to the National Assembly of Guinea.
56. Oral information, thanks to the kindness of General Lansana Diane, Guinean Minister for National Defence.
57. Up till 1950, the R.D.A. was affiliated to the French Communist Party with the French National Assembly. At that time, after a period of coercion by colonial administrators, the party's parliamentary representatives under Felix Houphouët-Boigny broke the alliance.
58. Toure, op. cit., p. 10.

Africans' with a board of teachers or agricultural monitors and two notables 'at odds with the canton chief.'[59] In the first quarter of 1948 it was 'reduced to a few units', despite the appearance of Sekou Toure who set up a local trade union federation.

When, in September 1951, *La Guinée française* inserted a communiqué from the secretary of the 'phantom section' of Dalaba announcing the collective resignation of its members, Madeira Keïta, then the Secretary-General of the R.D.A. in Guinea, responded[60] that there had not been any R.D.A. section in Dalaba for a long time. The quarterly report of the subdivision chief confirmed this.[61]

The Dalaba situation was repeated in many inland areas. 'This period', noted Sekou Toure, 'was filled with resignations of numerous militants and leaders of the movement, each one wanting to demonstrate his loyalty to the colonial regime.'[62] Except for a few isolated examples, the officials, who in 1947 made up the main body of the R.D.A., abandoned their struggle when they saw their careers threatened. Chieftaincy thus kept or regained its position with the support of the administration. But from now on, its moral authority was deeply impaired. Despite prosecutions and condemnations, the Guinean R.D.A. confronted chieftaincy, while consolidating its position in the towns through the unions. In 1950, the mimeographed R.D.A. newspaper *Coup de Bambou* launched an attack on the canton chief of Kebali, Alfa Bakar Diallo. Administrative accounts indicated that Diallo, 'appointed in 1933, . . . had displayed brutality and blundering' in 1934–5 in tax-collecting and after 1954 had continued war effort methods.[63] Diallo came to Conakry in the company of the young chief of Dalaba, Thierno Ibrahima Ba, to lodge a charge of libel.[64] The attacks in the *Coup de Bambou* came up against the 'united front of the chiefs', and its editor-in-chief was denounced in strong terms. In 1952 a complaint was lodged in Conakry against the same Alfa Bakar Diallo, canton chief of Kebali, by his villagers,[65] but it was not followed through. In the official view, the traditional position of chieftaincy was intact, but this, superficial judgment did not take into account either the moral discredit caused by the war, or the tension resulting from its increased demands at a time when subject people were no longer disposed to endure even traditional demands.

What, in fact, were these 'traditional dues'? They included work on

59. Archives of Dalaba, Political Report, 1947.
60. *La Guinée Française*, 15 Sept. and 19 Oct. 1951.
61. Archives of Dalaba, Quarterly Reports, Sept. 1951.
62. Toure, op. cit., p. 11.
63. Archives of Dalaba, 'Dossiers des chefs de canton'.
64. He succeeded his father Thierno Umar Ba on 2 Feb. 1948.
65. Archives of Dalaba, Quarterly Reports, 1st Quarter, 1952.

the chief's fields by the people of his canton, the upkeep and repair of his huts, taxes on the harvest, and taxes on inheritance which were also added in the name of 'tradition'. These taxes 'vary considerably according to the canton and even within the same district, for they are a function of the personality and greed of the chief and his entourage.'[66] The author of the report from which these lines are extracted remarked that the '*batulabe*' (the chiefs' agents sent into the countryside to collect taxes or at harvest-time) were 'the affliction of the Futa'. The new needs of the chiefs in the post-war period caused them to multiply 'special' taxes: to build a house, buy an American car, or finance a pilgrimage to Mecca. These taxes were no longer 'justified by the obligations of aid, protection or hospitality which originally justified them'. The thick file of complaints against the chiefs of the subdivision of Dalaba (filed but with no follow-through) tells us of these extortions. The chief of Kankalabe was criticised for collecting – in addition to the tithe on the harvests – a tax 'for the meal on the chief's birthday (10 frs. per married man); and another tax for his entertainment (in money and goods)'. The money provided for the workers employed to construct the road from Dalaba to Konkoure was shared between the chief and his entourage.

A signed complaint against the chief of Dalaba noted the following demands that he had made: 50 frs. per family for each festival;[67] 15 frs. a head at census time; 25 frs. a head for Bastille Day and Armistice Day; gifts when he went to Conakry; and additional contributions for the purchase of cars and houses. Other complaints cited women being abducted and oxen confiscated. An anonymous complaint of 1 April 1954 indicated that for every death of a man or woman aged more than 25, the inheritance 'tax' demanded was 10,000 frs. or two oxen. If the heir could not or would not pay, the possessions of the dead person were sold, the proceeds going to the chief. If the dead person had no children, the chief demanded the whole herd, and indeed had his granaries emptied, leaving nothing for the surviving spouse. A tax was levied for dead children aged seven or more. If the money was not paid in the time allowed, the livestock of defaulters was seized; they were beaten, their clothing was torn off, and they were left for two days tied to a tree without food as a warning to others.[68] The lifestyle and expenses of the chiefs were ever more disproportionate to the resources of their subjects. The report quoted above mentioned their monthly expenditures as being the following: Kebali, with 20,000 inhabitants had to pay 200,000 frs. a month, Bodié (7,000) 40,000 frs.; Dalaba

66. Archives of Dalaba, Report of Circle Commander, Dalaba, 9 Jan. 1955.
67. Probably for each Muslim holiday.
68. Archives of Dalaba, 'Dossiers des chefs – plaintes'.

(40,000) 150,000 frs.; Kankalabe (20,000) 150,000 frs.; Fugumba (3,000) 30,000 frs. a month.

The three most important chiefs (especially the Dalaba chief), sensing the danger, sought additional sources of revenue in trade, transport and plantations. Some months earlier, the circle commander of Dalaba had observed:

> The chiefs, whose wealth is in rather too stark contrast with the misery of most of their subjects, still have the people under control. But they will soon have to reconsider their way of life, or the means of supporting it, because the country is becoming ever poorer and their subjects also show more and more resistance to the payment of traditional dues.[69]

So, when the crisis had already begun, senior administrators blindly ignored these warnings. Up till 1954, their political reports noted a satisfactory political situation. Even though the R.D.A. in Guinea followed Houphouët-Boigny in his 'switch' of 1950, the colonial administration continued to see it as Enemy Number One, if not the actual agent of international communism.[70]

In fact, the decision of the R.D.A. to make a new alliance in Paris imposed certain tactical priorities on its Guinean branch, the P.D.G., notably not to break the unity of the movement, and to note that the political situation in France made the prospect of a government with Communist participation remote and thus made a parliamentary alliance with the Communists less attractive. The fate of Africa had ultimately to be settled in Africa itself and not in the French National Assembly.

From now on, the P.D.G. leadership set out to make their party a *party of the masses*. Their abstract proclamations against colonialism and capitalism and their thoughts on foreign policy was not something that would mobilise the masses, for whom these were not concrete issues; their policy was to strengthen the *union movement* by means of the struggle against discrimination in salaries, civil rights and so on. The bases of organisation which were then created in the cities (especially in the quarters occupied by workers, minor civil servants and craftsmen) would then proceed to the *conquest of the countryside*, and the militants of the towns would search the villages in order to create R.D.A.

69. Archives of Dalaba, 'Quarterly Reports, 3rd Quarter 1954'.
70. An astonishing report of the information services of the French Overseas Ministry conveyed confidentially under no. 710 APA/BTLA on 13 Sept. 1950, that the new base of the 'Kominform' in Africa was Liberia, 'where arms are sent along a series of roads to subversive Guinean elements . . . which the Administrator of N'zerekore points out, do not exist!' (Archives of N'zerekore, Confidential – Liberia. Message and answer, 17 Oct. 1950.)

committees based on local demands (roads, schools etc.) but above all on the *struggle against chieftaincy*.

The years 1951–4 were a particularly difficult period. The 'sudden change' at the R.D.A. summit had disoriented a large number of militants, without easing the pressure against them. The administration continued to persecute them and support 'administrative' parties opposed to them. It denounced the contradiction between 'the promises of collaboration made at the summit and the inflammatory remarks pronounced in the villages'.[71] In the 1951 legislative elections the R.D.A. did not field a successful candidate. The administrator of Kurussa noted: 'The R.D.A. and pro-R.D.A. elements took part in the elections, but then lost their enthusiasm'.[72] Transfers and dismissals contributed to this cooling off of the militant civil-servants. In 1952 this administrator mentioned some local parties: the *Union du Mandé, the Union franco-guinéenne* and the *Union de Kouroussa* (an electoral committee of the territorial adviser Keïta Ouremba). Union activity was almost nonexistent: 'The R.D.A. section was completely dislocated by the departure of most of its members.'[73] And in 1953 he wrote: 'Like last year, the general spirit of the population was encouraging.' The associations mentioned above were more or less defunct, except for the *Union de Kouroussa* which held two meetings. The R.D.A. had not been revived.

The situation was much the same in the forest region. Here the chiefs' authority had undoubtedly been disputed from the very beginning, which explains the early appearance of local opposition. The allegiance of Deputy Mamba Sano to the R.D.A. did not last, but it continued to be supported by territorial councilman Camara Kaman in Macenta, and Sekou Toure was elected councilman for Beyla in 1953. The isolation of the forest region, 'the end of the earth', allowed the old methods to continue until the Monrovia road was opened in 1952. Even in 1949, Camara Kaman denounced the obligation on the taxpayers of Macenta circle to provide 20 kilos of rice each. The rice was collected, transported on men's heads to selected centres, and sold there by the 'administration at 11 frs. a kilo to the European merchants, who resold it for 16 frs. The Macenta market was supervised to prevent the producers from coming directly to the consumers.[74] Two years after the abolition of forced labour, those who refused were still being punished with imprisonment. The Macenta circle commander wrote as follows to the local magistrate on 12 January 1948:

71. Archives of Kissidugu, Political Reports, 1955.
72. Archives of Kurussa, Political Report, 1951.
73. Ibid., 1952.
74. *Le Réveil* Dakar 4 April 1949.

*Subject*: Refusal to obey the canton chief. The accused [nine names follow] have refused to obey the canton chief of the village of N'Zapa (Guizima canton) who asked them to maintain and clear the paths. I shall be grateful if you will apply the sanctions provided in Articles 471 and 474 of the Penal Code for their opposition to duties involving the canton and its chiefs. . . .[75]

Thus the suppression of 'administrative justice' and the *indigénat* had not altered their methods, and the magistrates, who were mostly drawn from the administrative cadres, knew how to get around the law. The village chiefs themselves did not escape the *indigénat* system, 'judicial' confinement replaced its 'administrative' equivalent, as the following communication shows. Also from the circle commander to the district judge of Macenta, it is dated 16 June 1948:

The village chief of Sessu has given clear evidence of ill-will over the collection of taxes, and has opposed the canton chief's authority. Instead of coming to Macenta with the canton chief, he presented himself only after having been especially summoned, and after a delay of several days. I hereby lodge a complaint against him and I shall ask you to impose on him a prison sentence as provided by Article 483, 87 of the Penal Code for deeds of this nature. . . .[76]

In an animist area, solidarity between the chiefs and the leaders of initiation societies effectively terrorised the peasants. Certain Toma chiefs introduced the usage of a '*gris-gris*', which had as its basis blood and oils extracted from the human body. Thus, from time to time, *gris-gris* required victims. A police report gave the following account of the matter:

People in the canton often disappeared. In addition, no weapon can protect the ingenous traveller from the hold of the *gris-gris*. To act effectively, the *gris-gris* calls for human blood from time to time . . . It is placed at the bottom of the *cocosaleï*, a wooden vessel similar to a household water-pitcher. All around the vessel are carved wooden statuettes in human form, standing upright and clothed. To prepare the *cocosaleï*, you take the *gris-gris* from the bottom of it and put it in the middle of some decomposed human flesh. Human skin cut from various parts of the body (the cheeks, the forehead, the neck, the palm of the hand, the genitals, the nose or the sole of the foot) is then burned with some palm oil. The human oil obtained in this operation is distributed in little perfume bottles. The *cocosaleï* is of course [*sic*] previously coated with human blood, which makes the human oil powerful and efficient. Anyone who possesses some of this oil undeniably acquires influence over people. . . . The *gris-gris* was said to have been first introduced in French territory under the reign of chief Dialawoï Beavogui, father and predecessor of the canton chief Beavogui Wogbo.[77]

75. Archives of Macenta, cantonal archives.
76. Ibid.
77. ANG, 'Fonds de l'inspection des affaires administratives de Haute Guinée (non classé).' Cf. on the same matter, E. Rau, 'Le juge et le sorcier', *Annales Africaines*

Wogbo was exposed, arrested and found guilty of murder. But he was not alone in possessing the *cocosaleï*:

> Since then, other chiefs have been interested in the *cocosaleï* . . . But the one who has been most frequently accused during the last seven years is Kapero Inavogui, the present chief of the Uziamai canton . . . There might be other murderers in other cantons, but in fact the hired criminals come from the Uziamai canton.[78]

This report, which dates from 1955 or 1956, points out, with details presented on these murders, that the administration was thoroughly acquainted with the movements of this 'faithful servant'. But the chief was never concerned with it. We have been able to gather some data on Lower Guinea, where the situation seemed little different, except that chieftaincy, instead of being reduced to traditional dues, was strengthened by the establishment of agricultural domains, notably in banana plantations.

## *The R.D.A. offensive*

The election of Sekou Toure in 1953 as councillor of Beyla, despite lively opposition from the chiefs, gave a sign of approaching change. The by-election of 27 June 1954 after the death of Deputy Yacine Diallo was the beginning. Barry Diawandu, son of the *almamy* of Dabola, was elected in preference to Sekou Toure, but the R.D.A. used the election campaign to put down roots everywhere, and, although beaten, successfully continued organising.

> 1954 has shown, if there was any need, that, owing to the credulity of the people, the atmosphere of this country could be rapidly changed if their hopes and appetites were flattered a little.

The preceding years had been comforting, 'despite the all-too-heavy tax burden in proportion to the weak resources of the masses'. The poor rice harvest of 1953 forced peasants in some cantons to sell some of their sheep and oxen in order to pay the tax. The sub-section of the R.D.A. was revived, and their propagandists, including Sekou Toure himself, visited many villages, arousing a good deal of excitement. The

---

(Dakar, 1957), pp. 305–20. Denounced by a dismissed servant, Beavogui Wogbo and his accomplices were referred to the Assize Court in 1953, for a total of six known murders between 1942 and 1950. The *gris-gris* seems to have been introduced between 1920 and 1940 from Liberia or Sierra Leone (cf. my *Afrique Noire — L'ère coloniale*, p. 546. Cf. also the Archives of Kissidugu, the file on animism; one report points out that the canton chief of Duku (Gueckedu) was accused of possessing the '*kokozale*' [*sic*].

78. Ibid.

R.D.A.'s action was directed against chieftaincy. The office of the sub-section was almost exclusively made up of craftsmen (tailors, jewellers and shoemakers). There was obvious success in the villages, especially with the women and young people. However, the Union du Mandé, which supported the candidacy of Barry Diawandou, was passive.[79]

At Dalaba, the fief of Ba Thierno Ibrahima, the situation developed more slowly, but in the same way. The Association Gilbert Viellard was inactive.[80] In the 1954 election, the majority of votes went to Barry Diawandu, but his rival, Barry Ibrahima, called Barry III, the leader of the local socialist party (*Démocratie socialiste guinéenne*), polarised the hostility to chieftaincy. Meanwhile, the administrator, though a personal friend of the canton chief of Dalaba, sounded the alarm early in 1955:

> They [the chiefs] would no doubt want us to go on concealing their corrupt practices - their extortion and plundering - because that, unfortunately, is what most of them do.
>
> How many files containing the records of such extortions were buried in the circle offices during the period of administrative justice? How many generally dubious cases are still treated with indulgence in the Futa district? The moment of truth will come, however, to give these chiefs a final solemn warning - these chiefs who live opulent lives in contrast to the sordid poverty of their malnourished subjects who have to live on a fistful of fonio and a bowl of soured milk. Take two examples: the chiefs of Yambering and of Timbi-Medina (not yet condemned), - how often did they carry out that well-known plundering and worse, with the knowledge of the administration and the law, and remain unpunished? In this the administration - at all levels - bears a great and absolutely unquestionable responsibility.[81]

However, opposition was still concealed. 'I believe Dalaba is the only circle in the territory not to have a sub-section of the R.D.A.,' an administrator noted in mid-1955.[82] But at the end of the year it was a 'conflagration' thanks to a young teacher, Samba Lamine Traore, assigned to create a R.D.A. sub-section.[83] Throughout Guinea, the year 1955 marked not only the implantation of the R.D.A. among the rural masses, but also a massive change of political orientation among Guineans. This became clear in the legislature elections of 2 January 1956, the first to take place under universal suffrage. The administration, although hostile to the R.D.A., was bothered by the presence of its leader Félix Houphouët-Boigny in the government, and for the first time maintained relative neutrality. The overwhelming victory of

79. Archives of Kurussa, Political Report, 1954.
80. Archives of Dalaba, Quarterly Reports - 2nd Quarter, 1953.
81. Archives of Dalaba, Report of 9 Jan. 1955 on the condition of chieftaincy.
82. Ibid., 2nd Quarter, 1955.
83. Ibid., 3rd Quarter, 1955.

the R.D.A., which returned two out of the three Deputies, rang the death-knell of chieftaincy. The canton chiefs had not expected such a tidal wave, and had supported all the opposing candidates. Their defeat, in their own cantons, proved their political bankruptcy. In his political report for 1956, the circle commander of Kurussa noted:

After the 2 January 1956 ballot, which marked the victory of the R.D.A. in the circle as well as in other districts of the territory of Guinea, this party in one year has taken root in almost the entire circle, setting up village committees with a responsible person in charge, dividing the circle into sectors, headed by a militant from Kurussa, and interfering more and more in the administrative life of the district.

Likewise, the Secretary-General is increasing his tours in the bush, which is easier for him than for the circle commander or his assistant, who are detained in Kurussa by paperwork and the growth of technical services.

The two other parties represented in the circle, the B.A.G. of Barry Diawandou and the D.S.G., do not have either organisation or authority.[84]

In Faranah, the circle commander noted that the R.D.A. victory led to many legal complaints being lodged against the canton chiefs, who looked for support to the Administration, which however remained neutral. 'These matters did not often turn out to the chief's advantage'.[85] A violent demonstration by the 'rabble of the city' took place on 28 March 1956 against the canton chief of Kuranko, Layba Camara. Feelings were calmed somewhat, but 'the dismantling of chieftaincy in the circle was greatly advanced. Without administrative support, [the chiefs] collapsed, and the actual value of their authority became apparent. It would have been imprudent at this time to support chieftaincy, which was discredited by former customs.'

Here is a typical example, Layba Camara, condemned later on for murder and sentenced to hard labour for life. In 1944, the Administrator noted on this subject: 'A very good chief . . . punctually meets all administrative requests (products, laborers, livestock).'[86] In 1956, it's another story:

Since 1940, when he received his appointment, Layba Camara has ruled in an extremely harsh fashion. We have proof that he exacted ransom from his subjects, and always acted as a ruler, creating and destroying village chiefs at will, negotiating the chieftaincies of his canton, and regulating all matters of custom in return for large compulsory payments. The unconditional support that he received from the administration, which was happy to be rid of the irksome task of governing a turbulent region with constant palavers, allowed him to become a dreaded chief, who was able to terrorise the Kurankos into submission for fifteen years. He thus accumulated resentment which came to

84. Archives of Kurussa, Political Report, 1956.
85. Archives of Faranah, D., 'Procès verbal de passation de service', 22 Dec. 1956.
86. Ibid., report of 26 March 1944.

light immediately after the January 1956 elections, when he unwisely tried to dictate his conditions to the victorious R.D.A. [He had tried to forbid any R.D.A. demonstrations or meetings in his canton, where the party received 80 per cent of the votes.]

The complaints against him filled an enormous file. The administrator concluded:

If condemned, Layba's fate would be settled. And so we would see the last of a chief who could not adapt to new conditions, although he gave excellent service by maintaining calm, through fear, in a canton which was in a troubled state for fifteen years. Today, he is more embarrassing than useful.[87]

In many regions canton chiefs, especially those who were most hated, took refuge in the towns. An administrator's memorandum from Macenta, dated 31 August 1957, reported to the Governor that the canton chief of Guizima had been in Macenta for two months, and had not found it necessary to justify himself. He proposed his dismissal.[88] Those who remained often had to admit their powerlessness.

In certain places, especially the forest region, where authority passed to village R.D.A. committees, canton chiefs had to hand over their accounts: 'After the elections of 1956, the masses revolted and drew up an inventory of the chiefs and their men. The latter had to give back what they had taken, in one case amounting to 200,000 frs'.[89]

We have some evidence of the situation in Futa-Jalon. In Dabola the circle commander observed: 'At present the R.D.A. has total political domination in the circle, due more to hatred of the *almamy* and his family than to political opinions. The customary tribunal hardly functions any more. Many slaves have been freed.[90]

The struggle was bitter in Dalaba. In the 2 January 1956 elections, the majority of the canton voted for Barry III (the D.S.G. candidate), 'the personal and declared enemy' of the canton chief Ba Ibrahima. They 'vote D.S.G. because they are against the chiefs.'[91] A C.G.T.-affiliated trade union was created by Samba Lamine Traore. The latter, described in an earlier report as a 'fanatical marxist, all the more dangerous because he is irreproachable at the professional level', was 'removed for professional incompetence in Dabola' along with two of his colleagues in neighbouring R.D.A. sub-sections.[92] Then something extraordinary happened. Thierno Ibrahima, the most severe but

87. Ibid., 22 December 1956.
88. Archives of Macenta.
89. Oral testimony of M. Mamady Sagno, former Mayor of N'zerekore (1959) concerning the N'zerekore circle.
90. Archives of Dabala, 'Rapport de passation de services du 31 December 1956'.
91. Archives of Dalaba, Quarterly Reports, 1955–6.
92. Ibid., 2nd Quarter, 1956.

also the most intelligent of the Fouta chiefs, publicly announced that he was joining the R.D.A. (not without difficulty, for the Dalaba section demanded a declaration of self-criticism), and the R.D.A. put him up as a candidate. The R.D.A. won everywhere in the circle, with a narrow but clear majority. The territorial elections of 31 March 1957 gave the R.D.A. 58 out of 60 seats. The 'Government Council' of the *loi-cadre* thus entirely went over to the R.D.A.

## *Conclusion*

Although the Guinean chieftaincy suffered a severe blow on 2 January 1956, the Governor of Guinea was still hoping in a circular dated 14 April 1956, 'to regild the banner of chieftaincy with a reform'.

> [He acknowledged] that it is seriously compromised by the success of a party ostensibly opposed to it and that it is no longer admissible to support, against all opposition, chiefs who no longer represent anything; their authority would gain nothing by this, and ours would break down. In many cases we must admit our guilt, and recognise that for several years, for administrative convenience, we have closed our eyes to the behaviour of the chiefs who possess no legal power under our laws, but who are our principal collaborators and have performed many services for us. Let us recognise the hypocrisy contained in this not very strange acceptance of their means, so long as the chief fulfills his duties.[93]

Thus the Governor repeated - in almost identical terms - the views expressed by the clear-sighted Dalaba administrator early in 1955 - views which had not been understood, and for which he was reproached as needlessly alarmist.

The considerable upgrading of the chief's pay in 1956 did not resolve the problem: on the contrary, it made them appear even more parasitic and in no way justified their salaries.[94] The chiefs organised themselves, first in Guinea then on the federal level, into 'unions', but it was in vain.

The 1957 elections, which installed the *loi-cadre* government, also demonstrated the futility of hopes of restoration. It was no longer the man but the institution itself which provoked hostility, even in the Futa-Jalon region, and perhaps there more than elsewhere, since chieftaincy there, however 'traditional' it was, was the most oppressive. At the end of 1957, an administrative secretary touring the

93. ANG, no. 26/CAB, 14 April 1956.
94. 'I regard their pay and allowances as revenue from which they profit, but the Territory and the Circle do not. I do not hesitate to say that the chieftaincy of Mali is a heresy which costs four million a year' (speech of the circle commander of Mali, in *Guinée: Prélude à l'indépendance*, p. 44).

cantons of Kebali and Kankalabe, whose chiefs had just been dismissed, observed: 'There is a mood of hate and passion in the country which is relentless in its desire for the total destruction of everything concerning the customary chieftaincy of the cantons'.[95]

When the conference of the Guinean circle commanders chaired by Governor Jean Ramadier was held on 25, 26 and 27 July 1957, with the participation of the vice-president of the Government Council, Sekou Toure, the president of the Territorial Assembly, Diallo Saifoullaye, and the minister of the interior, Keïta Fodeba, the demise of chieftaincy was a foregone conclusion. By challenging chieftaincy as an institution, and emphasising its 'decay', the *loi-cadre* government persuaded the administrators themselves, with some exceptions, to admit that the abolition of traditional chieftaincy had become unavoidable.

Here is some significant evidence from the circle commanders:[96]

FUTA-JALON

*Labe*: 'For the last eight months, I have not dealt with a canton chief. To me it's the same thing whether they are there or not.'

*Mamou*: 'These chiefs made the mistake of descending into the political arena; they tied their fate to the defeated parties, and collapsed with them.'

UPPER GUINEA

*Kankan*: 'Abolition of the chieftaincy is desirable from an administrative viewpoint. Certainly if the tax brings in so little, that is because the people do not want to hand it over to the current chiefs. At least, that is what is being said.'

*Kurussa*: 'For almost four months, the canton chiefs have been absolutely useless. They are living off the state. . . . In the canton of Sankaran, all goes well despite the dismissal of its chief.'

LOWER GUINEA

*Boffa*: 'For more than a year and a half, the canton chiefs have been chiefs in name only.'

*Boké*: 'The people did not wait for our decision to reject the institutions of the chiefs. In seven cantons, the chiefs represent absolutely nothing, and they show up only on pay day.'

THE FOREST REGION

*N'zerekore*: 'Out of twenty-one [cantons] two of the chiefs have been in prison, and one of those is now allowed out on a temporary pass.

95. Archives of Dalaba, Quarterly Reports, Memo of 4 Oct. 1957.

96. *Guinée: Prélude à l'indépendence* (a report on the Conference of Circle Commanders), pp. 23–49.

Actually, the chiefs have been ineffective for a long time. They are useless.'

These few extracts are enough to show that the decree of 31 December 1957 abolishing the traditional chieftaincy in Guinea was not a simple administrative decision that changed nothing, but the legal consummation of a popular revolution.

And what became of the canton chiefs? Some idea can be obtained from an inquiry made in 1959 in half of the regions of Guinea. Those who belonged to an administrative cadre resumed their civil service posts and were assigned outside the regions where they had had power. This was the case with the former chief of Dalaba, Thierno Ibrahima Ba, who became a Regional Governor. By joining the R.D.A. at the last moment, he was able to keep his 'concession' (his lands), despite bitter protests from the villagers.

For others, dismissal was accompanied by loss of their ability to raise a workforce, as well as loss of lands which they had appropriated or usurped at the expense of the village community. In Dabola, where the *almamy* 'had suggested that his subjects surrender some of the richest lands of the circle',[97] the lands of the valley of Tinkisso, which the canton chief had monopolised and often left fallow, were put at the disposal of the people. In Beyla, most of the chiefs, deprived of their income and their women, most of whom except for some older ones rejoined their families, took the *'daba'* and went out to the fields like everyone else. One particularly hostile chief fled to the Ivory Coast; one from Damaro, nicknamed 'the red devil of the mountain', did not dare to leave his house. In Faranah, there was some opposition from the canton chief Calaban Ulare, who was arrested after an assault at a market in November 1957, which left 33 wounded and a fifteen-year-old child dead, and which had been made because his men wanted to oppose an R.D.A. demonstration. In the district council elections of 18 May 1958, the fallen chiefs tried to present a list, but they received 50 votes (their own and those of their families) against 20,000 for the R.D.A. In Banya, an enraged Layba Camara banned R.D.A. meetings in his village, and on 17 June 1958 attacked his opponents, leaving one dead and dozens of huts burned. He was arrested and condemned by the criminal court to hard labour for life. Two coffee plantations belonging to chiefs in the South were nationalised, along with Layba Camara's house, which was turned into a dispensary. Elsewhere, the chiefs had no plantations and there was nothing to take back.[98]

97. Ibid., p. 41.
98. Oral testimony by the Secretary-General of the PDG of Faranah, 1959.

In Macenta, the struggle was equally violent. With the exception of Chief Zeze Onivogui, an early supporter of the R.D.A. who died before its final triumph,[99] and two who rallied at the last minute, 'all the canton chiefs fought us to the last'.[100] On 24 August 1958, a touring delegation of the territorial assembly was attacked by followers of the ex-canton chief of Ziama; two died and many were wounded, including the secretary-general of the Macenta section, Massa Koïvogui. The people wanted to 'nationalise' the plantations and houses that had been built by forced labour, but this step was only taken in the cantons of Ziama, Balizia and Lee.

In N'zerekore, the 'nationalisation' of 1960 carried out by the district chief provoked some excitement. It was necessary to call a halt because of division among the people; some objected that since the chiefs had already been 'fined' it was unjust to deprive them of their means of existence. On the other hand, in the circles of Gueckedu and Kissidugu, the agricultural office had set up collective plantations in the main centres of the canton when they introduced coffee cultivation in 1936. These plantations entrusted to the 'management' of the chiefs were later appropriated by them. Together with the buildings that belonged to them, they were 'nationalised' at independence.

In Lower Guinea, where private property had a relatively long history, some ex-chiefs kept their plantations, some of which were quite large. Whatever the circumstances, where the former chiefs were able to hold on to their estates, they became integrated into the bourgeoisie of planters or businessmen of all backgrounds without constituting a separate social category.

For Guineans today [1966, eight years after Independence], chieftaincy seems like an institution of the remote past, even more so perhaps than feudalism seemed to the French in 1797, eight years after their Revolution. In those days in France, there were supporters of the *ancien régime* who believed in the possibility of turning the clock back. It is possible that some chiefs in Guinea dream sadly of the past, but I doubt that any of them can imagine, even in their innermost thoughts, that it could ever return.

99. In 1955, when the R.D.A. leaders of Macenta were arrested, he was bold enough to bring them 3,000 frs. and some rice in prison.

100. Oral testimony of the district chief Savane Moricandian, 1959.

# 8

# COLONISATION, DECOLONISATION AND THE TEACHING OF HISTORY: THE CASE OF BLACK AFRICA[1]

Since its origin, history has found itself torn between two vocations, which are complementary yet appear at the same time to contradict each other. The first of these vocations is objectivity: to reconstruct the truth, beyond the subjectivity of the evidence, as Thucydides was the first to attempt consciously. The second is the vocation of forming the mind, and - why not say it frankly? - the moral vocation: to understand the lesson which events provide, illuminate errors so that they will not be committed again, and bring out the human successes so that they will serve as an inspiration.

These vocations are complementary: because to reconstruct the past objectively implies, whether one so wishes or not, a value judgment on the facts, if only through the choice that is made in retaining certain ones as essential (this process is of greater value when it is conscious than when it is not). All the same, there is no disembodied history, and those who strive not to make judgments make them none the less without being aware of it - just as Monsieur Jourdain, in Molière's *Le Bourgeois Gentilhomme*, discovered that he had been speaking prose all his life. Inversely, to draw lessons from a falsified version of history would be a wasted enterprise, at least when one is faced with deliberate mystification. In short, reconstructing the past as it was and judging it correctly - far from being contradictory - are merely different aspects of the same undertaking; the same difficulties are met with and, as in all human activity, perfection is unattainable. There will always be gaps in our information, and always risks of error in our judgments. All the same, the undertaking is not merely possible; it is indispensable.

In France at the end of the nineteenth century and the beginning of the twentieth, the teaching of history was conceived as being part of a person's training in citizenship. It was meant to nurture patriotism and attachment to the institutions of the Republic. This intention was not, in itself, discreditable; it was even legitimate. But the conditions in which it was carried out contributed to discrediting it. Wishing to teach children through history to love their country and appreciate its

1. Lecture given to the Belgian association of teachers of history, Brussels, 1968 (published in *Cahiers de Clio*, 17 (1969), pp. 57-74).

national values was right and proper. But unfortunately, in the context of national imperialisms, this exaltation had to yield too often to chauvinistic exclusivism, and to the temptation to propagate contempt and hatred for other nations - especially the 'traditional enemies', the English and the Germans. The cost of this was, inevitably, the deliberate falsification of historical fact.

Our textbooks, and those of neighbouring countries, are still far from having rooted out defects of this kind - as is clearly shown by the efforts over two decades of our national associations of history teachers to remedy them by means of reciprocal criticism. Still, the desire to turn the school pupil into a sentient citizen, with an attachment to democratic and republican values, was not an unworthy one. But the identification of these values with the Third Republic as it was had to be pregnant with consequences; it had been an oligarchical republic of unscrupulous big business, the diametrical opposite to the image fostered by its promoters before 1870 ('What was good under the Empire?', they used to ask with good reason). The Republic and democracy were identified with the bourgeois republic and that alone. It was permissible to extol 1789 and the Girondins, but Robespierre, Marat, the days of June 1848 and the Paris Commune of 1871 were seen as stained with infamy. And one extolled with equal enthusiasm, in the 'work of the Third Republic', the laws guaranteeing the exercise of democratic liberties; lay, free and compulsory schooling; and the civilising and beneficent work of colonisation. . . .

The war of 1914–18 and the use made of nationalism between the wars by the different fascist movements led to the discrediting of a particular trend, but the trend was not suppressed for all that, but merely had to renounce its more obviously shocking manifestations. And, as often happens, one excess led to another. For the sake of the necessary objectivity, which had been ridiculed not long before, a history drained of all formative intention came to be proposed, often reduced to a jumble of more or less ill-digested economic abstractions (down with factual history!), completely incomprehensible to children aged between ten and fifteen. As a result, history gained the reputation in some quarters of being a discipline of 'memory', tedious and stodgy, burdening the mind with useless knowledge - and crying out to be drastically cut in order to relieve overloaded syllabuses and timetables. But the truth is the exact opposite to this: it was history's content of civic formation which was partly responsible for the hostility felt towards it. But the dedicated enemies of our discipline know how to make use of any weapon at their disposal.

Most of our textbooks have remained bastard compromises between routine and the passing fashion. On the whole they have sloughed off the jingoistic style which now arouses either fury or laughter; but it is the form that has been affected more often than the basic content. The desire for 'impartiality' had led, in the textbooks, to some dubious rehabilitations, which are not always free from ulterior political motives (Napoleon III, for example). In some matters, such as the appraisal of the fact of colonialism, nothing had changed till very recent years.

The chapters in our textbooks which dealt with it - beyond recapitulating a certain quantity of facts and dates - repeated a series of clichés within the ambit of colonial propaganda. For example, it was understood that the history of black Africa only began with colonisation; before that, it had lived in a state of grim barbarity under petty kings whose massacres depopulated the continent. And the pupil, like the teacher, was all the more convinced of this for never having heard anyone mention, for example, the empires of Ghana and Mali in connection with West Africa. Only certain specialists (administrators, moreover, not members of university history departments) were initiates in this domain, which for everyone else was completely closed. It was understood that colonialism had been beneficial; it had suppressed slavery; and it had ended the internal wars that had ravaged Africa, and established the 'French (or British or Belgian) peace'. In place of anarchy and bloody chaos it had instituted justice, mediated by the colonial administration. It had built ports, roads and railways, and established schools and hospitals. By those means, it was said (with little supporting evidence), colonialism had improved the living standards of the natives.

Doubtless the political rights and freedoms judged to be indispensable in Europe had not found their way to Africa; but this was for the good of the natives, who were not 'mature' enough for such institutions. It was a question of 'grown-up children' who had to be progressively educated to the point where they would be capable of benefiting from them. This at least was the theory of the more liberal, who placed this eventuality in a very distant future - several generations away - while others (I believe this was the case with Belgian colonisation), implicity or explicity, espoused the racist thesis, refusing ever to envisage this eventually occurring at all, and basing itself on a supposed congenital incapacity of the black race.

What has been called decolonisation - I prefer to speak of the crisis and collapse of the colonial system - gave a thorough shake-up to these dogmas. But the result has seldom been a radical change of vision. The authors of textbooks, and often historians too, content themselves with touching-up and adding to the traditional conception a little more often. It is admitted that colonisation was not, in its entirety, beneficient and civilising. There were shadows in the picture - resulting from the human error of individuals: for the more conformist, the exceptions that proved the rule. For the hardier spirits, the picture was a diptych with one panel showing the good and the other the evil – the two forming a balance. In any case, polemic on this subject is pointless, since colonisation now belongs to history; we have passed on from the oil lamp and the sailing ship, and therefore insistence is inappropriate, the sign of a partisan spirit in conflict with historical objectivity.

Can one be satisfied with this? For myself, I have to answer no. Historical objectivity rests above all on examination of the facts, and cannot proceed from a compromise between competing prejudices. Undoubtedly many things are acknowledged today which were formerly glossed over in silence, and which it was considered criminal to bring into the open. I remember that having spoken (in 1948) during my course on French West Africa at the Van Vollenhoven lycée in Dakar of the role of the commercial companies, and examined the mechanisms of what has come to be a standard concept under the name of the 'trade economy' (initiated by the geographer Jean Dresch a few years before), I was complained of by the parents of some of the pupils (among whom were several directors or agents of these companies), and accused of having brought politics into my course, and advanced propositions that were 'racist and anti-French'. The complaint was welcomed by the university authorities, and earned me a reprimand from the rector, Monsieur Capelle, then also director-general of education for the whole of French West Africa. The substance of what he said was that I had to understand that there were things which, at a pinch, one could say in a lycée in Paris or Marseilles, but not in Dakar, especially in front of Africans – of whom there were two among the forty-one pupils in my *classe de première classique*.[2]

We still have not reached a point where certain unpalatable truths can be stated with freedom. But in any case, have the underlying prejudices disappeared? In an article published in 1967, Jean Bourdon took up the cudgels on behalf of certain authors of African history textbooks, and cited with approval the opinion of Raymond Mauny expressed in an article by Governor-General Delavignette:

> The financial and other efforts which are being made for the benefit of the young states of this continent will be in vain if history books and, even more, school textbooks teach young Africans hatred of the former coloniser, seizing upon all that can make the remembered past appear unhappy, and delib-

2. The non-French reader may wish to know that the French system of secondary education has seven classes, from the *sixième* (entered at 11 or 12 years old) to the *terminale* (which follows the *première*), the *baccalauréat* examination occurring (in two parts) at the end of the *première* and the *terminale*. All classes from the *première* to the *sixième* are divided into *moderne* (no Latin) and *classique* (with Latin and Greek).

erately remaining silent on the immense achievements.[. . .] Why dress up Samori and other slave-hunters as heroes of African independence? And why, after denouncing Leopold II's exploitation of the Congo, refrain from recognising the civilising work accomplished over half a century by the Belgian constitutional government?

Leaving aside the very one-sided appreciation of the content of the textbooks in question, it is necessary to realise that the appreciation does not seem to stem primarily from concern for historical objectivity, but from political considerations (for which the authors are blamed!). Is this a sound method?

However, the time has come to drop generalities and to look at individual questions. As there is no possibility of tackling every question here,[3] we will concentrate on four which have been the subject of debate in recent years:

1. Were the European discovery of black Africa and the colonial enterprise fundamentally *interested* enterprises, i.e. determined by economic motives?
2. Who were the true heroes of the colonial conquest, the colonial heroes or the African heroes?
3. Can one speak of a 'civilising mission' when one recalls the methods of exploitation and of colonial administration that were used? And. . . .
4. Was decolonisation granted, or was independence achieved?

### *The geographical discoveries and the colonial conquest*

The theme of the disinterested, humanitarian or scientific character of the work of discovery and conquest was often advanced, at the time when they were taking place, by the active protagonists and the propagandists for the colonial enterprise. According to this view, it would be false to see in the great work of exploring the interior of the black continent in the nineteenth century a phenomenon essentially linked to the triumph of industrial capitalism in Europe. Disinterested scientific preoccupations were predominant, as the meagre support given to the explorers by their governments testifies.

To see the matter clearly it is necessary first to clear away some misunderstandings. That the explorers themselves were often entirely disinterested, and inspired either by scientific preoccupations or by the passion for discovery, cannot be denied. They risked and often lost their lives in an enterprise for which fame was the only possible reward.

3. Two other questions eminently worthy of debate were deliberately left out of consideration here as belonging to a more remote past: the re-evaluation of pre-colonial African history and the problem of the slave trade.

But the personal and historical determinants of a general phenomenon (in this case, the discovery of the interior of Africa) do not necessarily coincide.

An observation one has to make at the outset is that a leading part in the work of discovery was played by Great Britain – either by Britons or by men in British service. The latter was true of Heinrich Barth and Rene Caillié fell into the latter category; before undertaking their voyages on their own account, they had tried several times to obtain British support, failing that of their own countries. Britain was the only country with an 'infrastructure' of support for journeys of exploration. It was in 1788 that the Association for Promoting the Discovery of the Inland Parts of Africa was founded in England, and from 1805, when the Napoleonic wars were at their height, the British government began to subsidise expeditions sponsored by the Association. The date 1788 is not immaterial; it can hardly be considered pure chance that the beginning of major voyages of exploration coincided with Britain's defeat in the American War of Independence – and with the take-off of the campaign for the abolition of slavery, again in Britain. Certain individuals explained the matter very clearly at the time. American colonialism, one part of which was slave-owning, had had its day, and a time had to be anticipated when what it had had to contribute could be re-deployed by developing the African market, which had hitherto been limited to ebony, and given over to African intermediaries on the coast. The explorer Golberry wrote in 1802: 'It will not be enough, after having civilised and instructed [Africa], to succeed in exporting from it no longer men but a mass of precious articles, which will allow us to demand much less of our colonies [by implication, America]; it will also be necessary to find a compromise between absolute freedom and an excessively severe form of slavery for these necessary workers.'[4] This prophetic vision, a whole century ahead of its time, stated very exactly the economic and social system of the colonisation established at the end of the nineteenth century. Later, throughout the travel writings of Heinrich Barth, a work of pre-eminent scientific value, it is remarkable to note how minutely the German explorer scrutinises and appraises the nature and importance of the markets: a godsend for those today wishing to study the pre-colonial economy, but of great practical use to his contemporaries.

The interest shown by the explorers in reconnoitring the great river systems, by means of which they would penetrate and then move around in the interior of the continent, was also not purely geographic. It was a matter of finding out how to obtain direct access to markets

4. Golberry, *Fragments d'un voyage en Afrique fait pendant les années 1785, 1786 et 1787*, Paris, 1802, II, pp. 363–4.

over which African middlemen on the coast, who specialised in barter, had previously kept a profitable monopoly for themselves. And it was also not by chance that England, leading the way in the industrial revolution and enjoying unchallenged commercial and maritime supremacy, played a leading role in these activities. In England was to be found the greatest concentration of men and interests for which this enterprise had meaning, even if the interest (and understanding) was only shared by a few, and even if this was very largely a gamble on the future.

And the conquest? Henri Brunschwig[5] questions Lenin's interpretation in *Imperalism, the Highest Stage of Capitalism* by having accorded too little importance to the 'non-economic aspect of the question', Lenin had gone off the track, at least as far as French imperialism was concerned. French colonial imperialism was not to be explained by economic facts: 'It is in the pressure of nationalist fever following on the events of 1870–1871 that one has to look for the true cause of the expansion.'[6] Thus one comes back to a classical interpretation. And the supporting evidence? This was classical too. The colonial enterprise was not 'interested', economically speaking, because up till 1914 the costs had been greater than the returns. It was thus fundamentally nationalistic and political.

For the most part, the facts advanced are accurate, but their interpretation is questionable. If the true (albeit indirect) cause of the expansion was the defeat of France by Germany in 1871, can one reasonably conclude that if France had been victorious in that war, there would have been no French colonial expansion? Can one find in a fact peculiar to France the explanation for a phenomenon which was not peculiar to France but which involved most of the European great powers? Or must one seek in this expansion 'true causes' (by which one should understand 'fundamental causes') that apply to all the countries? Would this not reduce the causes that were peculiar to France – which were real and anything but negligible – to *accessory causes*?

The hesitation, incomprehension and even hostility regarding colonialist policies shown by certain governments and certain groups (sometimes dominant ones) in capitalist circles were not peculiar to France. Bismarck only came round to a colonialist viewpoint late in the day, and Leopold II had initiated Belgian colonisation in spite of Belgium. . . . Colonisation was no more the result of a premeditated plan by the representatives of high finance in the countries concerned than the 1789 Revolution was the result of deliberate actions by the

5. In *Myths and Realities of French Imperialism*, New York: Praeger, 1965.
6. Ibid.

French bourgeoisie. But the emergence of the colonial phenomenon at that time, and the nature of the phenomenon, were determined by the evolution of capitalism and by the new characteristics it acquired in the last quarter of the nineteenth century. This link - initially, at least - has not been grasped and consciously expressed by any but a few pioneers.

As for the economic 'balance-sheet of colonisation', it is only significant in the light of two basic considerations:

(*a*) In all 'capitalist' enterprise, it is necessary at the beginning to advance sums of money and take 'risks' (these famous 'risks' which some economists invoke to justify the 'rewards' of capital, namely profit). And so it comes about that the one who takes the risks goes bankrupt. . . . But this did not happen with French colonialism, which produced sufficient revenue between 1914 and 1945 to justify the investment.

(*b*)The balance-sheet only has meaning if one makes it clear who did the paying and who reaped the profits. In this enterprise, as in others, it was above all the taxpayer (i.e. the mass of the population) who paid, and certain private interests that profited. From this point of view, colonisation was a profitable affair for these private interests, and it was profitable too before 1914 (as Paul Louis pointed out in 1905 in his pamphlet *Le Colonialisme*).

*The colonial conquest: colonial heroes and African heroes*

French colonial historiography used to present the French protagonists of the conquest as heroes, pure and simple. The textbooks did likewise, and sometimes they still do. On the other hand, this hagiographical presentation had strict national limits. It is admitted that many of the colonial conquerors used cruel methods and committed atrocities, but these were the others - the English, the Germans and the ferocious H.M. Stanley - in contrast to the gentle Brazza.

In this version of history many facts have to be camouflaged. Naturally there would be no question of ignoring personality and temperament. Some of the colonial conquerors were honest and disinterested men, who believed that they were taking part in a great work which indeed had a purely national perspective in the present but which in the future would benefit the conquered peoples. Among these I shall cite General Meynier, the 'conqueror of Chad', who denounced certain excesses and deplored the destruction of African civilisation; and in the following generation, when colonisation had been firmly implanted, Governor Maurice Delafosse, who initiated African studies in France. But however good their intentions, they served a cause whose aim was the subjection of entire peoples against their will. . . . A word should be added concerning the myth of Brazza. There can be no doubting his devotion to his adopted country (he was of Italian origin) or his personal disinterestedness: as to the second of these qualities, he was ruined financially through trying to ensure the success of his earliest missions, for which the government of the day had not been prepared to extend sufficient credit. His methods were 'peaceful', due to his temperament possibly, but also because they were the only methods suited to the regions in question, and above all because, like Stanley, he was not materially equipped to use other methods. When, in 1905 – seven years after being dismissed for incompetence as an administrator – he returned to conduct an official inquiry into the actions of his successors, the latter did not fail to remind him that he was not above reproach himself, and that he had used, or allowed to be used, just such methods as they were being charged with as if they were criminal. Thus Monsignor Augouard, the turbulent bishop of Brazzaville, let him know that he had not been 'in the Congo for twenty-eight years without having acquired some grim documents', and that 'he would know very well how to use them to defend himself.'[7] His successor De Lamothe emphasised that the 'peaceful conquest' of the Congo had 'in fact been nothing but a fairy tale. Fighting, killing and burning had taken place there as elsewhere, only there were orders to say nothing about it.'[8] Mme Coquery has shown that Brazza contributed more than had been supposed to the establishment in the Congo of the big concession companies, which he later denounced relentlessly.

Two men, Voulet and Chanoine (whom we encountered above, pp. 95–6), were indeed removed from the gallery of heroes but they vanished from the historical record at the same time. Even in 1923 General Meynier, an eye-witness of their crimes, wished to relate them in his book *Les conquerants du Tchad*, but his superiors obliged him to refrain. The two young captains had distinguished themselves in the conquest of the Mossi territory, and if their story had ended there they would have had some right to be included in a roll of honour, although the archives show that they committed atrocities on that campaign similar to those which led to their subsequent downfall. In 1898, thanks to their connections in high places, they were given the command of a column that was to march from the Sudan to Chad to affirm French rights there, and meet the Foureau-Lamy mission coming from Algeria and the Gentil expedition from the Congo. Because the atro-

7. M. Augouard, *Mémoires*, vol. 2, pp. 153–4.
8. Letter of 15 June 1898 quoted by M. Blanchard, 'Administrateurs d'Afrique Noire', *Revue d'histoire des colonies*, 1953, p. 404.

cities they perpetrated held up their advance, Colonel Klobb and Lieutenant Meynier were sent to replace them. Furious at being robbed of their mission, they shot the two officers, killing Klobb and seriously wounding Meynier, and decided to continue the mission on their own. Voulet said afterwards: 'I renounce my family and my country. I am no longer a Frenchman – I am a black chief. . . . I regret nothing I have done. . . . In fact, my action is no more than a *coup d'état*. Today, if we were in Paris, I would be the master of France.'[9] His crime had not been to massacre thousands of Africans – he would have been forgiven for that had it not slowed down the progress of the expedition (the most severe punishment being considered for this was close arrest) – but to kill a superior officer. Voulet and Chanoine were soon to be shot by their men, whom they had told that they would never again return home. Officially their deed was put down to an 'attack of madness' due to the heat, which had quickly been put to rights by the soldiers loyalty to France! Well-informed contemporaries formed a different opinion.

A colonial administrator wrote pseudonymously in the *Revue blanche*, after denouncing the massacres carried out during the conquest of the Sudan and the sharing-out of thousands of 'captives' among officers and soldiers (this in the name of the fight against slavery!): 'The exercise of the most absolute arbitrary power and the possibility of the most outrageous abuses, without the slightest penalty, make [the officers] hard in their dealings with the natives, and unmanageable by their seniors. . . . The Voulet affair is entirely typical in that it is the monstrous but quite normal result of a similar morality.'[10] During the debate on the Voulet-Chanoine affair in the Chamber of Deputies in 1900, the following was said by Le Myre de Vilers, a former French Resident of Madagascar: 'Governments cannot be unaware that because they entrust their officials with excessive powers and give them no guidance and no directives, subject them to no control, and even allow them to bribe newspapers at home to sing their praises, these officials – these mere agents – lose all sense of proportion, believing themselves called to a higher destiny; they sacrifice everything else to their own interests, and have no other guide but their own whims.'[11]

Let us leave this subject here; the collective biography of the colonial 'heroes' awaits revision. But are not the 'decolonised' Africans mistaken in rehabilitating the 'petty kings with blood on their hands' so reviled by colonial historiography? Were they slave-hunters? That is undoubtedly what they were, as were all the chiefs in the African states.

9. From the Joalland report, quoted by Decrais, minister of the colonies (*Annales de la Chambre des Députés*, session of 30 Nov. 1900, p. 582).
10. J. Rodes, 'Un regard sur le Soudan', *La Revue blanche*, Nov. 1899.
11. *Annales de la Chambre des Députés*, loc. cit.

And by conforming to the morality of the country, the colonial conquerors were slave-hunters too, sharing out the captives they had taken among their soldiers or indeed, for the more scrupulous, selling them for the benefit of the public treasury, or 'freeing' them – having first made them enlist in the army. Gallieni himself had invented 'freedom villages', which Africans, without appreciating the irony, called 'villages for the commandant's captives'. They became a reservoir for the labour needed for porterage and work gangs. Escape was forbidden on pain of imprisonment, and the system was so attractive to certain administrators that, in order to force a village to pay its taxes, they had the idea of placing some of its inhabitants in a 'freedom village' till the taxes were paid. Usually, the mere threat was enough.

Neither Samori nor Behanzin was a model of humanity as we understand that term today, but nor were they the brutes and idiots portrayed by colonial historiography. Their colonial contemporaries – their enemies – respected their qualities as statesmen and strategists (cf. Baratier's judgment on Samori), qualities that were the more remarkable for having somewhat mitigated the overwhelming inferiority of the material means at their disposal. It is proper that the Africans should shed light on what till not long ago was forgotten or denied, and challenge a historical perspective designed to support the presumption that the black race was fundamentally inferior, capable only of producing savages and killers. And European historians should help them to alter this perspective. It was legitimate for Africa, at the moment of its independence, to rehabilitate men who were undoubtedly typical of their time and the society which produced them (a slave-owning one), but who had fought with indomitable courage against colonial subjection. They were precursors of national independence to the extent that they rejected foreign domination, although they did not, for all that, conceive of the nation in the modern sense – such a conception had no currency among them in their time.

Is there not something rather scandalous here? Is it unacceptable to give prominence to the roles of Louis XI and Louis XIV in forming the French nation as we know it today, because their morality is not our morality and their concept of the nation is different from ours? Must the Romanians be blamed for honouring their Prince Vlad 'the Impaler' (a sobriquet he richly deserved) because he fought fiercely against Ottoman domination although he was not at the same time a model of humane behaviour? And must we follow the example of those who see Napoleon only as cynically ambitious and a mass-killer – which he was – and forget his extraordinary capacity as a statesman and strategist, and the mark he left on the evolution of Europe? Las Cases' *Mémorial de Saint-Hélène* quotes him as reproaching his enemies among the European *ancien régime* for having seen him as no more than a Robespierre on horseback: this was not what he wanted to be, but it was what he became, to the extent that he contributed to the triumph in Europe of the ideas and institutions born of the French Revolution.

Certainly there is a risk, not always avoided, of a nationalistic distortion taking place which tends to idealise historical figures and make out that they represent values which did not even exist when they were alive. Different prejudices can lead to the opposite errors, for which there is equally little justification. And the serious and scientific study of these figures, so long unknown and so long misrepresented after the manner of all African chiefs who resisted the colonial conquest, must exclude either of these two deviations. In the case of Samori, the monumental work of Yves Person, based on oral evidence and study in depth of the various colonial archives, certainly makes a contribution in that direction. Other such contributions will certainly follow, allowing the gradual substitution of history for myth.

### *The methods of exploitation and of colonial administration*

Until after the Second World War, the different colonial historiographies – and certainly that of France – regarded the presentation of the beneficent and civilising character of colonisation as a matter of dogma. Today this one-sidedly optimistic presentation is scarcely accepted any longer: the development in all parts of Africa of anti-colonial independence movements, and the violence to which these movements sometimes resorted, made it untenable. It is as well to acknowledge that something must have been amiss in the colonial system for movements of equal scope to have risen against it.

But mostly what happens is that the traditional assertions are moderated, and that is all. Colonisation, it is said, was a factor for progress, and improved the lot of the natives, but unfortunately there were mistakes as well as positive results, and sometimes crimes were committed by isolated individuals. Clearly colonisation brought with it elements of technical progress, but again it must be emphasised that up till the final years this progress did not reach beyond the towns. For the vast majority of the peasants nothing had changed; they slept on the same mats and ate the same rice or millet as they had done before colonisation; they knew no roads and no railways, and had neither schools nor dispensaries. In 1945 the proportion of children at school in French West Africa had reached 5 per cent. Two years later, Professor Auguste Chevalier, one of the pioneers of tropical agronomy, toured the groundnut country of Senegal which he had discovered forty years earlier, and when he found the same misery, the same wattle-and-daub huts, exclaimed indignantly: 'What became of the millions of gold francs realised by the sale of nuts?'[12] Here and there, the enamelled iron container had replaced the terra-cotta *canari*, the petrol lamp had replaced the traditional oil lamp, and Manchester cotton fabric the local material (not always a change for the better), but in the general conditions of life there had been no basic change. It is necessary to say that even today studies of the subject either skim the surface or refrain from examining those aspects of the colonial institutions which affected the actual material condition of the indigenous peoples.

A primary aspect was the much closer and more open connection in the colonies between certain big agglomerations of financial and economic interests and the administration than ever existed in the mother-countries. The role of these big interests in the Belgian Congo and the specific and direct way in which they were involved in the political and administrative bodies themselves (e.g. in the special committees of Katanga and Kivu) are well known. From 1899 to 1929, French Equatorial Africa was shared out between several dozen 'concession companies' which, despite the steady reduction of their privileges, retained exorbitant rights up to the very end. In French West Africa, three big companies, which had a firm hold over three-quarters of the export trade, completely dominated the economy, sticking to the maxim 'buy little cheaply, sell little for a high price'. Thanks to the co-operation of the administration - this was one of its main tasks - primary products were provided for them at very low prices, often by obligatory or forced cultivation; at the same time, they provided the population with imported goods which were sold at twice the going rates in the metropolitan market - which certainly could not be justified by the freight cost. In Chad, the forced cultivation of cotton brought the peasant 20–30 Belgian francs for a year's work. The company with the monopoly of purchase (Cotonfran) made profits, on a capital of 11 million francs in 1936, of 6 million in 1938 and more than 10 million in 1943, and never made less than 2 million in any year between 1937 and 1945 (average profit 5–6 million).

To the obligatory growing and selling at controlled prices one must add the general application of forced labour in many and various forms: the upkeep of roads and bridges, erection and maintenance of government buildings, massive long-term recruitments for major public works such as laying down new roads or railways, or to provide labour for European plantations. The building of the Congo-Ocean railway in Equatorial Africa in 1921–34 cost between 10,000 and 20,000 lives, and in 1927 the death-rate on the work-sites rose above 47 per cent. In addition, before 1914 there was the crushing forced labour for porterage, later transferred to maintenance work on the motorable

12. *Revue de botanique appliquée*, nos 295–6, 1947, pp. 173–92.

roads. And again, forced labour was extracted by the intermediate native chiefs forming part of the administration, whose arbitrary actions wore the mask of custom.

Men had to be provided not only for labour but for war: in French Africa, after the First World War, a term of three years' military service was imposed, and these conscripts were certain to be the first to be drafted to any theatre of war, notably in colonial expeditions. There were wars in Syria and Morocco after 1918 and in Indochina and Algeria after 1945. This would seem to reduce to the minimum the happy results of the 'French peace', so often mentioned as one of the beneficent features of colonisation, to say nothing of the expeditions sent against African populations in revolt (e.g. the Baya revolt in French Equatorial Africa in 1928–31).

After the tribute in goods and labour, there was tribute to be paid in money, i.e. tax. Generally this was a poll tax (sometimes, in the early days, levied as a hut tax), seemingly modest but in fact particularly unjust and onerous because of its uniform rate (the poor thus being the hardest hit), and because it affected populations whose money income was desperately weak. Taxes often siphoned off most of a people's money income, especially in the regions least touched by trade.

In short, at the same time as continuing to produce their subsistence with the quasi-prehistoric tolls and methods as in the precolonial time, the Africans also had to practise cultivation for export (to deliver the quantities of produce needed to provide for tax payments) and to give a part of their labour for other tasks. Such obligations could, of course, only be imposed by force and as such were incompatible with any form of democracy or local self-rule. With the co-operation of the chieftaincy – itself at the beck and call of the white administrator – the colonial government exercised an absolute power, within a framework of laws and regulations promulgated by the mother-country. The *indigénat* not only excluded civil rights (the right to vote) and political rights (association, assembly, the press), but suppressed personal liberty. The native would in effect suffer penal sanctions without trial, by a single administrative decision and without the right of appeal – except to the officer who had handed down the punishment; imprisonment and fines within the French possessions; and corporal punishment in the Belgian Congo (illegal in the French possessions but carried out none the less).

Finally the question has to be asked: what did the system aim to achieve? Did it have humanitarian ends, or were the very limited technical advances made solely in the interests of European capitalist enterprises which gained their profits from colonial development? Was the object of the work carried out in education and sanitation to advance the progress of human beings or to have a workforce in a condition that would enable it to fulfil its appointed functions?

An enlightened colonial, Maurice Delafosse, wrote in 1921:

If we are prepared to be honest with ourselves, we have to admit that altruism did not bring us to Africa, at least not as a nation. . . .

Sometimes we wanted to find markets for our commerce, and resources of primary materials for our industry; sometimes we needed to protect the security of our nationals or prevent ourselves from being outdistanced by our foreign rivals; sometimes we were moved by an obscure and unconscious desire to obtain a little glory for our country - and sometimes we simply obeyed the whims of chance or followed in the footsteps of an explorer because we did not believe we had a choice to do anything different. Nowhere can I find, as the motive of our colonial expansion in Africa, a genuine and reasoned wish to contribute to the wellbeing of the populations whom we went to subjugate. That facile excuse was one that we gave ourselves retrospectively, but it was never part of the design.[13]

He ended with this warning:

It is absolutely necessary that our intervention should be a cause and an element of progress and wellbeing for them [the African societies - J.S.-C.]. If those things were not present, all colonial endeavour would stand condemned. By the same token, its eventual bankruptcy would be foredoomed.

The wish of Maurice Delafosse remained a wish, and what he feared came to pass: the colonial enterprise was condemned and it became bankrupt.

### *Granting of decolonisation or the winning of independence?*

It is clear that decolonisation was not always granted in a sudden flash of lucidity and goodness of heart on the part of the coloniser, but rather submitted to because there was no alternative. The Belgian Congo is a case in point so well known that it does not need to be laboured.

In certain French textbooks, especially those intended for Africa, it is sometimes claimed that decolonisation was a plan long pursued by General de Gaulle following the Brazzaville conference in 1944, and which triumphed when he took power for the second time in 1958, despite setbacks caused by the ability of public opinion to understand what was involved. Very similar appraisals are sometimes made of British policy as well, decolonisation being represented as a task that had been pondered and carried out deliberately. This, as it stands, is not in accordance with historical fact and therefore has to be rejected.

The Brazzaville conference in 1944 and the speech that General de

13. Maurice Delafosse, 'Sur l'orientation de la politique indigene en Afrique noire', *Afrique française. Renseignements coloniaux*, 61 (1921), pp. 146–7.

Gaulle made there certainly had great historical consequences. But what exactly were they? The war, then about to enter its final phase, was fought by the anti-Hitler allies in the name of the right of peoples to self-determination (the Atlantic Charter). An important contribution in men and resources had been asked of the overseas peoples for the sake of these objectives, so was it possible for those peoples to be denied the benefit resulting from victory in the struggle? Because of the United States attitude, notably in Morocco, there were grounds for the fear that advantage might be taken of the fact that France, the mother-country, was under enemy occupation in order to break up the empire. The essential objective of the Brazzaville conference was to scotch any such idea. It envisaged neither independence nor autonomy for the French colonies, either in the long or the short term. Such a possibility was, indeed, expressly ruled out in the following statement which was included among its recommendations (the capital letters reproduced below appeared in the original):

> The objectives of the work of colonisation accomplished by France in the colonies RULE OUT ANY IDEA OF AUTONOMY, ANY POSSIBILITY OF EVOLUTION OUTSIDE THE FRENCH BLOC OF THE EMPIRE: THE EVENTUAL SETTING UP OF SELF-GOVERNMENT IN THE COLONIES, HOWEVER DISTANT, IS RULED OUT.

The conference contented itself with envisaging the suppression of forced labour five years *after the end of hostilities*. It was not the Provisional Government (led by General de Gaulle) but the Constituent Assembly of 1945–6 which scrapped this step-by-step advance under pressure from French public opinion and the elected representatives from overseas. But de Gaulle, in his speech, affirmed the necessity of allowing the overseas peoples to 'rise by slow stages to the level where they would be capable of *participating in the conduct of their own affairs*. This is the end towards which we have to move. We will not conceal from ourselves that the stages will be long ones.' Despite the vagueness of this declaration of principles, and the delays it envisaged, it created an undeniable shock. It marked a decisive change from traditional colonial policy. At one stroke it raised the hopes of the peoples concerned, and traditional colonial circles reacted with furious protests.

But 'decolonisation' was still far off. In his speech at Bayeux in 1946 after renouncing power, General de Gaulle spoke in favour of France continuing to maintain her presence in the colonies. His opposition to the two constitutions adopted successively in 1946 was based, among other things, on what he judged to be over-liberal arrangements regarding the colonies. He supported a policy of force in Indochina, and we know what his Algerian policy was up till 1961. In 1958 the constitution proclaimed that its membership of the French Community did not imply a right to independence. The inevitability of later change was accepted, but it was not a change that was willed.

In fact, where both French and British policy over colonial independence was concerned, one can say that whether the people resorted to armed resistance in an independence movement or accepted peaceful evolution was dependent on the circumstances. There was military repression in Algeria and Kenya, where a substantial population of Europeans were fiercely opposed to independence; and there was peaceful evolution - with sometimes more and sometimes less goodwill - in Ghana and Guinea, because the colonial power could identify no local forces which it could rely on to obstruct the way to independence, or because in an extremity the independence movement might make it impossible for the colonial power to intervene. Guinea's independence, grudgingly recognised as it was, could never have been accepted at all if it had not been for the war in Algeria, and the impossibility of fighting on a second front in black Africa.

The metropolitan power always submitted to decolonisation, and never willed or genuinely prepared for it. This is a fact which it behoves us to recognise. Needless to say, my few remarks on the four questions on page 183 above fall a long way short of exhausting the subject. The elaboration of a scientific history on these questions, which are still so heavily charged with passion, is something that still remains largely to be pursued; sometimes it has not yet even been attempted. But what has been achieved - even if it is in the form of unanswered questions - must be introduced into history teaching if the latter is to fulfil its task of civic education. The latter assumes an exact knowledge of the immediate past and present realities of the Third World, which is coming more and more to appear in its true colours: as the greater part of the actual world.

# 9

# AN UNRECOGNISED PIONEER OF THE DEMOCRATIC AND NATIONAL MOVEMENT IN AFRICA: LOUIS HUNKANRIN (1887–1964)[1]

This study was in draft at the time of Louis Hunkanrin's death, and it may be useful to recall briefly how it came to be written. While writing *Afrique noire – L'ère coloniale*,[2] I became aware, through studying various books and administrative papers, of the important political role Hunkanrin had played between 1914 and 1940. There was nothing more than an occasional short reference, an acknowledgment of his existence which had slipped out inadvertently; over matters of this nature, the orders of the colonial administration were to keep silent.

But with difficulty I succeeded finally in contacting Hunkanrin when the French government requested me to leave Guinea on pain of forfeiting my French nationality. He was prompt in sending me the documents needed to establish his biography, but they arrived during the holidays and only came into my hands several months late. The book had by then been completed, and no major alterations were possible; therefore, because I had been unable to give proper attention to the role of Hunkanrin in the book, I promised to devote a special study to it, and in a letter written on 2 May 1964 Hunkanrin mentioned that he would send some further documents. But only a few weeks later I heard instead that he was dead.

So, not having been able to pay Hunkanrin the tribute due to him when he was alive, we pay it now by recalling his honesty, uprightness and irrepressible energy, and at the same time his modesty and self-sacrifice.

## *Political life in the French colonies of black Africa before the Second World War*

For most observers, African as well as European, the age of politics in black Africa[3] begins with the elections of 1945. By stretching a point,

1. Published in *Recherches dahoméennes*, new series (Porto Novo), no. 3 (Dec. 1964, pp. 5–30, and reprinted in A.I. Asiwaju, G.L. Hazoumé *et al.*, *La vie et l'oeuvre de Louis Hunkanrin*, Cotonou: Librairie Renaissance, 1977, pp. 31–45.
2. Paris: Eds Sociales, 1964; published in English as *French Colonialism in Tropical Africa, 1900–1945*, London: Hurst, 1971.
3. It is only that part of black Africa ruled by France that we are referring to here: the

one can say that there were certain preliminaries taking place in 1936–8; but it has to be acknowledged that the necessary conditions for a genuine political life had not been created in the French colonies of tropical Africa till the end of the Second World War.

Nevertheless, this political movement in our own time had some precursors: not only in movements of armed resistance or religious movements, the form of which continued that of political life in the pre-colonial era and the resistance to colonial conquest, but in secular forms and with an essentially modern character. What these precursors achieved was undoubtedly of limited scope; in the objective conditions prevailing in this part of the French colonial empire, it could not have been otherwise. First there was the power of the colonial administration, its autocratic principles dating from the time of Faidherbe[4] and based on legislation passed under the authoritarian Empire of Napoleon I. The statutes relating to the *indigénat*, the 'native justice' which it wielded and the whips of the circle guards gave the administration the means it needed to stifle the slightest attempt to voice a political opinion. Such was held to be inadmissible *a priori*.

But above all the economic and social situation was unfavourable. In French West Africa there was no industry, no vital economic centre where ideas, along with people and commerce, could ebb and flow. Dakar was a centre of economic and political authority, not the hub of the federal economy. The social categories that were likely to provide support for a political movement in the modern style were essentially *évolués* – 'evolved persons' who in fact were African civil servants educated in the European schools – and skilled workers. At that time they were very few, and besides most were employed at isolated posts in the bush; the administration never failed to send the 'strong-minded' ones – i.e. potential leaders – to such places. And except on the railways (to be exact, at Thies on the Dakar-Niger system, the scene of the first strike movement), there were few genuine workers and those few often possessed skills and a mentality comparable to that of the artisan (masons, carpenters and the like), with little or no literacy – thus limiting their political role.

The rather more numerous *évolués* were isolated by the ambiguity of their position. Educated and moulded by the colonial power, they were intended to serve it as executive staff – as a channel for its policy. This role, coupled with the life-style they had acquired and the contempt with which they were said to regard their 'savage' and illiterate

---

'modern' political movements in Ghana and Nigeria before the Second World War are well known.

4. Louis Faidherbe (1818–89), governor of Senegal in 1854–61 and 1863–5, founder of Dakar, and a major architect of the French colonial empire in Africa.

brothers, placed a barrier between them on the one hand and the peasant masses and the traditional chiefs on the other. The colonial administration sedulously cultivated all the feelings of mistrust and contempt between the various social levels. Yet the members of this *évolué* circle bitterly resented all the humiliations inherent in the colonial condition. At school they had listened to the republican principles of liberty, equality and democracy being exalted, and colonialism being justified on the grounds that it had freed the slaves and destroyed the tyranny of 'petty kings who had blood on their hands'. Then, suddenly, once their schools had fired them with the ambition to be 'French Africans', the colonials would give them brutal reminders that, whatever qualifications they might have, they were still 'natives' and 'only in one or two generations could they presume to reach the level of the white, the inheritor of a thousand-year-old culture' – regardless of how crude and uncultured the white might be! An African graduate of the École Normale d'instituteurs (the teacher training college) or of the medical school remained subject to the *indigénat* – in the administration's eyes, he was no more than a clerk with a certificate of education.

In such a setting it was natural that the desire for emancipation should have shown itself for the first time. What would be its programme? The claim of national independence seemed utopian at that time, but it cannot be said that the thought of it was absent from people's minds.[5] But the collapse of nearly all the old independent African states had left no doubt as to the overwhelming military superiority of the colonisers. Above all, there was no *national* spirit. And finally, anyone publicly voicing a claim to independence would have been imprisoned instantly.

So it was on the political territory of the colonisers themselves that the battle would have to be waged. The radicals, converted to the colonial idea since Doumergue had become minister of the colonies,[6] and other 'republicans' strove to convince the left-inclined section of the French electorate of the civilising, democratic and liberating character of colonisation. In the name of a policy known as 'assimilation' (which true 'colonials', with cynicism mixed with naivety, denounced in horror – they could not see behind the sleight-of-hand that was being performed), colonisation, by increasing the number of schools, would transform little savages into 'French Africans'. So here were these *assimilés*, educated in French schools but still subject to the *indigénat*; and here too, under the motto 'Liberty, Equality,

5. This is clear from the passages, dating from 1921, in the *Messager dahoméen* quoted below (p. 209).
6. In the first radical government – that of Combes (1904).

Fraternity', some of the worst abuses of power were being perpetuated.

Thus it was in the name of 'republican principles' that the first campaigners set about their struggle. They took those principles literally and demanded that the colonisers' actions should correspond with their declarations of principle: abolition of the *indigénat* and the granting of French citizenship and political freedoms were the watchword. At the same time, the whole colonial regime was denounced: exactions by chiefs, protection by the administration – in the name of 'respect for customs' – of practices which it pretended to banish (including slavery), the arbitrary behaviour of the administrators, and the sheer brigandage of the colonial trading companies.

This policy gave the movement the widest possible mass support. The *évolués* were unanimous in considering that they, at least, should have political rights. And those who felt contempt for their 'uncivilised' brothers and acknowledged that, as far as *they* were concerned, the *indigénat* retained its validity, had too high an opinion of themselves to be able to regard their own submission to that regime as acceptable. Certain colonials – petty officials or employees in the business houses – who believed in colonisation but reacted with disgust when they saw its real character, were liable to support that point of view (this happened only very rarely from the 1930s onwards). And, finally, this policy made it possible, as a last resort, to appeal for the support of democratic opinion in France.

Inspite of its narrow outlook, this 'assimilative' democratic movement had an objectively *national* content in the sense that it achieved the broadest front against imperialism and its basic political institution, the *indigénat*, that could be achieved at that time. But this is not to say that action was easy, even on this basis. The autocratic principles of the French colonial administration induced a habit of intolerance in its governors and administrators. The slightest criticism was taboo, and even colonials who proved refractory were quickly put in prison or shipped home. But when it came from 'natives' it was doubly inadmissible, and became treason against the administration or the *indigénat*. Freedom of assembly, association and the press did not exist.

French laws did not apply automatically in the colonies; they had to be promulgated anew by the Governor-General – at his discretion, since he was not under any obligation to do so. But even where certain laws had been made applicable in the colonies, there were ways of deflecting them. Without freedom of association, the collecting of contributions and subscriptions was termed a 'swindle' by the administration, and prosecuted as such. As for the press, having the right to publish was not enough in itself; it was also necessary to have the use of a printing press. Thus colonials, from missionaries to officials who were Freemasons, were almost unanimous in rejecting the *évolués*' claims, however modest; the few individual exceptions were eliminated from the colony as soon as they showed themselves. As for the *évolués* who voiced such claims, they were termed 'enemies of France' or, after the First World War, 'agents of Moscow'.

Let us now look at the framework in which this first beginning of political life was able to find concrete expression. The conditions for a normal, legally permitted political life could hardly be said to exist outside the four municipalities *de plein exercice*[7] in Senegal - St Louis, Dakar, Rufisque and Goree. Those who 'originated' from these municipalities (*originaires*) had voting rights, and in 1916 they were unequivocally accorded French citizenship. Up till 1914, whites and people of mixed race dominated Senegalese politics, using the votes of the African masses for their own personal ends, but in the elections of that year the Africans for the first time dominated the political arena. The St Louis half-caste Carpot was defeated by Blaise Diagne, a Catholic from Goree who also happened to be a pure-blooded African.

In the preceding years, Diagne had campaigned actively in his newspaper *La Democratie du Sénégal*, attacking the 'sharks' of colonisation (the big Bordeaux companies), and demanding the extension of the *plein exercice* to the principal towns of Senegal. Electorally he brought racial solidarity into play. However, once elected he forgot his programme. The restriction of the right to vote to such a tiny fraction of the population made it easy for its significance to become distorted. Diagne had obtained confirmation from Clemenceau of the citizenship of the *originaires*, but he allowed himself at the same time to be made a recruiting agent for French imperialism in its quest for cannon-fodder. In 1923 he made the 'Bordeaux pact' with the big commercial interests of that city: in exchange for the electoral support of the trading houses (which sent circulars to this effect to their agents in Africa), he undertook to defend their interests in parliament. When the International Labour Office held its fourteenth meeting at Geneva in 1930, he advocated forced labour.

Thus Diagne became caught up in the system. His new local newspaper had a title, *La France coloniale*, which was a programme in itself. In 1928 he only managed to keep his seat by an electoral fraud. But a large part of his electorate remained loyal to him. Privileged in the matter of military service (eighteen months in a home station, instead of three years) as in the electoral franchise, this electorate was more concerned to consolidate its privileges than to do battle for the rights of

7. Literally, 'of full mandate'. These municipalities were specially chosen following the French law of 1884. The colonies had only 'mixed' local councils, consisting partly of nominated members and with the over-riding power in the hands of a nominated mayor-administrator. This regime also affected certain district centres and other important towns.

Africans generally. . . . The opposition, even if it occasionally denounced the abuses of the regime of which Diagne formed an integral part, insisted above all on the claims of the *originaires*: the right of those employees born within the municipalities, possessing French citizenship, to the 'colonial supplement' in addition to their basic salaries, and other advantages usually reserved to Europeans; the land rights of the Lebu in Dakar; and the re-establishment of the General Council of Senegal in its earlier form, with a majority of representatives of the municipalities with *plein exercice*. Thus the existence of an electorate in Senegal and the presence in the French Chamber of Deputies of a black parliamentarian (who from time to time became an under-secretary of state) served as window-dressing for the benefit of foreigners, proclaiming the democratic and non-racist character of French colonialism.

After 1945, this aspect of Senegal's history had an oppressive effect on the political life of the country, it also explains the suspicious reactions of the other territories. There were indeed few other places where a sufficient number of *évolués* were concentrated to create suitable conditions for political activity. However, a notable concentration did exist on the littoral of Togo and Dahomey. Here, since before the colonial conquest, there had been a well-educated bourgeoisie in the trading factories, with a European style of living, even while they remained faithful to local family organisation and traditions. These families, whether of local or Brazilian origin, sent their children to missionary schools - Portuguese and then French - until the conquest introduced secular schools. Largely excluded from the commercial world, the members of this bourgeoisie were left no choice but to enter the administration. Thus Dahomey, like Senegal, was soon providing clerks and civil servants, many of whom had to settle outside their own country in order to find jobs. But while economically blighted, like the black and half-caste bourgeoisie of Goree and St Louis, this group did not even have the illusory compensation of political rights. Hence this was a much more favourable setting for the birth of a political protest movement linked to the masses, even if the *indigénat* made it that much more difficult for such a movement to express itself.

## *First struggles, 1907–1918*

Louis Hunkanrin was born on 25 November 1887 at Porto-Novo, then a French 'protectorate'. Colonisation had to make use of the old rivalry between the two brother-kingdoms of Porto-Novo and Abomey to conquer the whole of Dahomey. If Abomey had remained 'traditional', the town of Porto-Novo, which had long been in contact with commerce, was already partly europeanised - like Lagos, not far away.

The young Louis Hunkanrin attended a missionary school, then a completely new secular school, from which he emerged as the star pupil of his year. It was in 1903 that Governor-General Roume - at the suggestion of his Secretary-General Camille Guy, a graduate in history and geography who had entered the colonial administration - created the educational system which, with a few modifications, remained in force in French West Africa till Independence. This system envisaged the training of native teachers, and among the first year's students enrolled in 1904 at the teacher training college at St Louis (formerly the school of 'hostages'[8]) was the brilliant schoolboy from Porto-Novo. Graduating as a teacher in 1907, he was appointed to the school at Ouidah in Dahomey.

Hunkanrin's character was already formed, and we can go over its essential traits as they became apparent throughout his career. For him the role of educator was inseparable from civic action: he considered it his duty to place at his people's service the means imparted to him through his privileged education - whatever the consequences for him might be. Hunkanrin was able to combine inexhaustible energy with a highly developed sense of justice. If he had been able to accept a few compromises with the established order, he could have had a tranquil, honourable and profitable career for himself; but on matters of principle he would not compromise, and to that end did not hesitate to sacrifice his career and his freedom, and even risk his life. Only through his extraordinary physical resilience did he manage to survive his various terms of imprisonment and ten years' exile in Mauritania.[9]

The young teacher had hardly taken up his new post at Ouidah when he put himself at the service of his fellow-townsmen to defend them against colonial high-handedness in its various manifestations. To provide an organisational base for resistance against this high-handedness, he created the first branch in Dahomey of the French Ligue des Droits de l'Homme (League for the Rights of Man). Retribution followed quickly: in March 1910, for the first time, he was found guilty, sent to prison and deprived of his teaching post. He was to suffer

8. The colonial authorities, following the example of African kings and of European nobles in the Middle Ages, obliged African chiefs who were in alliance with - or in submission to - them to hand over one or more of their sons as a guarantee of their father's loyalty. These young men thus received a French education with the intention of consolidating their attachment to the regime.
9. Governor Angoulvant, who caused some 100 chiefs to be deported there from the Ivory Coast, regretted that he had not been able to obtain the death sentence for them, but consoled himself by observing that, according to past statistics, deportation to Mauritania would achieve much the same result.

especially from the vindictiveness of Noufflard, the Governor of Dahomey from 1912 to 1917, a typical colonial careerist who had risen quickly in the hierarchy thanks to his connections, and a former propagandist among high school pupils for the *Comité de l'Afrique française*. Hunkanrin himself gives us this picture, which is typical of the colonial morality of the time:

Under the reign of Noufflard, the natives of Dahomey were treated as inferior beings, as *animae viles*. An order of the Governor-General, approved by the ministry of the colonies, gave administrators the right to inflict on native French subjects, for so-called 'slurs on the honour due to French authority', disciplinary penalties of up to fifteen days in prison and a fine of 100 francs (gold francs – let there be no mistake!). The Governor had the power to extend these punishments to a month in prison and a further fine of 100 francs. Along with these formidable disciplinary powers went abuse of power; what crimes were committed by administrators and the Governor to the detriment of French 'subjects', who were liable to be arbitrarily taxed and subjected at any time to forced labour!

When the Resident, Maria, passed by in his rickshaw, it was obligatory to remove one's hat, stand to attention and make a military salute. Whoever did not want to comply with this discipline was dragged away, beaten up, put in prison and given 'disciplinary penalties'. Resident Brot, who lounged in a portable hammock escorted by circle guards, did the same, and his escort, who were utterly ruthless, struck with all their might at any native, literate or otherwise, who by a lack of the proper attention and promptitude had 'cast slurs on the honour due to French authority'. The whole population lived in terror.[10]

It was difficult, on the spot, to defend the people's cause. Hunkanrin continues:

The first press organ which defended the cause of the people was the *Écho de Dahomey*, founded in 1900 by a French merchant at Porto-Novo called Valez. The managing director of this publication was a restaurant-owner at Porto-Novo called Crescent. The paper ceased to appear because of Valez's business problems which forced him to go back to France, never to return. Crescent followed him. Only Europeans at that time would have been able to take his place, but none was prepared to take risks to defend the population.[11]

10. Louis Hunkanrin in *Litteris*, 8 June 1963. These practices lasted as long as the colonial regime. In 1938 I witnessed the methods used by an administrator in North Dahomey whose name I forget, a manic sadist whose mere presence struck such terror into the Africans that they became incapable of uttering a single word. He went riding on horseback wearing white gloves with two 'boys' at his side – one with a box in which he collected up the soiled pairs of gloves, and the other with a box containing clean pairs. . . . I am not aware of what he did to the people, but because of the terror he inspired and his manic behaviour one can only suspect the worst. He ticked me off sharply for letting down 'European dignity' by not wearing a tie. I took this rebuke seriously to heart.
11. Hunkanrin, loc. cit. There is no copy of the *Écho de Dahomey* to be found in the newspaper files at the Bibliothèque Nationale. We have not found any local newspapers

Unable to express his views locally, Hunkanrin did so through newspapers in France.

There were many good French people who were indignant at the acts which they saw committed, but living in the colony they could do nothing openly to denounce them and have them checked. Having found a spokesman in me, they supported me by every means possible, and gave me information which enabled me to write articles and send them secretly to our defenders in France.

Some of those whose hostile acts towards the Governor became known to him through his spies paid for them with their lives. One of these was Ulysse Cros, inspector of education. Invited by Governor Noufflard to have supper with him at Government House, he was poisoned during the meal and taken back *in extremis* to his own house, where he died. Another was Fournier, manager of the C.F.A.O. shop in Porto-Novo: a circle guard shot him at point blank range while he was taking an evening bicycle ride, close to the government lines.[12] A further French companion-in-arms, M. Paulme, director of Chargeurs Réunis at Cotonou, was only able to escape death by returning hurriedly to France.[13]

Hunkanrin's articles were published thanks to Maurice Violette, Deputy for Eure-et-Loir, in the *Annales Coloniales*; by Raoul Briquet, Deputy, in *L'Éclaireur Africain*, and by J. Lemaire, Deputy for Indre and a former governor-general, in *La France d'Outre-Mer*. These politicians, as the titles of their journals show, were not generally opposed to the colonial principle; far from it. But before 1914, while at the very heart of the 'colonial party', they did not hesitate to denounce severe abuses in the colonies. This current of opinion disappeared – at least, it was no longer able to find expression – after the 1914–18 war.

'Besides these journals', wrote Hunkanrin, 'I caused powerful lampoons to be stuck clandestinely on walls in Porto-Novo, Cotonou, Ouidah and Allada denouncing the baseness of Governor Noufflard and attempting to galvanise the people's energies.'[14] Repression made

---

there dating from before 1914, except for some copies of the local edition of the *A.O.F.*, which was edited by Scapula, a lawyer, and printed by the printer Ternaux at Conakry.

12. Some may be inclined to doubt these assertions of Hunkanrin's, but the account of this murder given by Governor Noufflard himself in his 'eulogy' at Joseph Fournier's funeral is extremely strange. According to his version, Fournier was hit 'accidentally' by shots fired by a sergeant of the native guard who was in a state of 'drunken fury' (*délire alcoölique*). Previously a 'model of discipline and devotion to duty', this sergeant happened to be a Djerma Muslim, and as such someone who never drank alcohol. . . . (*Journal Officiel du Dahomey*, 1 Jan. 1914, pp. 23–5).

    How did this model soldier suddenly come to be drinking himself into a frenzy? And how did this frenzy lead him to fire those shots, and finally, how did those 'accidental' shots happen so precisely to hit a political opponent of the government?

13. Hunkanrin, loc. cit.
14. Ibid.

it necessary for Hunkanrin to leave Dahomey, so during 1913–14 he lived at Dakar and became one of the editors of *La Démocratie du Sénégal*, then under the direction of Blaise Diagne; the newspaper's campaigns resulted in Diagne being elected to the legislature in 1914. Back in Dahomey again, Hunkanrin was subjected to new legal actions, and had to 'go underground'.

Numerous sentences were pronounced against me in my absence by the tribunal at Cotonou, on the orders of M. Noufflard, for my campaign against him (alleged conditional death-threats, serious political disturbances of a kind to compromise public safety etc.) – sentences totalling more than fifty years in prison and seventy-five years' local banishment.

Hunkanrin's campaigns finally caused Noufflard to be recalled, since his actions had passed all bounds of acceptable conduct; and he had to embark at Lagos to avoid the hostile demonstrations he would have faced in Dahomey . But before Noufflard's recall, Hunkanrin had to endure further ordeals. The First World War had broken out, and to escape the Governor's henchmen who made a determined attempt to find him, he was compelled to hide out in the scrublands near the frontier with Nigeria. But even from there, he made secret journeys to Porto-Novo and continued to bombard the Governor with open letters of denunciation, some of which were pinned up in his office.

From my solitary hide-out, which my supporters called *Banuso* – meaning, in our language, 'only speak to your heart' – because there are no honest people and all men are liars, I founded with Paul Hazoumé a clandestine handwritten journal entitled *Le Récadaire* [the name of the messengers of the ancient kings of Dahomey]. . . . M. Noufflard, scanning the maps of Dahomey and Nigeria, did his utmost to track down the *Banuso* where I was in hiding.[15]

Noufflard's departure did not ease Hunkanrin's situation, since the new Governor, Fourn, did not revoke the arrest warrant.

The organised movement led by Hunkanrin relied on the traditional élites for its main support. Although Toffa, the king of Porto-Novo, had been the ally and faithful supporter of the French, particularly during the two Dahomey campaigns, he had been brought to heel once he had ceased to be regarded as useful. At his death in 1908, his son – while retaining the honorific title of *chef supérieur* (paramount chief) – had his role reduced to that of a cantonal chief, a mere agent of the governor and the local administrator, whose orders he had to promise to carry out. The bitterness felt in these traditional circles can be imagined. On this aspect, Hunkanrin wrote to me:

The political awakening of Dahomey was the work of the movement of

15. Ibid.

notables who were aged between fifty and sixty-five just after the First World War. The young men, mostly civil servants and clerks in business houses, feared for their jobs because they were liable to be dismissed, imprisoned or otherwise maltreated for the merest trifles. 'Keep your mouth shut' was their motto.[16]

Among those who inspired the movement, Hunkanrin mentions Paul Hazoumé, its secretary-general, who later gained literary fame for his ethnological work on the blood pact in Dahomey and for his historical novel *Doguicimi*, and became, after 1945, a counsellor of the Union Française; Ony Bello, a notable; Sognigbe Micpon, prince of Porto-Novo; Tolli Toffa, prince of Porto-Novo, heir to Toffa and an active chief; Gandonu Kly, village chief of Vakon; Aminu Balogun, a merchant and notable, president of the Porto-Novo section of the Comité franco-musulman; Etienne Tete, an army sergeant and secretary of the movement; Jecha, prince of Porto-Novo and a notable; Yessufu Adjorin, a merchant; and the Porto-Novo notables Adande, Awanto, Aplogan, Aplogan Vedji *et al.*

## *The war and after, 1918–1923*

Louis Hunkanrin thus lived in hiding from 1914 till 1918, the year when Blaise Diagne arrived in Dahomey. Diagne had been sent to West Africa by Clemenceau with the title of 'Commissioner of the Republic in West Africa' and the rank of governor-general, to step up the recruitment of infantry soldiers for the army.

Having been, during my stay at Dakar in 1912–13, a co-editor of the publication *La Démocratie du Sénégal*, of which Diagne was the political director, I took advantage of his arrival in Dahomey to make my situation known. I was taken to Government House by Lieutenant Galandou Diouf, aide-de-camp to Diagne and later Deputy for Senegal, and ushered into the Governor's office, which the Commissioner-General for colonial manpower [Diagne] was occupying. The latter had Governor Fourn called and said to him: 'Hunkanrin has only defended what are clearly French interests, closely linked to those of our African brothers. He has not committed any crime, and it would ill become us to persecute him in order to conceal Noufflard's crimes.'

He then telephoned the public prosecutor and requested him to bring him all the arrest warrants against me so that I should be able to move about without fear. Holding all the warrants in his hand, M. Diagne said that I was to find him some recruits in Porto-Novo. I had no trouble in finding twenty the

16. There was another French organisation besides the 'Ligue des Droits de de l'Homme' which served as a base of operations for Dahomeyans: the 'Comité franco-musulman' (French Muslim Committee). It had its headquarters in Paris at 110 rue Demours, and among its leading lights were Edouard Herriot (twice Premier of France between the wars) and Lavenarde.

same day, and I myself enlisted as a volunteer for three years. This example was followed by other compatriots, friends and relatives, and when we embarked at Cotonou there were 120 of us – all due to my activity – on our way to join the 90th Senegalese rifle battalion at Rufisque. A month later I was sent to the eastern front, where my duties were to do with rations and the guarding of Austrian, German and Bulgarian prisoners of war at a camp at Mikra, 10 km. from Salonika.

At the end of the war, Diagne had me appointed to a secretaryship at the headquarters of the General Commissariat for colonial manpower in Paris . . . where I was put in charge of Dahomeyan affairs, and kept Diagne informed of everything that might be of interest to him. Through my intervention, many abuses of power to which Senegalese and Dahomeyan soldiers were subjected were made known and stopped. Up to this point, Diagne and I were on good terms and there was nothing with which we could have reproached each other.[17]

The above testifies to Hunkanrin's honesty and candour – the latter a quality that was once again to be his undoing later. Being without ulterior motives himself, he was unable to impute them to others. But it is clear that there were such motives on the part of Diagne, who had undoubtedly rescued his old collaborator only to help him in his task of recruitment. With great loyalty, Hunkanrin emphasised that he himself had only been recruited voluntarily; but it was clearly Diagne's understanding that the two of them had concluded a deal, which made Hunkanrin into a tool of his personal policy. It did not take long for the misunderstanding to come out into the open. Here is Hunkanrin again:

Diagne was a powerful man at that time, and was hand in glove with Clemenceau, the 'Tiger', who refused nothing that he requested. He had firmly resolved to obtain for me a job in Dahomey as administrative assistant to the chief of police so that, being always under the government's thumb, I would keep quiet about abuses to which I might be a witness. It was a pact with the colonialists. The rehabilitation of Noufflard, and my own reconciliation with that bandit, were also part of his intentions.

If I had accepted, I could have had anything I wanted, but it would have been at the expense of my friends and the local people who trusted me and had never ceased for a moment to support me in the struggle. I declined the offer – hence our estrangement.[18]

Estranged from Diagne, whose colonialist attitude was continually in evidence, Hunkanrin founded in Paris a newspaper called *Le Messager Dahoméen* to defend the interests of Dahomey. Its political director was Maître Max Clainville-Bloncourt, an advocate in the Paris court of appeal. As has already been mentioned, I have not been

17. Hunkanrin, loc. cit.
18. Ibid.

able to trace any copies of this periodical in Paris; the only copy I consulted was one preserved by Hunkanrin himself, which was almost entirely devoted to the campaign against the *indigénat*, and for 'subjects' to receive citizenship.

Writing under the pseudonym 'Eké-l'oju-ti', Hunkanrin showed, in an article entitled 'How citizen's rights are acquired in West Africa', the full absurdity of the system of naturalisation, which was doled out in driblets at the Governor's discretion:

According to a decree of 25 October 1912, a French subject who wishes to avail himself of these rights must serve for ten years in a government department so as to be thoroughly policed and shaped in the government's mould. He must be of blameless conduct and morals, renounce his ancestral customs, and – most tricky of all – obtain good reports from the government. These reports are confidential and are merely the preliminary. . . . And they alone can cause the unhappy subject's request to be rejected.

Not without malice, he shows where the privilege of the four municipalities can lead:

The numerous children of the Governor of Dahomey, M. Fourn (a Frenchman!), are in fact subjects because they were not born in one of the four municipalities of Senegal, and because M. Fourn omits to recognise them by a legal act.[19] By contrast, the children born of a union between a foreigner – say a German – and a woman who is a native of either Dakar, Goree, Rufisque or St Louis are French citizens, entitled to vote and be elected to parliament.

Let us take the example a little further. Here is Mamadu, a Bambara infantryman, from deep in the Sudan, who has come to Dakar with his wife, a Bambara like himself, through accident of military service. While there she gives birth to a son, who is declared and registered at the town hall in Dakar with the name of Mussa. This son of Mamadu is a French citizen, who has the vote and can be elected to parliament, while Mamadu himself remains a foot-soldier and a French subject. When Mussa is old enough to bear arms, he will be enrolled in one of the metropolitan corps. . . . If he is a sergeant, and his father is a sergeant too, he will have a subsistence and equipment allowance of 1,000 francs a month, while the man who begot him, who is only a native, an *anima vilis*, will have only 40 francs a month. Mussa will have access to all forms of public employment while his father – poor Mamadu! – will only have the right to hold his tongue in the face of the *manigolos*[20] of French civilisation.[21]

The following editorial by Max Clainville-Bloncourt in the same issue of the paper expresses the hope which the prospect of an age of revolution in Europe was capable of arousing:

19. He did so subsequently, perhaps influenced by this article and others.
20. *Manigolos* were whips made of hippopotamus hide, carried at all times by circle guards.
21. *Le Messager dahoméen* no. 4, 15 July 1921.

We already felt that four years of war, after staining the world with blood, had troubled every conscience. Each day brings us a greater certainty that the internal structure of European states, like international relations between peoples, are about to undergo a radical change. And these revolutions will not occur unless the political and economic organisation of the colonies feels the repercussions. [. . .] Every happening has its appointed time. Voltaire makes Mohammed say: 'Arabia's time has come at last.' The time will come for the Congo and Dahomey as well. [Quoting Marcus Garvey, the author concludes:] We will not ask England or France or Italy or Belgium why they are here. We will simply order them to get out. The democracy and freedom which are good for the white man to experience are good for the black man too.

At the same time Hunkanrin took part, with Diagne and Dr W.E.B. DuBois, in the second Pan-African Congress held in London, Brussels and Paris in August and September 1921.[22] He returned home in 1922, and resumed the leadership of the organisation set up in 1914. Meanwhile, the radical lawyer and Deputy, Maurice Violette, had managed to have Hunkanrin's fifty-year prison sentence and seventy-five years' banishment cancelled by the ministry of the colonies. But having returned to a colonial country, he was not going to be left for long without suffering repression once again.

## *Deportation to Mauritania, 1923–1933*

On 17 February 1923 some notables gathered in Porto-Novo and drew up a petition against the institution of new taxes (market dues) and the abuse of forced labour, pointing out how discouraging these practices were for the population, and that they created the risk of a mass exodus to Nigeria.

The pretext for repression was to hand. The following account of the ensuing events was given in the French press:

### *An Act of Sedition Occurred in Dahomey Last Month*

The energetic measures taken by M. Merlin [Governor General of French West Africa] immediately restored calm.

*Paris, 16 March.* We drew attention some time ago to a strong agitation taking place in Dahomey. From Porto-Novo we have received the following intelligence.

On 12 February, the day after the departure of M. Henri Michel, former Senator for Basses-Alpes and elected delegate of Dahomey [elected exclusively by French citizens, officials and the military, i.e. by the colonials] in the High

22. The first Congress was held in Paris, at the Grand Hotel, on 19–21 February 1919. In his correspondence with me, Hunkanrin made no reference to it, and it would seem that he did not attend; at that time, he was probably still serving in the army.

Council for the colonies, who had been on a visit to the colony, a demonstration took place in Porto-Novo, followed by a strike at several workplaces.
An assembly of strikers a few days later, which gave rise to a tumultuous demonstration, had to be dispersed, and there was no choice for the police and army but to intervene. At this the agitation, far from subsiding, became more intense. The trouble reached the outskirts of Porto-Novo and our native police were chased from their posts by insurgents armed with rifles.
The administrator Chassériau sent riflemen to restore order. The crowd surrounded them, and they were obliged to use their weapons. One corporal and four natives were wounded. M. Merlin, . . . when informed of these facts, ordered Governor Fourn to proclaim a state of siege, which he accordingly did. At the same time, he had a machine-gun company and a mortar section sent from Togo, led by a battalion commander. Meanwhile the Minister for the Navy, warned by M. Merlin, ordered the gunboat *Cassiopée* to sail for Cotonou.
The deployment of forces on this scale had an immediate effect. Ten of the ringleaders, headed by two known agitators Oni Bello and Etienne Tete, were arrested; the other rebels were disarmed. Today the colony is calm once again.[23]

*The Bulletin de l'Afrique française* of April 1923 was much less precise. It mentioned incidents having taken place in February and early March at Porto-Novo, and the refusal to pay duty and taxes, and stated that the movement had 'somewhat' (*tant soit peu*) reached the regions of Adjohon and Ueme. Of the Parisian report quoted above, Hunkanrin writes:

Everything related in this article is a mere tissue of lies. . . . 'Insurgents armed with rifles': the carrying of weapons was forbidden for the native, and permits to buy guns were only granted to very few people. How could the so-called insurgents have found weapons and armed themselves?
What is true is that considerable forces were deployed, a state of siege was declared without any justification, and a gunboat was sent to Cotonou which had no revolt to quell and nothing to do. Its crew strolled quietly around Porto-Novo with their hands in their pockets, making fun of the Governor and all his works.[24]

Governor-General Carde, in his address to the Governing Council, let it be known why the affair had been blown up: it was to find a pretext for getting rid of trouble-makers:

Some agitators belonging to certain advanced circles in France have sought to implant their extremist doctrines among the most *évolué* of the natives of the

23. It has proved impossible to identify the newspaper from which this piece was extracted; the clipping was found in one of Louis Hunkanrin's files.
24. Hunkanrin, loc. cit.

coast and to recruit adherents there. They have had no success.

. . . It is undoubtedly to this propaganda that we owe the agitation that was produced last February at Porto-Novo, a region where for quite a long time it has been believed for some time that the population have an insubordinate attitude. The pretext of the agitation was the levying of new taxes and the recruitment of the annual military contingent.

Our intervention was as prompt as it was firm, and a few days were enough for order to be restored without any bloodshed. The sanctions pronounced on the ringleaders had a salutary effect on their compatriots, and demonstrated our relentless will not to allow malcontents to imperil the supreme authority of the state.[25]

What were the 'sanctions' against the 'ringleaders'?

Except for ten or a dozen members of the movement [see above, p.206] who were able to escape the repression, we were all arrested and condemned, some to terms in prison ranging from six months to two and five years, and others to deportation (i.e. internment in the most arid regions of French West Africa). Prince Sognigbe Micpon and I were interned in Mauritania, he at Tichitt and I at Kiffa.[26]

The decision for our deportation - an administrative measure - was contained in an order dated 14 April 1923, issued at the request of Fourn. This was the '*guillotine sèche*' (dry guillotine) which Governor Angoulvant considered to have the same result as a death sentence. *La Dépêche africaine*, describing the affair, had this to say on that particular subject:

Prince Sognigbe Micpon did not long survive his sentence. Ill, and deprived of medicines and sometimes of food as well, the prince soon died - in effect, because of the physical and mental sufferings brought about by his internment. This outcome had been foreseen, because the prince had been advised before his departure to draw up a will.

Hunkanrin owed his survival to his robust health and fierce energy. The account he gives of his journeys and of his time in exile cannot fail to be moving: 'At Kiffa, my first halt on the desert road, I endured the terrible sufferings of solitary confinement for several long months, day and night, and deprived of fresh air and light. At the end of my agony I was taken to a camp right in the desert itself. There I experienced life in a tent, open - as if ironically - to the air and the light, but also exposed to all the elements and, in addition, to the arbitrary behaviour of my Moorish armed guards, who applied themselves to the task of increasing the hardship of my life in the desert, which was already hard enough anyway.[27]

25. *L'Afrique française. Renseignements coloniaux*, no. 12 (1923), p. 431.
26. Hunkanrin, loc. cit.
27. *Dépêche africaine*. The cutting is probably taken from an issue which appeared in 1930, but the file of this paper held at the Bibliothèque Nationale does not include the issue in question. The *Dépeche africaine* was published in Paris by a West Indian, Maurice Satineau.

Despite the terrible conditions in which he was forced to live, Hunkanrin carried on the struggle by every means at his disposal. On 21 September 1923 he lodged a complaint against various individuals in the Dahomey government, whom he accused of having instigated the measures against him. Three months later the president of the court of justice at Cotonou claimed that he had never found 'any trace of his complaint' at the court; Hunkanrin's mail was in fact heavily censored at Dakar. The complaint, which he renewed, was now investigated by a professional magistrate, but the Governor-General quickly replaced the magistrate by a member of his administration, who dismissed the matter as requiring no further action.

After the death of Prince Sognigbe Micpon at Tichitt, Hunkanrin was transferred there, and then moved from one fortress to another: Akarijitt, Tidjikja, Tamchakett. In 1930, while at Tadjikja, he intervened many times on behalf of slaves ill-treated by the Moors, and had a number of them freed by a court's decision. But Moorish feudal lords and the local administration were able to allege that Hunkanrin was endangering public safety and have him removed, by order of the Governor; he was then sent to Tamchakett. Two slaves who succeeded in following him there were arrested, condemned to fifteen days' 'administrative' imprisonment, and then returned to their former masters.

Hunkanrin complained to the public prosecutor at St Louis (10 April 1931), and was then able to send to France the complete dossier he had established on slavery in Mauritania and the way in which it was protected by the colonial administration in defiance of official proclamations. His own cause had never ceased to be pleaded in France, mainly by the *Ligue des droits de l'homme*, in which he had long been a conspicuous militant.

> At first the *Ligue* intervened energetically and strikingly in our favour with the Minister for the Colonies. The colonial despots, who did not expect this, took fright and made arrangements to bar our way. Some retired senior officials insinuated themselves into the central committee and it was their baneful advice which won the day, and led to our complaints being hushed up.
>
> Their unfortunate machinations ended by causing a schism in the inner councils of the *Ligue*. Several important members, including Félicien Challaye, a teacher of philosophy at the Lycée Condorcet and one-time collaborator of Brazza in the Congo [on his mission of 1905], and Elie Reynier, teacher of history and geography at Privas (Ardèche) and president of the *Ligue*'s Ardèche branch, resigned in anger at the *Ligue*'s conduct when confronted by the victims of injustice and high-handed action. . . .[28]

It was Elie Reynier who published Hunkanrin's dossier in a booklet

28. Hunkanrin, loc. cit.

entitled *L'esclavage en Mauritanie* (Slavery in Mauritania).[29] In the preface he wrote:

> With documentation to hand, [Hunkanrin] exposes the trade in blacks which is practised, and officially protected and guaranteed by administrators and judges. Thus, in these times when there are colonial disturbances which are only too fully justified, and with a megalomaniac and imperialistic colonial exhibition in progress, Hunkanrin's narrowly focused and precise testimony is well-timed.

The copies of the booklet which were mailed to Hunkanrin were confiscated, and he was obliged to pay the resulting fee (reimbursed on his release!). However Chazal, the Governor of Mauritania whose complicity with the slave traffickers he had denounced, was replaced.

### *The Dahomeyan press; deportation to Tougan, 1941–1947*

In 1933, after ten years spent in the desert, Hunkanrin was at last set free and allowed to return to Porto-Novo. In the hope of keeping him under his personal control, Governor-General Brevié brought him back into the administration and assigned him to the department of political affairs to study local customs, as part of the great work of writing up the customs of French West Africa, which he had ordered at that time.[30] But Hunkanrin set about this task in his own way. He received his compatriots and listened to their complaints; and his report tended not so much to codify retrograde 'customs' as to make them evolve in a liberal direction. . . . This was not appreciated in Dakar, where it was noted in the margin of the report that Hunkanrin had not done the work for which he was being paid, and he was consequently discharged.

After his return in 1933, he resumed his journalistic activity, but not openly on account of his government employment. In the previous ten years the number of newspapers in Dahomey had increased. Before 1923, the legal requirement that the manager should be a French citizen had made it impossible for an African press to exist, but in that year a chance of history suddenly opened the way for it: the public prosecutor in Porto-Novo, immediately after the pretended 'sedition', authorised the publication of newspapers under the responsible management of French 'subjects' and gave each one his support *vis-à-vis* the administration. It was never possible later to revoke this right.

29. Privas: Imprimerie Moderne, 1931, 30pp. The colonial exhibition referred to in the preface took place at Vincennes, near Paris, in 1931.
30. The outcome of this enterprise was published in the three volumes of *Coutumiers juridiques de l'A.O.F.*, Paris: Larose, 1939.

The quite large number of well-educated people and the existence of several small presses operated by craftsmen made it possible for sheets to be published, which often ran for only a short time due to lack of finance, but serving as a channel for denunciation and agitation such as no other colony possessed.[31] There were never less than half a dozen, and those which appeared for the first time in 1933–5 were Auguste Nicoue's *Le Phare du Dahomey*, Blaise Kuassi's *Le Courrier du Golfe de Benin* (Kuassi became Hunkanrin's son-in-law), *La Voix du Dahomey, L'Étoile du Dahomey*, and *La Presse porto-novienne*. They played an important part in denouncing the repression which followed the demonstrations at Lome, Togo, in January-February 1933.[32] Faced with a common danger, they united and in May 1933 the six papers published a joint declaration in reply to their detractors: 'In the eyes of those wretches, the journalists of Dahomey are pretentious and contemptible people. They call them "black scribblers", and find that they do not know how to write. . . . Even if they don't know how to write, they do know how to tell the truth.'[33]

The administration had to resign itself to acknowledging their existence, and, joining in the game itself, caused an organ to be set up that was devoted to its interests, with the bizarre title *Vers la suprême sagesse* (Towards the supreme wisdom). Its editor, a former schoolteacher, had his salary paid from a secret fund.

Hunkanrin was an active contributor to *La Voix du Dahomey* and the *Courrier du Golfe de Benin*, an activity which caused him fresh difficulties. On 11 September 1934 the offices of *La Voix du Dahomey* in Cotonou and the private house of the manager were searched. This was as the result of a paragraph accusing a senior official of having received a personal gift of 14,000 francs from various canton chiefs, with the circle commander acting as intermediary. The administration were well aware that this could only have been ascertained from confidential official documents. Needless to say, the priority now was not to upset the senior official in question but to teach a lesson to the impudent people who had exposed the scandal. Five men were arrested – one for 'possession of arms' because some cartridges had been found at his

31. At this time, opposition newspapers in Dakar found themselves refused the use of the printing presses, which were a monopoly of the Grande Imprimerie Africaine, a subsidiary of the Delmas trust. Two publications were duplicated: the *Périscope Africain*, an organ of the anti-Diagne faction edited by Galandu Diuf, and the reactionary *Stegomya*, produced by the European businessman Louis Girard mainly for 'poor whites'.
32. Hunkanrin was still in Mauritania at this time. On the Lome affair and the role of the Dahomeyan press, see J. Suret-Canale, *French Colonialism in Tropical Africa*, op. cit., p. 446.
33. *Courrier du Golfe de Benin*, no. 33, 1 May 1933, p. 33.

house, the four others for 'misappropriating official correspondence'. One of them who dared to protest was summarily sentenced to a year in prison for 'contempt of court'.[34]

Meanwhile, the fascist-inclined French government of Pierre Laval placed new repressive measures in the hands of the colonialists through the Regnier-Rollin decrees. The Rollin decree of 10 April 1935, which applied to the colonies other than the West Indies and Réunion, provided in its first article for prison terms of between three months and a year and fines of 500 to 5,000 francs for 'whoever, by any kind of publication, incites resistance to the application of laws, decrees, regulations or orders of the public authority'. Article 2 punished with three months to a year in prison and a fine of 100 to 3,000 francs 'those who, by any means whatever, cast aspersions on the respect due to French authority'. For officials these penalties were doubled, and the offender would be banned from holding any public office for between five and ten years. Thus a blow was struck against any criticism of the authorities.

On 7 November 1935, the manager of the *Courrier* was sentenced to a year in prison and a fine of 1,000 francs for 'insults and defamation' concerning the assistant administrator Maupoil.[35] Finally, between 29 January and 9 April 1936, the 'big trial' of the *Voix du Dahomey* was held – the final result of what had begun in 1934. The verdict, announced on 10 June, imposed twenty-eight fines for 'illegally setting up an association', two for 'theft and concealment' (of documents), and ten for 'aspersions on the respect due to French authority' – the retroactive effect of the Rollin decree! Among those condemned was Hunkanrin, who was ordered to pay a fine of 100 francs.

However, in the course of this affair the esteem and trust in which Hunkanrin was held by his compatriots suffered a blow. In the eulogy he delivered at Hunkanrin's funeral, his old comrade Paul Hazoume said: 'The administration, misjudging this period of calm in the life of the veteran fighter, wanted to take advantage of it to make him play a dishonourable role during the *Voix de Dahomey* trial.'[36] In the period that followed, Hunkanrin was generally criticised, and consequently removed himself from the political arena. How did this happen? The documents consulted in Dakar by the American scholar Spiegler suggest that Hunkanrin did not act reprehensibly in any way but was once again the victim of his own candour. He was discredited because he had established close relations with a French official, and this caused people to suspect that he had gone over to the administration's side.

34. *La Phare du Dahomey*, no. 105, Sept. 1934.
35. *La Phare du Dahomey*, no. 118, Nov. 1935.
36. *Aube Nouvelle*, no. 174, 6 June 1964.

The police reports reveal that this official was on a special assignment to establish contact with Hunkanrin, and tell him that he completely shared his convictions. Hunkanrin, who was always ready to believe well of others, became enthusiastically devoted to this unexpected friend. This was what the administration wanted: by publicising his close relations with the official, Hunkanrin was bound to become distrusted by his compatriots. The trick succeeded, and put out of action for a time someone whom prison had failed to subdue.

Still further ordeals awaited Louis Hunkanrin. In 1940, France was defeated by the Nazis, and the spirit of the collaborationist French government in Vichy was triumphant in French West Africa. Hunkanrin unhesitatingly took the path of resistance.

> Because my house in Davié [a suburb of Porto-Novo] was on the road that led to British Nigeria, administrators, government clerks, merchants, sailors - patriots who supported the continuation of the fight against Germany and her allies - hid there to put on disguises before rejoining the Free French at Lagos. . . . I was given the task of distributing in Porto-Novo and other towns of Lower Dahomey tracts produced by the Free French forces in Lagos and brought from there in canoes which we had built.[37]

The Vichyist authorities - Governor Truitard and an official named Moulère - decided to implement a policy of repression. Gbehinto, the king of Porto-Novo and heir to Toffa, who had lent his car to French officials travelling to Nigeria, was arrested and committed suicide. On 1 January 1941 Hunkanrin was arrested. So also were Adewale, a Nigerian policeman who had come to make a reconnaisance at Porto-Novo; Wabi, a Dahomeyan who had lent him some clothes; and Albert Idohu, the manager of the John Holt establishment at Porto-Novo. A court-martial presided over by Colonel Verrier condemned these three to death, and they were shot on the Fann rifle range. Although Hunkanrin had sheltered Adewale in his house at Davié, nothing could be proved against him.

Embarked for Dakar on 11 September 1941, Hunkanrin appeared before an intelligent military examining magistrate, Captain Chacun, who decided to dismiss the allegation against him of having committed a breach of state security. But the Vichyist prosecutors had had the foresight to magnify the charge by adding that of uttering falsehoods in the public press; they did this with the connivance of a shady lawyer who subsequently took refuge in Dakar. Hunkanrin was sentenced to eight years' hard labour and sent to the penal settlement at Tougan in the Sudan, and when he protested he was given an additional sentence for contempt of court.

37. Louis Hunkanrin, *L'Éclair*, no. 8, Dec. 1947.

Hunkanrin denounced the machinations of which he had been the victim and demanded that his case be reopened, but in vain. Vichy fell, and in 1944 France was liberated, but Hunkanrin stayed in detention and his complaints were classified as calling for no further action.

## *Last years of struggle, 1947–1964*

The colonial administration had achieved its object of keeping the old campaigner out of circulation during the pre-election period in 1945–6. Only on 25 September 1947 did the public prosecutor at Bamako decide to order his release, and he was freed on 1 November. But an order of 2 November banned him from residence in any of the territories of French West Africa.

A 'Louis Hunkanrin Defence Committee' was set up in Dahomey to have him rehabilitated and to open a case against the perjurers who had mounted the common law accusation against him in 1941. The *Secours populaire de France* (a mutual aid organisation), with the support of Apithey, the Deputy for Dahomey, started a campaign to this end and intervened with the Minister for the Colonies. Hunkanrin was finally authorised to return to Dahomey. There he founded a new newspaper, *Le Trait d'Union* (The link), in which he pursued his campaigns and again denounced high-handedness, abuses and plundering by government.

In 1949 he was visited by Jacques Mitterrand, a member of the *Assemblée de l'Union française*,[38] who wrote of him as follows in *La Défense*, the organ of the *Secours Populaire*:

'What do you think of Hunkanrin?' I said to the aged African who received me at his home in Dahomey with that delicacy and that impulsive hospitality which are among the great distinguishing marks of Africa.

'Ah', he said, 'there is an upright man, without a blemish on his character, a man who hates injustice. He cannot tolerate a disloyal act, and in a question of honour he would rather kill himself that make a compromise with dishonesty.'

The next day we went to see Hunkanrin at his old house in Porto-Novo. His desk is covered with books, newspapers and sheets of paper blackened with his handwriting. On the wall I see, with emotion, framed photographs of former heads of the *Ligue des Droits de l'Homme*: Francis de Pressensé and Ferdinand Buisson . . . these are Hunkanrin's silent but eloquent companions. Before this man with his unwavering gaze I feel shame for the French colonial administration which in recent years rained unjust and perfidious blows upon him.[39]

38. One of the three parliamentary assemblies under the 1946 French Constitution (the others being the National Assembly and the Council of the Republic, later the Senate). It was of a consultative nature.
39. Jacques Mitterrand, 'L'Affaire Hunkanrin, illustration de l'arbitraire en Afrique noire', *La Défense*, 22–29 May 1949.

Worn out by age and the hardships of two deportations, Hunkanrin continued the fight as far as his strength allowed. On 8 June 1963 he responded with great kindness to my own request for information about his life and career. This article depends for its data essentially on the documents he sent me.

When the revolution in Dahomey took place in October 1963, he joined in the work of national reconciliation, and not long before his death the authorities once again sought him out to arbitrate in a dispute between some merchants.

In the last letter he wrote to me, dated 2 May 1964, he excused himself for a delay in attending to our correspondence on the grounds of illness, and the failure of a French friend to carry out a commission entrusted to him: 'At that time we were living under the Maga regime, when everyone lived in fear of being sent to prison or thrown into a concentration camp. I would not have wanted my friend to suffer that fate. . . .' He promised to send more documents, but death came before he had had time to prepare them, on 28 May 1964.

The Dahomeyan government honoured him with a state funeral. His old comrade Paul Hazoume delivered the eulogy, and the issue of *L'Aube Nouvelle*, the government's official newspaper, for 6 June was given over to a description of the ceremony and recollections of his career. I still regret that this essay - which I dedicate to his memory - could not be submitted to him personally, as much to correct errors as to give him the satisfaction of seeing that due honour was being done to his life of struggle and hardship.

Louis Hunkanrin's struggle and life now belong to history. I am confident that others will soon devote to him works of greater depth, and will immortalise the humane spirit of this great fighter, whose only object in life was to vindicate the rights of Africa and the rights of humanity.

## *Afterword*

The above text, like the other essays in this collection, is dated. Written and published in 1964, it was based exclusively on printed sources and on documents from his personal archives communicated to me by Louis Hunkanrin. I was unable to consult the archives which were accessible at that time - either those of the former government-general of French West Africa (now preserved in the National Archives of Senegal at Dakar) or those of the former government of Dahomey (today the National Archives of the Democratic Republic of Benin). However, the American researcher Spiegler - who visited me in 1963 when I was at the high school of Kindia in Guinea and put me in direct touch with Hunkanrin - consulted these archives himself and had the great kindness to let me know what he had extracted from them concerning Hunkanrin. At the time the above essay was published, the archives of the former French Overseas Ministry (today Archives Nationales de France - Section Outre-Mer, rue Oudinot, Paris) had not yet been opened for the period after 1920.

Among relevant works published or otherwise made available since, we will mention the following:

Anignikin, S.C., 'Les origines du mouvement national au Dahomey, 1900-1939', doctoral thesis (3rd cycle), University of Paris VII, 1980.

Asiwaju, A.I., G.L. Hazoume *et al.*, *La vie et l'oeuvre de Louis Hunkanrin*, Cotonou: Librairie Renaissance, 1977. This collection, which includes my own article, contains, among a variety of studies and contributions, extracts from the file on Hunkanrin preserved in the National Archives of Benin, and the text of Hunkanrin's pamphlet on slavery in Mauritania.

Codo, C.B., 'La presse dahoméenne face aux aspirations des "évolués": *La Voix du Dahomey*, 1927-1957', doctoral thesis (3rd cycle), University of Paris VII, 1978.

Djivo, J., 'Hunkanrin', notice in *Dictionnaire bio-bibliographique du Dahomey*, Porto-Novo, I.R.A.D, 1969.

Glele, M.A., 'Naissance d'un état noir (L'évolution politique et constitutionelle du Dahomey de la colonisation à nos jours)', *Droit et Jurisprudence*, Paris, 1969.

Hazoumé, G.L., 'La presse dahoméenne et le système colonial, 1919-1939 (Rôle historique et thèmes idéologiques)', DESS Sciences politiques, University of Paris I, 1977.

Langley, J.A., *Panafricanism and Nationalism in West Africa, 1900-1945*, Oxford, 1973.

Lokossou, C., 'La presse au Dahomey, 1894-1960. Evolution et réalisation face à l'administration coloniale', doctoral thesis (3rd cycle), EPHE, Paris, 1976.

Moseley, K.P., 'Indigenous and external factors in politics: Southern Dahomey to 1939', Ph.D. thesis, Columbia University, New York, 1975.

# 10

# THE GEOGRAPHY OF CAPITAL IN THE PARTS OF TROPICAL AFRICA UNDER FRENCH INFLUENCE[1]

In earlier works of a more general nature,[2] we have analysed the origins and method of functioning of colonial capital - on the grand scale - in the French domain of tropical Africa, excluding the Indian Ocean zone. This collection of territories - the former French West Africa and French Equatorial Africa, Togo and Cameroon - constitutes what we can today call the French sphere of influence in tropical Africa. The thirteen states other than Guinea which emerged from the old colonial territories have remained predominantly under French influence - through a multiplicity of ties, of which the most decisive is membership of the franc economic zone. Colonialism in its classical forms has been replaced by neocolonialism, of which the basic characteristic is the massive presence in the economies of those countries of French industrial and finance capital, from both private and state sources.

Up till the 1950s, the economy of these African countries had remained a 'trade economy' - to use the term first proposed by Jean Dresch in 1946 and later adopted by economists. On one side of this 'trade' was raw agricultural and (to a smaller extent) gathered produce, obtained by traditional methods within an economic and social framework which, with some exceptions, was also traditional. On the other side were imported 'trade goods' - such things as textiles, hardware and low-quality tools. These were exchanged, mainly on a seasonal cycle, at warehouses in the bush. The 'trade' had only the most superficial resemblance to free commerce. It could not have functioned except under the compulsion of the administrative apparatus. There was a personal poll tax, payable in cash, which the producer had to find from the sale of his crops; and there were various forms of forced labour or compulsory cultivation, the sale price being fixed according to price lists established by administrative diktat. All of this combined to make the African peasant a participant in a system of commerce which provided him with little return, but which

1. This essay is the official résumé of the Author's doctoral thesis, presented at the University of Paris VII in 1984 and now published in book form (for the bibliographical details, see p. 235).
2. See J. Suret-Canale, *French Colonialism in Tropical Africa*, op. cit., pp. 159–293, and *Afrique noire occidentale et centrale. III: De la colonisation aux indépendances*, Paris: Eds Sociales, 1972.

was highly profitable for the commercial establishments known as 'trading houses' – not because of the volume of their business but because of the size of their profit margins, their investment being minimal.

This archaic and rudimentary system of exploitation blocked the way to any economic development, which would have required the diversion of an important part of the population from its 'traditional' organisation, involving the gathering or production of export goods, into other activities. Because of this, exploitation of the capitalist type – which demands a body of workers earning wages – barely exists at all, having no space in which it can achieve an 'economic' existence, since the lowest wage greatly exceeds the cash reward of the 'independent' peasant. Capitalist-type exploitation only occurs in a few cases: timber (Gabon and Ivory Coast), gold and diamonds (mainly in equatorial Africa), and some plantations in the coastal regions of Guinea, Ivory Coast and Cameroon. Even this is not capitalist in the full sense of the word because the workforces employed are not true wage-earners – 'free workers' – but are made up largely of unskilled labourers recruited by the administration, in other words forced labour.

As long ago as the end of the nineteenth century a virtual *de facto* monopoly was established in the colonial trade, for the benefit of a number of family firms – mainly those from Bordeaux in Senegal and those from Marseilles in Guinea and Dahomey (now Benin) – while in the French Congo (subsequently French Equatorial Africa) the monopoly enjoyed by the concession company was *de jure*. From around 1907 till 1920, the capital of these companies became integrated with metropolitan finance capital, while the companies themselves kept their provincial links. The Protestant banking fraternity, represented chiefly by the Banque de l'Union Parisienne, extended its influence to embrace the Bordeaux firms, while the Banque de l'Indochine established itself in the 1930s, taking advantage of the current financial crisis. From then till the time of Independence, three mighty trading companies or groups of companies exercised effective control over the French-ruled parts of black Africa. These were the Société commerciale de l'Ouest africain (S.C.O.A.), its capital derived from Switzerland and the city of Lyon; the Compagnie française de l'Afrique occidentale (C.F.A.O.), its capital mainly from arming naval vessels and from industry in Marseilles; and the subsidiaries (known by a variety of names) of the Anglo-Dutch conglomerate Unilever, founded in 1929.

The transitional period 1945–60 introduced a number of changes in economic structure. Parallel changes were occurring at the same time in France, of which these were merely the overseas extensions; they consisted largely of a massive public investment in the economy. As in France, within the framework of economic plans of several years' duration, an independent fund was set up: the fund for investment and for economic and social development in the overseas territories (Fonds d'investissement et de développement économique et social des Territories d'Outre-Mer – F.I.D.E.S.). F.I.D.E.S., primed by the metropolitan budget, financed massive investment (which would have been illegal not long before), and many state-owned companies or public institutions intervened in a wide variety of areas, also as investors. Investment and intervention were directed essentially towards infrastructural projects – communications (roads, seaports, airports), energy production, urban development; to the development of export crops and of previously neglected mineral resources; and, as accessories to these, to the 'social' sector. This involved the extension of primary schooling, which had hitherto never reached 5 per cent in French West Africa, and was even lower in Equatorial Africa; the starting of secondary education; and the building of hospitals. The initial effect of these investments was to increase both the spread and the intensity of the trade economy: an increase in groundnut production in parts of the interior where access had previously been difficult (Mali and Niger) and a veritable explosion in the production of (mainly) coffee and cocoa by African farmers in regions with a humid tropical climate (the Ivorian forests and southern Cameroon). At the same time, a specialisation and diversification of commerce began in the main centres. The mechanisms of the franc economic zone and a general regulation of markets turned the French-ruled parts of black Africa into the equivalent of a licensed game park for French companies and economic institutions. There were beginnings of industrialisation, strictly controlled by the trading houses and certain specialist firms (often subsidiaries of the former); and the new industries were plugged into a well-established 'circuit' of economic activity, with import substitution and the initial (and usually partial) processing of export products. Almost all were located in ports or political capitals – Dakar, Abidjan, Douala, Pointe-Noire, Brazzaville.

The changes brought about by Independence were not of the same fundamental nature as those of 1930–46, and their effects were only felt gradually. Essentially the new economic structures that had been established in the previous period stood their ground and developed further, always with a heavy involvement of public funds from abroad ('aid') and a growing role for state institutions (at first French, but increasingly those of the new nations). Of this the principal end-result was to allow private capital – largely foreign (above all, French) finance capital – to reproduce itself, always at a sufficient margin of profit. These were the structures and the corresponding phase in the history of capitalism that certain Marxists term 'monopolistic state capitalism'

Leaving aside debates on points of doctrine and sticking to easily verifiable facts, there can be no denying the massive intervention in all aspects of the economic process by the state - rather one should say *states*, since we are talking of the French state, some other developed capitalist states, some transnational corporations, and increasingly the new African nation-states. As in the years before 1960, the intervention manifests itself, on the one hand, by contributions of funds ('aid') in the form of subsidies or loans on easy terms aimed at securing the profitability of the operations of private capital (infrastructure, development of export crops, mining, oil exploration); and, on the other hand, in the state (one should properly say 'states') taking over increasingly large and diverse sectors - those sectors, indeed, which are indispensable for the functioning of the economy (and thus for the realisation of private profit) but which are considered either unprofitable or insufficiently profitable by private capital, which then concentrates on certain sectors which return high profits while abandoning the rest to the public domain.

On the French side, the policy of investing public funds overseas was pursued using the same instruments as ever: F.I.D.E.S., now transformed into F.A.C. (Fonds d'aide et de coopération - aid and cooperation fund), and C.C.F.O.M. (Caisse centrale de la France d'Outre-Mer), which had the task of managing and distributing the fund, and was now transformed into C.C.C.E. (Caisse centrale de coopération économique). The same public institutions - state corporations, public utilities, companies with mixed private and public participation - continued to be involved in the most varied areas of activity while undergoing several changes of name. Being part of the franc zone kept the African economies closely tied to that of France, and gave French companies an unchallengeable lead over their international competitors. However, the days of the 'game park' were over.

This change had less to do with the coming of political Independence - although partly resulting from it - than with the effects of European integration, and here again the changes in Africa did no more than reflect those taking place in the former colonial power. We are talking of the effects of the Treaty of Rome (1957) which set up the European Economic Community, and the association in this community of the colonies of members of 'the Six', an association confirmed after Independence by the Yaounde accords of 1963. The opening of frontiers was quite as important for France as for its one-time colonies. The intervention of the F.A.C. and the Caisse centrale gave way to that of the F.E.D. (Fonds européen de Developpement - European Development Fund) and the B.E.I. (Banque européen d'investissement – European Investment Bank). The interventions of the International Bank for Reconstruction and Development (I.B.R.D.) and its subsidiaries, which had been limited before 1960, now began to multiply under its new title of 'World Bank'. State institutions of a similar kind in the United States and West Germany were involved too, though not on such a large scale. Whether of French origin or not, the investments were oriented mainly towards infrastructural works and big mining operations or schemes for the development of export crops.

Officially, the purpose of this 'aid' was to join in the struggle against underdevelopment, which would lead eventually to the African economies 'taking off'. As things turned out, the effect was to perpetuate and accentuate external dependence and growing internal imbalances. There were undoubtedly positive results from the population's point of view in education and social policy (although close examination might reveal shadowy patches in the sunlit landscape), but the true objective of the 'aid' – and its effect – was to allow transnational corporations established in Africa to extend their operations and their profits, at least up till the deepening of the world crisis triggered by the 'second oil shock' of 1979–80.

French finance capital in Africa, while retaining its predominant position, has undergone some structural modifications, again reflecting parallel occurrences in metropolitan France. Essentially, these are part of the tendency towards concentration which was a feature of the beginning of the Fifth Republic, and which was pursued up till the early 1970s. The big commercial houses have retained their power. As we shall see, their role has changed; but, because of their close association with monopolies in the forwarding business and in the fitting out of ocean carriers, they exert a continuing *de facto* control over external trade and over most import-substituting industry. The concentration first became apparent with the emergence in 1963 of a fourth giant conglomerate, Optorg. This firm, which had previously been interested in trade with Indochina (and, before 1917, in cereals from Russia), absorbed the Peyrissac company of Bordeaux and the former Gabonese concessionary company, the Société du Haut-Ogooué (S.H.O.). This reconstitution was completed in 1966 with the absorption of another Bordeaux company, Chavanel. Also in 1966, the old Banque de l'Union Parisienne was taken over by the Compagnie financière de Suez, which had been driven by Egypt's nationalisation of the Canal to involve itself in French business, and became in a few years one of the most powerful conglomerates in the French economy. Thus Optorg passed from the influence of the Banque de l'union Parisienne to that of the Suez company. The other group which holds a dominant position in the French economy, the Banque de Paris et des

Pays Bas (the Bank of Paris and the Netherlands – 'Paribas'), had an African presence dating back many years with its subsidiary, the Compagnie générale des colonies, which in 1958 became the Compagnie générale de participation et d'enterprises (Cegepar). In 1968, at one and the same time, it took the form of a holding company (under the title of Compagnie financière de Paris et des Pays-Bas) and gained control of one of the three pre-existing 'giants', S.C.O.A., to which it sought to add an international dimension, notably in the Caribbean and the Far East. The absorption of the Banque de l'Indochine by the Suez company extended the influence of the latter in another direction.

The C.F.A.O. remained, to all appearance, 'independent', but the ascendancy there of foreign financial interests based in the Marseilles region (the Lazard bank) became an increasingly decisive factor. Unilever, already a transnational with wide ramifications, reached the greatest degree of concentration that could have been conceived possible. And outside the big trading companies we also find, in several specialist areas, corresponding French groups (e.g. Pechiney, which had become Pechiney-Ugine-Kuhlmann, and Rothschild). The essential feature of the non-French 'foreign' interests was their involvement in extractive industries – as had already been the case before 1960.

We have already drawn attention to the role, from 1946 onwards, of French state-owned corporations, with their subsidiary bodies and the investments they made. They now expanded into new areas of activity and at the same time had their place taken increasingly by African state enterprises – this in 'liberal' as much as in more socialist countries. The new African state sector played what was in many ways a contradictory role. Initially, as in Senegal with the nationalisation of the groundnut trade in 1962, and most of all in states with a socialist orientation (like Mali and Congo-Brazzaville), it often came into being and then widened its scope with the intention of countering imperialism – in the shape of foreign private financial groups, particularly French ones. It was a matter of removing certain areas of commercial activity from foreign control and exploitation, or at least to be able to ensure, by right, that national interests would be safeguarded. However, what most frequently happened in practice, especially where the relationship with the old colonial power remained one of political and economic dependence, was that the extension of the public sector in the African state merely took the form of functions – and financial responsibility – being transferred from France to the state in question, and sectors of the economy that were considered uneconomic by large-scale private capital being nationalised. When the state took shareholdings in private companies, the companies often submitted voluntarily, and indeed the very largest private capital concerns would actively seek state participation, even to the extent of surrendering majority holdings. By such means, these companies could obtain guarantees against demands from their employees and against their eventual competitors. In other ways this state-owned sector provided sources of income – direct and indirect, legal and illegal – to the new administrative and political bourgeoisie, who thus became integrated into the system.

Let us now consider the area of intervention of monopolistic state capital – either that of a foreign state, usually France, or of the African state in question. The communication infrastructure – roads, railways, seaports and airports – had long been in the public sector. However, the actual *means* of transport remained largely in private hands. In the case of road transport, the subsidiaries of financial groups (e.g. S.A.G.A.[Société anonyme de gérance et d'armement]-Rothschild) suffered a setback, while more flexible small African concerns enjoyed a corresponding advantage. However, public or joint public and private corporations still exist in several countries.

The control of sea and air transport remains largely in private hands: the Chargeurs-Delmas-Vieljeux group in the former sector and U.T.A. (Union de transports aériens), a subsidiary of Chargeurs, in the latter. The Chargeurs shipbuilding concern is almost always the partner or 'technical adviser' of African firms (usually in joint state and private ownership) in the business of commissioning vessels. U.T.A. had the most profitable air routes assigned to it by Air France. Air Afrique operates alongside it: this entity is officially an African 'multinational' in the sense that the majority of African states concerned are participants, but U.T.A. is its private partner, responsible for 'technical assistance', and Air Afrique is, *de facto*, a subsidiary of U.T.A. As for the chronically loss-making local air companies, these are usually set up with mixed participation, with U.T.A. or Air France as partner.

In the energy and water-supply sector, the last private (French) companies disappeared after 1975, after which the sector came to be run exclusively by state or mixed state/private corporations – one or two in each country. The shareholders raised capital from the French public corporations C.C.C.E. or E.D.F. (Electricité de France – which has operated the nationalised electricity supply industry in France since 1946) or, in rare cases only and very much on a minority basis, from private sources.

Industrialisation followed along the same lines as before Independence – import-substituting manufacture or the part-processing of exportable commodities. Since the total absence of industrialisation, or its feebleness where it does exist, is rightly considered to be one of the chief symptoms of underdevelopment, the creation of new industries was seized upon rather too readily as the start of industrial 'take-off' so beloved by developmentalists. Hence each state wished to have its own full range of mini-industries serving a small market, to the detriment of the older industries which had been set up with a larger market in prospect than one country could provide. This process – which did not achieve its aim – slowed down considerably in the wake of the economic difficulties after 1974, but did not die out completely.

It is these processing industries, together with extractive industries (see below), which will benefit most from the tax and customs privileges envisaged in the various 'investment codes'. And those who will benefit most from the entire system will be the big commercial houses and the 'technical' companies with which they are generally associated for the purpose of setting up these industries, and which are entrusted with the task of marketing the resulting production. This happens both when the industry in question is regarded as a private concern, and when the state holding is 100 per cent and the private partner merely provides 'technical assistance'. On the whole, these industries only manage to survive with government support in the shape of tax concessions, subsidies and protectionism.

The extractive industries – mines, petroleum and gas – are a special case. Their first phase of activity was in the aftermath of the Second World War, in 1949–51, with a first generation of exploitations which were kept going less for the value of their output than for the exceptional ease with which the extraction process could be carried on. Quarrying was one such industry, and closeness to ports acted as an inducement. The second generation, which had a greater spread, was planned at the end of the 1950s and entered production after 1960. The latest developments, leaving petroleum aside, took place in the 1970s, but none of the projects that still exist came into existence in the ten years up to the time of writing. This has been due to political uncertainties and, of course, the world economic crisis.

The character of the capital employed in the mining industry has not changed since the 1950s. The French state, through credits from F.A.C. and C.C.C.E., and through its specialised institutions (the bureau of geological and mining research, the atomic energy commissariat, the bureau of petroleum research, Elf-Erap and others, has taken over the basic costs of prospecting and infrastructure. Outside the oil business, the capital structure of the exploiting companies brings together several elements. First there is French state finance, working through the state corporations already mentioned. There is French private capital – in a minority, but ensuring that it has a decisive position: e.g. Rothschild for Miferma (Société anonyme des Mines de Fer de Mauritanie – Mauritanian iron ore), Comilog (Compagnie minière de l'Ogoouré – Gabonese manganese) and Comuf (Compagnie des Mines d'Uranium de Franceville [Gabon]),

Comilog and Paribas for Taïba phosphates, etc. Finally, there are some other participants besides the French – e.g. North American and British – often with holdings of nearly 50 per cent, but still a minority compared with the French interests, both public and private. Since 1974, except for two instances of total nationalisation (Mauritanian iron ore and Togolese phosphates), the widespread acquisition of holdings by the African states has not altered the situation to any great extent; the state holdings have generally been acquired with borrowed funds. The wish of Mauritania and Togo to benefit from their own national wealth brought them up against the combined pressure of those in control of the international markets, and they had to reach agreement with their former partners. When it proved impossible to establish a structure for profitable operation, private capital held back – as in the case of the Holle potassium extraction company (a classic technical and financial failure), of which the entire capital remained in the hands of French state corporations and the Congolese state. The situation of petroleum (and of gas, with which it is often linked) is somewhat different; the big international petroleum companies were more often in competition with eachother than acting in concert. With petroleum in Gabon, the Congo and, more recently Cameroon, the vital role was played by subsidiaries of the French state company Elf-Erap, subsidiaries in which big private French combines – Rothschild and Paribas – were shareholders. This was so even before the Elf-Aquitaine merger transformed the main French state oil group into a mixed company owned partly by the state and partly by private capital. The other (non-French) 'majors' of the oil industry were not excluded, but they only had a secondary position (Shell-Gabon, AGIP-Congo etc.) The shareholdings of African states – hitherto always in a minority – have no influence on the way the companies' operations are managed.

There is large-scale public involvement in agriculture, as during the colonial period. It was exercised then through the medium of agricultural services and 'native provident societies', which contributed in varying degrees to the spread of modern methods and materials (selected seeds, tools etc.). Several large operations were launched by state enterprise: the Office du Niger, rice-growing units in Senegal, Cameroon and Chad, and mechanised oilseed production by the C.G.O.T. (general company of tropical oilseeds). The financial results of these operations were always disastrous, and the technical results sometimes so. State intervention in agriculture became general after 1960, the instruments being companies or agencies entirely or partly in the state sector – initially French but subsequently 'national'. These have the task of '*animation*' (bringing to life), 'management' and 'technical assistance' for the growing of export crops by African peasants, whether 'traditional' crops like cotton and groundnuts grown in the savannas, or items like coffee and cocoa which have a place in the commercial or capitalist framework.

Intervention is practised in various forms. The most complete form is that operated by the C.F.D.T. (French company for the development of textile fibres), a company of mixed participation with a majority state holding, which, even before 1960, followed the pattern established by the private concession companies set up in the Central African Republic and Chad between 1928 and 1932. Eventually, it will take over these concessions. In the savanna zones that are considered suitable, the C.F.D.T. manages the cotton crop as a monopoly - a monopoly of both purchasing and processing (ginning). In the 1970s, its operations were taken over by 'national' corporations, some completely, while in others a C.F.D.T. involvement still continued. All, however, were represented by C.F.D.T. in its annual reports as if they were its subsidiaries. In the ten states we are considering, production of cotton seed increased from 150,000 tonnes in 1957/8 to 620,000 tonnes in 1979/80. This was a success for technology, but from the point of view of the inhabitants' ability to enjoy a balanced diet and of the condition of the soil itself, the result was disastrous. Furthermore, the financial return was derisory: between 1974 and 1979, the cotton price in Liverpool actually decreased by 0.8 per cent. But this was much less than the decrease in the price of groundnut oil for the same period, which was 16.8 per cent.

In a less 'totalitarian' fashion, other bodies managed other field crops for export - e.g. Satec (company of technical assistance and cooperation) and B.D.P.A. (bureau for the development of agricultural production). Thus Satec managed groundnut production in Senegal, but was taken over by Sodeva (agricultural technical assistance and advisory company), which was nationalised by the Senegalese government in 1969. In Ivory Coast, public intervention is organised on the basis of a national enterprise, Satmaci (Ivory Coast technical assistance company for agricultural modernisation), which is mainly concerned with managing coffee and cocoa production, and has progressively switched its other responsibilities to specialised 'development companies'. As a general rule, all these bodies are responsible for the provision of selected seeds, agricultural equipment, fertilisers and means of controlling plant disease, and bring the producer into contact with a network of 'animators' or monitors responsible for ensuring that growing techniques recommended by experts are carried out.

Thus, as in the past, and now on an even greater scale than before, the 'independent' peasant is compelled, against his wish, to grow export crops in response to external demand. But while there is no longer compulsion in the forms used during the colonial era, it often persists, notably in cotton production. Chad did not hesitate to do what the colonial regime never dared to do: make it a *legal* obligation, and not merely a practical one, to grow cotton, with those who did not comply being punished. Any peasant needing to obtain cash has no way of doing so other than by growing cash crops, for which a framework and outlets exist, even though the actual monetary rewards are negligible. The states themselves have no choice; the taxes they levy on these products are their main source of income – sometimes their only ones – for priming their budgets and for repaying their foreign debts. However big the 'margin' taken by the states in taxation – and often it is enormous – the chief beneficiaries are those who have the international markets in these primary commodities under their control. The latter also engage in profitable speculation. And they do not bear the risk of their investment; the risk falls partly on the peasants, but the investments themselves are guaranteed by the countries that provide 'aid' and by those that receive it, and make payments under contract to the 'management' companies.

Despite the discouraging lessons of past experience, these forms of 'management' do not exclude the pursuit or actual realisation of large agro-industrial operations, sometimes within the public sector (e.g. the Office du Niger, rice-growing units and 'industrial' palm groves in Ivory Coast and Benin) and sometimes through the agency of private promoters. An example of the latter is market-gardening in Senegal with the US-Dutch B.U.D. concern; here agro-industrial units grow sugar-cane and produce refined sugar, oriented – in this case alone – to the home market. The results, both technical and financial, have been no better than in the past; B.U.D.-Senegal went bankrupt, and the running of the palm groves in Ivory Coast was handed over to the privately-owned Rivaud group. And so on. The unprofitable nature of these operations at the level of the states concerned does not mean that they were not rationally conceived; they produced yields, but only outside the borders of those states.

Here we come up against one of the major changes since the time of Independence: the dislocation of the traditional channels of trade. This is the culmination of a trend which began to evolve in the 1950s: the 'trading companies' ceasing to deal in 'products' (i.e. those for export) and, at the same time, detaching themselves from small-scale trading in the bush, which was given over to African retail traders. Not long ago, these two activities were carried on simultaneously at the warehouse of the trading post. In 1960 the economy of tropical Africa was still a 'trade economy'. By 1970 the trade had completely disintegrated, and no coherent economic system and replaced it.

The development of communications, the suppression of compulsory supplying of products not in the 'scheduled' range (this included mostly fruit rather than vegetables), the low quantity and equally low quality produced, the irregularity of supply, and, *per contra*, the peasant's weak purchasing power – all these factors have combined to make the bush trade uninteresting for the big companies. The process has perhaps been hastened by the nationalisation of the trade in primary products, such as occurred with the Senegalese groundnut trade in 1962, but the abandonment has come about more often on the initiative of the companies themselves. Almost everywhere the nationalised companies or state agencies, which have always made losses, have had to take on the collection and marketing of agricultural produce for export – indispensable if a minimum of disposable income is to be maintained for the peasant in the bush, and a major source of income for the state budget.

But where this activity has been abandoned or continued on too small a scale by the private sector, it has been necessary for these wholly or partly state-owned companies to set up or revive a sales distribution network in the bush – mainly for imported goods. Often the big privately-owned commercial companies had a share in their capital; they almost always obtained their provisions from abroad and not locally, and rendered 'technical assistance', pocketing the resultant profits and passing to the states the eventual costs of this 'social' commerce. They also kept for themselves vital elements in the economy: specialised retail outlets and services (motor-cars, mechanical engineering, electricity supply, industrial refrigeration, building materials, and machinery and plant for public works and tree-felling); and the French '*grande surface*' or '*Prisunic*' formulae became converted locally into the 'self-service' and supermarket (eventually the hypermarket). This took place only in the big towns, home of the privileged classes able to command the necessary purchasing power.

To varying degrees, the traditional trade economy integrated – or was on the way to integrating – the whole population within the colonial economy. But now the inequality of development is becoming accentuated by the concentration of investment and economic activity in the regions and centres of production yielding the greatest return, and the abandonment of the rest. Mining and oil-producing 'enclaves', which are virtually foreign territory as far as the country's economy is concerned and are only small employers of labour, accounted from this time onwards for a large proportion of export income, and indeed of national income. In many states – notably Mauritania, Gabon, Congo-Brazzaville, Togo and (since 1973) Niger – it accounts for the greater part. Development of agriculture is concentrated in the zones which are already rich – e.g. the forests of Ivory Coast and southern Cameroon – whereas the underprivileged zones of the Sudan-Sahel region in the interior became exhausted through cash crops (groundnuts and cotton) and other activity (large-scale animal rearing) which produce little cash and further degrade the environment and destroy the ecological balance. Their impoverishment increases, thus stimulating emigration to better agricultural areas (Ivory Coast, for the most part) and, above all, to the towns, where uprooted peasants accumulate on the outskirts and in shanty-towns, and even find their way to Europe unless police measures stop them. Everywhere social differences become more pronounced - between luxurious residential and business quarters, urban slums and the deserted countryside where a half-starved population hangs on with increasing difficulty.

The importance of the African bourgeoisie whose rise followed Independence should not be underestimated - although it should not be overestimated either. It is above all a political and administrative class, and no more than an accessory in the economy; even in Ivory Coast, one of the states where local private enterprise has received most encouragement, the proportion of local private capital in the total of investments still had not risen to 10 per cent by 1982. Certainly the demographic factor has played no small part in accentuating the imbalance: the population of the thirteen former French colonies in West and Central Africa had doubled from 31 to 62 million between 1960 and 1983.

With crop subsistence neglected or effectively penalised, a rural exodus and a population explosion, the problem of malnutrition is being magnified from several directions at once. And the climatic deterioration which began in 1968 and reached peaks in 1972-3 and 1983-4, hitting the Sahel hardest and then spreading south from 1977 onwards, aggravated the disaster.

All the thirteen countries, plus Guinea, imported less than 50,000 tonnes of rice in 1938. In 1959, without Guinea, they imported 190,000 tonnes; in 1978 Ivory Coast on its own imported 130,000 tonnes of rice; and the six 'least advanced' countries (Benin, the Central African Republic, Mali, Niger, Chad and Togo) imported more than 170,000 tonnes of cereals in 1975 and more than 280,000 in 1981. To that general decline in the economic situation were added the effects of the enormous oil price rises in 1973-4 and 1979-80. At the end of 1983, Senegal and even Ivory Coast had to negotiate the rescheduling of their foreign debts. If the indebtedness of African countries appears modest compared with that of other Third World states in Latin America and Asia, it nonetheless weighs heavily on economies which are already in a bad way. For these countries the establishment of a 'new international economic order' is not merely a question of justice; it is a question of survival.

# BIBLIOGRAPHY OF WORKS BY JEAN SURET-CANALE CONCERNING AFRICA

This bibliography is confined to books and articles dealing with Africa. It does not include numerous book reviews that have appeared in such publications as *La Pensée*, *Recherches africaines* (Conakry, 1959–69), *Cultures et Développement* etc.

*Books and independent publications*


*Afrique noire occidentale et centrale*, I. *Géographie, civilisations, histoire*, Paris: Editions Sociales, 288pp., 1958 (2nd edn 1961; 3rd edn 1968, 400pp). Spanish edn Buenos Aires; Chinese edn; Russian edn Moscow: Oriental Publishing House; Japanese edn Tokyo: Riron-sha; German edn Berlin (East): Akademie-Verlag.

*Afrique noire*, II. *L'ère coloniale* (1900–1945), Paris: Eds Sociales, 1964, 1 vol. in-8° 640pp., cartes et figures. German edn: Berlin: Akademie Verlag, 1969; English edn. *French Colonialism in Tropical Africa*, London: C. Hurst, 1971.

*Afrique noire*, III. *De la colonisation aux indépendances (1945–1960)*, part 1. Paris: Eds Sociales, 1972, 432pp.

*Documents EDSCO*, no. 91: *Afrique noire occidentale et centrale (géographie physique, peuples et civilisations)*, Chambéry, Edsco, 1963, and no. 92, 1964 (*Géographie humaine, histoire, états*, in collaboration with J. Cabot). *Afrique orientale et australe* (nos. 93 et 94) in collaboration with J. Dresch, B. Davidson, O. Guitard *et al.*

*La République de Guinée*, Paris: Eds Sociales, 1960, 432pp. Russian edn Moscow: Progress Publishing House, 1973.

*Historie de l'Afrique occidentale* (in collaboration with D.T. Niane), Conakry: Ministry of National Education, 1960 and Paris: Présence africaine, 1961, 224pp. German edn Darmstadt, 1963.

*Histoire de l'Afrique centrale* in collaboration with I.P. Kaké (and E. Maquet), Paris: Présence africaine, 1971, 258pp.

*Historia, A Guinee as ilhas de Cabo Verde* (in collaboration with Vasco Canral), P.A.I.G.C. Unesco, 1974, 184pp. In Portuguese.

*La Faim dans le monde* (in collaboration with J.-C. Mouchel), Paris: Eds Sociales, 1975, 250pp.

*Essais d'histoire africaine*, Paris: Eds Sociales, 1980, 270 pp. (Hungarian edn: Budapest: Kossuth Könivkiado, 1983).

*La Faim dans le monde* (in collaboration with Marie-Françoise Durand), Paris: Eds sociales, 1984, 200pp.

'Géographie des Capitaux en Afrique tropicale d'influence française', thesis for doctorat d'Etat ès-Lettres et sciences humaines, Université de Paris VII, 1984, 3 vols 975 + 77pp. (duplicated); 1 vol. Annexes, 98pp.; 1 vol. listing the French-influenced financial groups in tropical Africa, 1970–71, 189pp.; 1 Atlas (graphiques de groupes), Laboratoire de graphique de l'E.H.E.S.S., 1984, 43 pp., 30 maps and diagrams separate from the text.

*Afrique et Capitaux*, Paris: À l'arbre verdoyant, 1987, 2 vols. 861pp. The published version of the doctoral thesis of 1984.

### *Articles*

'Quelques aspects de la géographie agraire au Sénégal', *Cahiers d'Outre-Mer*, 1948, pp. 348-67.

'L'industrie des oléagineux en A.O.F.', *Cahiers d'Outre-Mer*, 1950, pp. 280-8.

'L'Almamy Samory Touré', *Recherches africaines* (Conakry), 1959, pp. 18-22.

'L'anticolonialisme en France sous la IIIe République', ibid., 1959, pp. 23-34.

'La Guinée dans le système colonial', *Présence africaine*, XXIX, 1959-60, pp. 9-44.

'Essay on the social and historical significance of the Peul hegemonies (19th-20th centuries)', *Studien zur Kolonialgeschichte und Geschichte der nationalen Befreiungsbewegung*, II, pp. 29-59, Akademie-Verlag, Berlin, 1960 (in German). French version: publ. in *Cahiers du C.E.R.M.*, 1964, *Recherches africaines* (Conakry), pp. 5-29 (1969).

'Les fondements sociaux de la vie politique africaine contemporaine', *Recherches internationales*, 22, XI-XII, 1960, pp. 6-56.

'Le régime des grandes concessions au Congo français (1899-1914) et ses conséquences', *La Pensée*, 93, Sept.-Oct. 1960, pp. 10-23.

'L'économie de traite en Afrique noire sous domination française', *Recherches africaines* (Conakry), 2 (1960), pp. 3-38.

'La conférence interafricaine des sols de Dalaba', ibid., pp. 54-9.

'La troisième conférence interafricaine des sols', *Annales de géographie*, LXIX (May-June 1960), pp. 302-4.

'La réserve naturelle intégrale des Monts Nimba', *Recherches africaines*, 2 (1960), pp. 69-76.

'L'Afrique à l'heure de l'indépendance et la "Communauté rénovée" ', *Cahiers du communisme*, 11 (Nov. 1960), pp. 1735-61.

'Brazza ou la dernière idole', *Recherches africaines* (1960), pp. 12-16.

'Les archives nationales de la République de Guinée', *Archivum*, XI (1961), pp. 155-8.

'Les sites archéologiques du Guémé-Sangan et Pété-Bonôdji' (in collaboration with C. Baldé and N.K. Camara), *Recherches africaines* (1962), pp. 51-68.

'A propos des Guinzé de Guinée', *Recherches africaines* (Conakry), 2-3 (1963) pp. 32-3.

'Les noms de famille toma' ibid., pp. 34-5.

'Deux échantillons de folklore contemporain', ibid., pp. 36-8.

'Un pionnier méconnu du mouvement démocratique en Afrique: Louis Hunkanrin', *Études dahoméennes*, n.s. (Porto-Novo), 3 (Dec. 1964), pp. 5-30.

'Un exemple d'industrialisation africaine: Fria', *Annales de géographie*, LXXIII (1964), pp. 172-88.

'Notes sur l'économie guinéenne', *Économie et politique*, 123 (Oct. 1964), pp. 74-96.

'Contexte et conséquences sociales de la traite africaine', *Présence africaine*, L (1964/2), pp. 127-50.

'Les sociétés traditionnelles en Afrique tropicale et le concept de mode de production asiatique', *La Pensée*, 117 (Oct. 1964), pp. 3-24.

'Revised version in *Sur le mode de production asiatique*, Paris: Eds Sociales, 1969, pp. 101-34.

'Les anciennes colonies françaises d'Afrique de 1944 à 1946', *Recherches internationales*, 44-45, pp. 280-302.

'La femme dans la société africaine', *La Vie africaine*,. March 1965, pp. 25-32.

'La fin de la chefferie en Guinée', *Journal of African History*, VII, 3 (1966), pp. 459-93. English version in M.A. Klein and G.W. Johnson, *Perspectives on the African Past*, Boston: Little, Brown, 1972, pp. 370-401.

'A propos du Ouali de Goumba', *Recherches africaines* (Conakry), 1964(1966), pp. 165-6.

'Le siège de Boussédou', *Recherches africaines* (Conakry), 1964 (1966), pp. 165-6.

'L'industrie en A.O.F. au lendemain de la Deuxième Guerre mondiale', *Revue économique de Madagascar*, 3-4 (1968-9), pp. 27-56.

'Colonisation, décolonisation et enseignement de l'histoire', *Cahiers de Clio* (Bruxelles), 17 (1969), pp. 57-74.

'Les forces motrices sociales et politiques de la révolution africaine', *Studien über die Revolution* (Festschrift for Prof. Markov), Berlin: Akademie-Verlag, 1969, pp. 511-21.

'Les origines ethniques des anciens captifs au Fouta-Djalon', *Notes africaines*, 123 (July 1969), pp. 91-2.

'The Fouta-Djalon chieftaincy' in M. Crowder and O. Ikime (eds), *West African Chiefs: Their changing status under colonial Rule and Independence*, New York: Africana Publishing Co., 1970, pp. 79-97.

'Touba in Guinea, holy place of Islam' in C.H. Allen and R.W. Johnson, *African Perspectives*, Cambridge University Press, 1970, pp. 53-81.

'Un aspect de la politique coloniale française en Guinée. Le mythe du complot féodal et islamique de 1911', *Bulletin de la société d'histoire moderne*, 14th series, 13 (1970), pp. 13-19.

'Die Bildung des Staates Guinea', *Zeitschrift für Geschichwissenschaft*, Berlin (East), 6 (1970), pp. 783-91.

'The Western Atlantic Coast, 1600-1800' (chap. XI) in M. Crowder and Ade Ajayi (eds), *History of West Africa*, I, London: Longman, 1971, pp. 387-440.

'Die Bedeutung der Tradition in den westafrikanischen Gesellschaftsordnung' in *Tradition und nichtkapitalistischer Entwicklungsweg in Afrika*, Berlin (East): Akademie-Verlag, 1971, pp. 107-38.

'L'Almamy Samory Touré', *Révolution démocratique africaine* (Conakry), 48 (May 1972), pp. 199-253.

'Grandeur et présence de Nkrumah', *Présence africaine*, 85 (1973/1), pp. 50-5.

'L'Afrique noire', in *L'Afrique*, Paris: Éd. Martinsart, 1973, pp. 81-128.

'Les relations internationales de la République de Guinée', in Kenneth Ingham, *Foreign Relations of African States*, Colston Papers, XXV, London: Butterworth, 1974, pp. 259-96.

'Qui peut écrire l'histoire de l'Afrique?' in Michel Amengual, *Une histoire de l'Afrique est-elle possible?* Dakar: Nouvelles Éditions Africaines, 1975, pp. 11-34.

'Économies et sociétés d'Afrique tropicale', *La Pensée*, 171 (1973), pp. 75-105.

'La crise du néo-colonialisme', *Revue canadienne des Études africaines*, VIII, 2(1974), pp. 211-33.

'Sécheresse et famine dans le Sahel', *Cultures et développement* (Louvain),VIII, 2(1976), pp. 327-34.

'La Sénégambie à l'ère de la traite', *Revue canadienne des Études africaines*, XI, 1(1977), pp. 125-34.

'Strike movements in French West Africa', *Tarikh* (Lagos), V, 3 (1977), pp. 44-56.

'Chronique de Guinée', *Cultures et développement* (Louvain), X, 2 (1978), pp. 297-314.

'Découverte de Samori', *Cahiers d'Études africaines*, XVII (2-3), 66-7 (1978), pp. 381-8.

'A propos de Vigné d'Octon. Peut-on parler d'anticolonialisme avant 1914?', *Cahiers d'Études africaines*, XVIII (1-2), 69-70 (1978), pp. 233-9.

'La grève des cheminots africains d'A.O.F.', *Cahiers d'Histoire*, 28 (1978), pp. 82-122; abridged English version in Peter C.W. Gutkind, Robin Cohen and J. Copans (eds), *African Labor History*, Beverly Hills, Calif. Sage, 1978, pp. 129-54.

'Réflexions critiques sur un certain nombre de théories relatives au Tiers-Monde' in *Classes sociales et lutte anti-impérialiste en Afrique et au Proche-Orient*, Berlin: Akademie-Verlag, 1978, pp. 42-8.

'L'apparition et le développement du capitalisme dans les pays en voie de développement' in *Impérialisme, solidarité avec les peuples du Tiers-Monde et lutte pour un nouvel ordre économique*, Paris: C.G.T., Centre confédéral d'études économiques, 1978, pp. 9-33.

'Le Bénin, une expérience originale', *Aujourd'hui l'Afrique*, nos. 14-15 (1979).

'Politica e società coloniale' in *Il Mondo contemporaneo*, IV: *Storia dell'Africa e del vicino Oriente*, Torino: La Nuova Italia, 1979, pp. 106-25.

'L'Afrique mal en point', *Civilisations* (Bruxelles), XXIX, 3-4 (1979), pp. 236-52.

'Afrika: Häuplinge gestern und heute', *Urania-Universum* (Leipzig), 25(1979), pp. 249-55.

'Hommage à Alioune Diop' in *Trentième anniversaire de Présence africaine*, Rome: Ed. des amis de Présence africaine, 1979, pp. 82-90.

'Sécheresse et famine dans le Sahel . . . et ailleurs', *Cultures et Développement* (Louvain), XII, 1(1980), pp. 137-41.

'Réflexions sur quelques problèmes d'histoire de l'Afrique', *La Pensée*, 212(May 1980), pp. 94-112.

'Vingt ans après les indépendances. L'indépendance réelle', *Aujourd'hui l'Afrique*, 21 (1980), pp. 5-9.

'Géographie, marxiste', *Espaces-Temps*, nos. 18-19-20 (1981), pp. 9-18.

'Le Sénégal à l'encan', *Aujourd'hui l'Afrique*, 22 (1981), pp. 2-6.

'Les Mourides', *Aujourd'hui l'Afrique*, 25 (1981), pp. 31-2.

'Africa: Prehistoria-Siglo XV. Introduccion, El Africa subsahariana y el mundo antico' in *Historia Universal*, Barcelona: Salvat, V (1981), pp. 147-57; 'El Imperio de Kanem-Bornu y los origenes de la civilización hausa', ibid., pp. 194-7;

'Ife y las civilizaciones del golfo de Benin', ibid., pp. 197-201.

'From Colonization to Independence in French Tropical Africa: The Economic Background' in Prosser Gifford and Wm. Roger Louis, *The Transfer of Power in Africa*. New Haven and London: Yale University Press, 1982, pp. 445-81.

'Résistance et collaboration en Afrique noire coloniale', in *Etudes africaines offertes à Henri Brunschwig*, Paris: Ed. de l'E.H.E.S.S., 1982, pp. 319-31.

'Les formes du capitalisme monopoliste d'État en Afrique tropicale d'influence française', *Tricontinental* (Habana), 84, 6 (1982), pp. 4-20.

'Africa: Siglos XVI-XVIII. Introduction - Los grandes descobrimientos maritimos y el comercio de esclavos' in *Historià Universal*, Barcelona: Salvat, VII (1982), pp. 135-60; 'La costa de Guinea de la "Rivières du Sud" al Congo', ibid., pp. 181-95; Sintesis de los Siglos XVI-XVIII, ibid., pp. 367-76.

'Quelques données sur les entreprises en République populaire du Congo (1970-1971)' in *Entreprises et entrepreneurs en Afrique*, Paris: L'Harmattan, 1983, II, pp. 519-34.

'Marx et les Balantes' (with Yves Benot), *Révolution*, 159 (18-24 March 1983), pp. 46-49.

'Théorie et pratique du "Parti-État" en République populaire et révolutionnaire de Guinée' (special issue: *Etat et société en Afrique noire*), *Revue française d'histoire d'Outre-Mer*, LXVIII, 250-3 (1981 [1983] ), pp. 296-310.

'David Diop à Kindia' in *David Diop, Témoignages, Études*, Paris: Présence africaine, 1983, pp. 142-4.

'La zone franc. Fonctions, avenir', *Recherches internationales*, 7 (1983/1), pp. 106-16.

'Africa, Siglos XIX-XX: Introducción' in *Historia Universal*, Barcelona: Salvat, X (1983), pp. 135-140; 'Etiopia y Madagascar: dos casos marginales', ibid., pp. 161-5; 'El Imperio colonial español', ibid., pp. 234-5; 'Etiopia', de la independencia mantenida a la independencia reencontrada', ibid., pp. 238-40;

'Sintesis de los Siglos XIX-XX', ibid., pp. 349-60.

'Le spectre de la faim', *Almanach de l'Humanité*, 1983, pp. 228-31.

'La Guinée, la Terre et les Hommes', and 'La Guinée dans l'histoire', *Aujourd'hui l'Afrique*, 27 (1983 [1984] ), pp. 2-12.

'La Conférence de Berlin' (Introduction to the edition of the protocols and General Act of the Berlin Conference, 1884-5), *Bremer Afrika-Archiv*, F, 19, Bremen, 1984, pp. 3-37.

'Où en est la géographie?' *La Pensée*, 239 (May-June 1984), pp. 5-8.

'La compétition franco-allemande en Guinée (1884-1885) d'après les archives coloniales françaises', *Asién-Afrika-Lateinamerika* (Leipzig), 13 (1984), pp. 33-43.

'De la traite coloniale au néo-colonialisme. L'impact sur les économies d'Afrique tropicale d'influence française', *Recherches internationales*, 13, July Sept, 1984, pp. 11-24.

'La conférence africaine de Berlin, 1884-1885', *La Pensée*, 241 (Sept.-Oct. 1984), pp. 103-21.

Preface to Paul Vigné d'Octon, *La gloire du sabre* (1st published 1900), Paris: Quintette, 1984, pp. 7-40.

'Les affamés du XX° siècle', *L'Humanité-Dimanche*, 258 (4 Jan. 1985), pp. 10 and 261 (25 Jan. 1985), p. 10.

'Géographie des capitaux en Afrique tropicale d'influence française' (resumé of thesis), *L'Information géographique*, 49, 2 (1985) pp. 84-8 and *Intergo*, 76 (1984), pp. 85-7.

'Dix ans de politique française en Afrique, 1974-1984', *Aujourd'hui l'Afrique*, 30 (1985), pp. 2-10.

'Tiers-Monde, Etat, et Libéralisme', *La Pensée*, 248 (Nov.-Dec. 1985), pp. 45-55.

'Conférence internationale sur le centenaire de la Conférence de Berlin - Brazzaville, 30 Mars-6 Avril 1985' (review) in Denyse de Saivre, *Il y a cent ans: La Conférence de Berlin*, Dakar-Abidjan: N.E.A., 1985, pp. 109-11.

'Chronique de Guinée' (II), *Cultures et Développement* (Louvain), XV, 4 (1983 [1985] ), pp. 743-65.

'Guinée: Incertitudes', *Révolution*, 308 (24 Jan. 1986), pp. 38-9.

'Signification de la conférence de Berlin', *Aujourd'hui l'Afrique*, 40 (1986), pp. 2-6.

'L'Afrique noire d'hier à aujourd'hui', *La Pensée*, 251 (May-June 1986), pp. 127-30.

Preface to Régis Antoine, *Histoire curieuse des monnaies coloniales*, Nantes: Eds A.C.L., 1986, pp. 7-10.

Preface to Raphaël Nzabakomada-Yakoma, *L'Afrique centrale insurgée. La guerre de Kongo-Wara*, Paris: L'Harmattan, 1986, pp. 7-11.

Postscript to Gaston Donnat, *Àfin que nul n'oublie. Itinéraire d'un anticolonialiste*, Paris: L'Harmattan, 1986, pp. 394-6.

*'Afrique, structure et milieu' (Géographie générale)*, *Encyclopaedia Universalis*, vol. 1, 1987, pp. 394-411.

'La politique coloniale française sous la IIIe République' in *Centenaire de la Conférence de Berlin. Actes du colloque international Brazzaville, avril 1985*, Paris: Présence africaine, 1987, pp. 199-228.

'Amilcar Cabral et l'analyse sociale' in *Pour Cabral* (symposium international Amilcar Cabral, Praia, 17-20 Jan., Paris: Présence africaine, 1987, pp. 99-109.

'Voyage au Rwanda', *Aujourd'hui l'Afrique*, no. 35 (1987), pp. 30-1.

# INDEX